URBAN LIFE AND URBAN LANDSCAPE SERIES

HIGH STAKES

Big Time Sports and Downtown Redevelopment

Timothy Jon Curry, Kent Schwirian,
and Rachael A. Woldoff

THE OHIO STATE UNIVERSITY PRESS • Columbus

Library of Congress Cataloging-in-Publication Data

Curry, Timothy J. (Timothy Jon), 1943–
    High stakes : big time sports and downtown redevelopment / Timothy Jon Curry, Kent Schwirian, and Rachael Woldoff.
        p. cm.—(Urban life and urban landscape series)
    Includes bibliographical references and index.
    ISBN 0–8142–0963–7 (cloth : alk. paper)—ISBN 0–8142–5125–0 (pbk. : alk. paper)—ISBN 0–8142–9029–9 (cd)
        1. Sports—Social aspects—Ohio—Columbus. 2. Professional sports—Social aspects—Ohio—Columbus. 3. Sports—Economic aspects—Ohio—Columbus. 4. Professional sports—Economic aspects—Ohio—Columbus. 5. Community development—Ohio—Columbus. 6. Urban renewal—Ohio—Columbus. I. Schwirian, Kent P. II. Woldoff, Rachael. III. Title. IV. Series.
        GV706.5.C869 2004
        796'.09771'57—dc22
                2004001100

Cover design by Dan O'Dair.
Text design by Jennifer Forsythe.
Type set in Times New Roman.
Printed by Thomson-Shore, Inc.

9 8 7 6 5 4 3 2 1

Contents

List of Illustrations   vi

Preface   vii

Acknowledgments   xiii

1   Sports Facilities, Public Funding, and
        Community Conflict   1

2   The Stadium Game   11

3   Sports and the Urban Redevelopment Game   28

4   Columbus: Facts, Image, Games, and Players   43

5   Issue 1: To Build an Arena and a Stadium   62

6   From Win-Lose to Win-Win   79

7   Beyond the Arena District: Downtown Columbus
        (with Benjamin Cornwell)   101

8   Other Cities, Other Games (with Benjamin Cornwell)   114

Appendix: The Ecology of Games Social Action Model
              (with Benjamin Cornwell)   135

Notes   167

Index   183

List of Illustrations

Figure 1   When Were the Stadiums Built?   19

Figure 2   Schematic Map of Columbus   46

Figure 3   Freeway System and Location of Nationwide
            Arena District   48

Figure 4   Photo of John H. McConnell   91

Figure 5   View of the Nationwide Arena   106

Figure 6   Changes in Taxpayer Costs for Cincinnati Stadium
            Projects, 1995–2001   128

Figure 7   Public Financing of Urban Professional Sport
            Facilities by Decade   130

Figure 8   The Ecology of Games Social Action Model   138

Preface

Journal Entry, February 28, 2001

On a clear cold evening in Columbus, Ohio, I made my way downtown. It was just 26 degrees outside when I picked up my neighbor Steve to go watch a major league hockey game. The game started at 7 PM and featured Columbus's new team, the Blue Jackets, playing the Phoenix Coyotes. The new hockey arena was all but sold out, with 18,136 fans in an arena with a capacity of 18,500 people.

We decided to take the freeway because we were in a hurry and wanted to have some time before the game started to check out the new arena district. The district consists of restaurants and shops that border the front of the Nationwide Arena, the newest hockey arena in the United States.

Choosing the freeway was a bad idea as the traffic was all backed up. At that time of night such a traffic jam was unusual. In Columbus most people tend to *leave* the downtown area by 6 PM to head home to the suburbs. Where were all these cars going? We could see their red taillights stretching into the distance.

As we inched along I remembered. Tonight the U.S. soccer team was playing Mexico in the World Cup competition. The game was being played in Columbus's new soccer stadium, home of the Crew, Columbus's Major League Soccer (MLS) team. The entrance to the soccer stadium is right off the freeway, so most of these cars were headed for the soccer game. Eventually we passed the soccer stadium, brilliantly lit and clearly visible from the freeway. From the car I could see people settling into their seats past the giant soccer ball that marks the entrance to the facility. I said to Steve, "Man, that team from Mexico is going to be freezing tonight! Who plays soccer in such cold weather?" Perhaps the Mexicans were affected by the cold because I later found out that they lost the game in a shutout—2–0.

We arrived downtown at the parking garage just minutes before the game. We parked and rushed through the corridors of the covered sky-bridges connecting the parking garage to the Nationwide Corporation's world headquarters building. The building's outside sign lets everyone know of its status in the downtown area. Unsure of the best route to the arena, we followed the crowds of people hurrying in the general direction of the arena district—right near the headquarters.

As we turned the corner onto the street, we suddenly saw the hockey arena. Bright spotlights illuminated the scene, and loud rock music blasted from the amplifiers outside the building. It was a typical scene in today's urban world and one that a person might dismiss in Boston or Los Angeles. However, we were in Columbus, Ohio—or Cowtown, Ohio, as some call it. Here, a big downtown arena was quite remarkable. Just a few years ago this patch of land was what urban planners of the 1990s and 2000s call a "brownfield," an undeveloped property that served as a rather grim welcome to the downtown of the sixteenth largest city in the United States.

As we entered the arena, activities were in full swing. Crowds surged through the gates and up the escalators and searched for their seats. The PA announcer introduced the teams, and the players skated back and forth on the ice before solemnly taking their positions for the opening formalities. The massive television monitors displayed the vocalist singing the national anthem. The crowd cheered wildly when she finished, and blue spotlights flashed around the ice rink to celebrate the start of another game in the Columbus Blue Jackets' inaugural season.

The Blue Jackets won the game 5–2. I was impressed that few fans in the sold-out crowd left early, even though the outcome of the game was fairly certain by the third period. People stayed in their seats, enjoying the scene to the end. Maybe it was the beer, pork sandwiches, popcorn, and Italian sausages that kept them there. Or perhaps it was the constant flow of entertainment on the overhead monitors, including orchestrated film clips, replays from the game, live action shots, and close-ups of fans.

Three hours after we had arrived, Steve and I headed back home. His voice was hoarse from cheering so loudly for so long. "Thanks for the evening," he said, "I enjoyed it." I agreed that the noise, pageantry, and excitement were invigorating, but tiring. I was so wired up from the night's activities that I didn't sleep well despite my fatigue. Little did I realize that the arena district might become a model for other cities in the near future.

The Columbus Model

This book tells the story of Columbus's rapid transformation from a town dominated by college sports to a national contender in major league sports. It describes how Columbus managed to acquire two professional sport franchises and two new sports facilities—each at a fraction of the cost that most cities have paid for just one new facility. It also tells the story of a successful urban redevelopment project—one of which Columbus is justifiably proud and one that was, for the most part, funded through private financing. Our goal in telling these stories is not to promote or boost Columbus's profile as a "world-class city." We leave that task to the city's growth-and-development lobbies. Instead, we chose to tell this story because such tales of success are all too rare. Typically, when sports are the avenue for urban redevelopment, the result is far less benign and much costlier to taxpayers than is the case with Columbus.

On the surface, the Columbus story is deceptively simple: The city gained an arena, captured a major league hockey team, and held on to a major league soccer team. However, understanding the processes and events leading to these outcomes is actually a complex matter that involves a commingling of national economic forces, local aspirations for the city to be seen as "big league," a downtown in desperate need of revitalization, and the folding of the entire set of issues into a local social system. The local system in Columbus has a sociocultural structure and historical tradition that is not well adapted to ventures of this type.

By the end of our research, however, we had seen the importance of Columbus's story to stimulating new ideas about stadium financing and encouraging the growth of new sports such as soccer. For instance, the National Hockey League's Phoenix Coyotes are preparing to move into a new arena in Glendale, Arizona. The Coyotes' current facility is the American West Arena, which is better suited for basketball. Their new facility is part of a 227-acre, master-planned development that will have retail, entertainment, and commercial components similar to Columbus's Blue Jacket arena district. The Coyotes created their financial plans for the development after surveying the Blue Jacket model. The expectation is that the arena-district concept will spur many other developments involving other sports.[1]

Columbus can also take credit for encouraging the construction of soccer-specific sport stadiums in the United States. The Hunt Sports Group and Major League Soccer have recently announced plans for the construction of two new stadiums. One is a $65-million stadium and complex for the Dallas Burn, and the other is a $140-million Home Depot Center for the Los Angeles Galaxy. While these new stadiums do not guarantee the survival of the league, they indicate a more stable base for future growth. Columbus, by providing the league's first practice facility and first soccer-specific stadium, has encouraged other cities to take the plunge.[2]

Two Main Purposes of This Book

In this book we tell the story of Columbus for two specific purposes. First, we describe and explain the reasons that contemporary cities have seized upon big time sports as a way to stimulate downtown revitalization. Second, we explain and outline the intricate ways in which community issues and decisions about sports and revitalization become intertwined with the community's social, economic, and political systems.

We aim this book at a wide audience. Those interested in city planning will be intrigued with the story because it provides an interesting case study of how decisions were made and unmade and made again as a result of unpredictable outcomes. Those interested in sports will be fascinated by the story of how Columbus obtained the first stadium built specifically for professional soccer and one of the newest franchises in professional hockey. Taxpayers interested in forcing the owners of professional sport teams to pay a fair share of the costs of construction of new facilities for their teams will be interested in the story of the opposition, who managed to win a political battle against the Titans of Columbus. And those interested in sociological theory will find the theoretical discussion and methodological details in the appendix especially interesting. We demonstrate the way Norton Long's ecology of games model (1958)—when used in conjunction with other urban theories—is a useful perspective for understanding the local dynamics of major revitalization projects.[3]

Theme of the Book

Professional sports have become a primary tool for the downtown redevelopment of large cities. Decisions about the construction of new sports facilities invariably raise the issue of who will pay for the development—the public or the private sport entrepreneurs? Inevitably, as community conflict develops between those wanting the public to pay through increased local taxes and those opposed to local tax increases. These issues are fought out in the overall context of the local political economy, culture, and history. When the public says "No" to tax increases, private sector entrepreneurs can profitably take on the construction costs of the sports venue if a bold developer folds it into a larger and imaginative neighborhood redevelopment project.

Organization of the Book

Chapters 1, 2, and 3 provide a discussion of the links among big time sports, urban revitalization, and the downtown redevelopment game. In Chapter 1, "Sports Facilities, Public Funding, and Community Conflict," we present an overview of (1) the explosion in sport facility construction, (2) the community trends that have resulted in professional sports coming to the fore in local development issues, and (3) the emergence of local opposition to the public funding of venues for professional sports. In Chapter 2, "The Stadium Game," we describe the emergence of big time professional sports and how the demands of sports franchise owners for new stadiums, arenas, and ballparks have created a "stadium game." In Chapter 3, "Sports and the Urban Redevelopment Game," we look at how the local, urban redevelopment game is structured and how professional sports fit into it.

In Chapters 4 through 7 we discuss (1) Columbus as a city ripe for professional sports franchises, (2) the Issue 1 battle over the public funding of sports venues for privately owned professional franchises, (3) the private sector entrepreneurs stepping forward to build the venues required for professional sports in the city, and (4) the way in which a successful sports-driven redevelopment project in one downtown neighborhood can have little effect on other downtown neighborhoods.

Chapter 4, "Columbus: Facts, Image, Games, and Players," deals with (1) facts about the city and its popular image, (2) the decline of downtown, (3) the city's redevelopment game and its players, and (4) the role of Ohio State University as a major force in local life. Chapter 5, "Issue 1: To Build an Arena and a Stadium," tells the story of a group of businessmen and political leaders who attempted to attract a professional hockey franchise to town by building a new arena. It also describes how they attempted to keep a soccer franchise by constructing a new stadium for it. We also describe the rise and actions of the anti-tax-increase opposition.

In Chapter 6, "From Win-Lose to Win-Win," we (1) show how and why the lightly funded opposition was able to defeat the progrowth group at the ballot box, (2) describe why the private sector entrepreneurs stepped forward to build an arena and stadium without the "necessary" funding from an increased tax, (3) detail how the arena project was incorporated into a winning revitalization project for the northwest segment of downtown, (4) describe the business elite falling-out and how and why they fought each other in a court battle that was far more rancorous than was their Issue 1 fight against the tax opposition. In Chapter 7, "Beyond the Arena District: Downtown Columbus," we show how and why the arena district revitalization project was a clear success while the rest of the downtown continued to slide.

Chapter 8, "Other Cities, Other Games," is a discussion of the quest in Pittsburgh and Cincinnati to build two stadiums in each city. We show that without the kind of private sector leadership that Columbus had, the Cincinnati and Pittsburgh taxpayers were left to pick up the financial burden of the new sports venues. The stadiums in those two cities were not incorporated into a comprehensive redevelopment project as was the arena in Columbus.

We conclude the book with a theoretical appendix. In it we (1) discuss this study in terms of Norton Long's ecology of games model, (2) add to our analysis insights from today's mainstream sociological theories of the city, and (3) present a general summary, social action model useful for looking at community issues and events.

Acknowledgments

WE THANK ALL of our interviewees for their time, information, and openness. Only a few revealed signs of defensiveness, and just one person centrally active in the Columbus arena/stadium tax issue refused to be interviewed (by making appointments with us but never keeping them). Most interviewees were helpful and shared their files, correspondence, blueprints, drafts of codes, and marketing studies. We would like to think that this had something to do with our interviewing skills, deportment, and appearance, but we think it had more to do with their genuine desire to help tell this story and share information about this very interesting and unique case. Several interviewees suggested that we talk with others that were not on our original list of people to be interviewed. These leads were important in helping us understand multiple sides of the debate.

Early on in designing this project, we had decided to publish the list of the interviewees in this section, as some studies do. However, upon further reflection, we have decided that this is not appropriate. Even though this particular controversy ended as a win-win situation, there may still be residues of hard feelings on both sides. Although we could try to protect the identity of an informant, public officials, opposition leaders, and others involved in the controversy might come to regret the fact that we made public the list of all those we interviewed. While Ohio State University's (OSU) Human Subjects Institutional Review Board approved this project and did not require us to maintain the anonymity of the interviewees, it did require that we honor any of our interviewees' specific requests for confidence.

In general, most people were comfortable talking with us, and only one interviewee specifically requested anonymity. Besides, as we researched the controversy, we found that the public record itself (in terms of interviews published in newspapers, letters to editors, feature articles, and comments made on radio and television shows) were adequate to capture the essence of what we needed to express through direct quotations.

We received support from several important sources. First, we are grateful to the Ohio Board of Regents' Ohio Urban University Program. We also thank OSU's Urban Affairs Committee for financial support. OSU's Center for Urban and Regional Analysis (CURA) was most supportive throughout the project, especially Morton O'Kelly, Leslie Smith, and Ed Malecki. We also thank the members of the CURA Urban Roundtable. These are faculty and graduate students from sociology, geography, city planning, economics, public policy and management, history, nursing, family medicine, African and African American studies, human ecology, community development, rural sociology, and other related disciplines who gather regularly to hear, discuss, and critique research presentations. They can be a tough group, but they are always pleasant, to the point, and very helpful. We tried to wear them down with a long presentation, but they still gave us relevant feedback.

We are especially grateful to Benjamin Cornwell, a graduate student in the Department of Sociology. He entered this project with enthusiasm after we had already gathered the material on Columbus. He helped to research and draft material contained in Chapters 5, 7, and 8 and the appendix and provided many hours of service editing the rest of the text. We are also grateful to Dr. Pat Schwirian of OSU's College of Nursing, Primary Care Research Institute, and Program in Gerontology and Geriatrics for reading, rereading, and critiquing versions of our manuscript. We also thank our friend, colleague, and supporter, OSU's Vice Provost for Curriculum and Institutional Relations, W. Randy Smith, who has been "Mr. Urban Affairs" at the university for many years.

The final shaping of the manuscript for publication owes much to the experienced hand of Dr. Zane Miller, reviewer for the urban studies area of The Ohio State University Press. Along with Heather Lee Miller, Acquisitions Editor, Dr. Miller was instrumental in turning our drafts into a publishable document in a timely fashion.

It goes without saying that much of what is positive in this book comes from the influence of all of these fine people, but they bear no responsibility for any of the book's shortcomings.

1

Sports Facilities, Public Funding, and Community Conflict

The Red Sox are asking for $275 million in public financing for their $627-million ballpark plan—$140 million from the city to purchase and clear land for the new ballpark by the current Fenway Park and $135 million from the state to build parking garages and improve roads and subway stations.

Residents said at a City Hall hearing Monday that it is unfair for the city to consider spending so much on a baseball park, when other plans to build new schools, community centers, and other city improvements have been put off for financial reasons.

"We have a housing crisis, we have a healthcare crisis, we have a transit crisis, we have an open space crisis," said Helen Cox, a resident of the Fenway neighborhood since 1958. "We do not have a baseball crisis."

City Councilor Maura Hennigan, from the Jamaica Plain section of Boston, agreed. "This is a terrible deal for taxpayers," she said.

The Associated Press
June 6, 2000

THE BOSTON BALLPARK issue is not an isolated event. In the last fifteen years, many U.S. cities have debated the topic of publicly funded arenas and stadiums. In many cities, sport facility issues have set off a remarkable amount of political conflict, and these conflicts—themselves—are interesting to observe. However, the explosion in sport facilities construction in American cities—along with the public's investment in them—reflects larger trends in American society.

The Explosion in Sport Facility Construction

In recent years the public has spent more than $17 billion on the construction of more than one hundred new arenas, football stadiums, and baseball parks in the United States.[1] In most cases voters agree to spend tax dollars on the construction of these facilities to support privately owned, major-league sports franchises. In many cases, teams, investors, and politicians make a deal that will combine tax dollars with private funds to pay for a project, and the public usually picks up the tab for more than half of the costs. Upon completion, governmental entities usually lease the facility to the professional franchise that operates it as a for-profit enterprise. The franchise collects the parking and concession revenues and rents for other uses of the facility. New facilities typically contain luxury boxes and suites catering to the business community and wealthy individuals, families, and groups. They also feature season-reserved, well-positioned seats that require a license fee to purchase (see Chapter 2 for more discussion of this topic). These arrangements provide the franchise with far greater revenues than were possible in the old facilities that lacked such luxurious accommodations.

Most major-league sports entrepreneurs desire new facilities for their organizations. They claim that they cannot operate profitably without a new facility *and* a favorable lease arrangement. They also claim that *they* cannot afford to build these facilities, so the public must provide most of the funds. Team owners argue that this is only fair because the public greatly benefits from the presence of a major-league team in the local community. In addition to this advantage, team owners claim that the public also benefits from the presence of a new, first-rate facility that will attract a wider range of entertainment to the community than was possible with the old facility. In the end, if the public resists these appeals, many team owners threaten to relocate their teams to a more "hospitable city."[2] In fact, numerous entrepreneurs have actually moved their teams to other cities, demonstrating to local sports fans that they should not dismiss such a threat as a bluff.[3]

In most cities, local pro-growth coalitions attempt to mobilize support for stadiums, arenas, and ballparks by framing sport facility issues in terms of urban redevelopment. Formulated as such, sport facility construction often competes for scarce public dollars with more conventional redevelopment efforts, such as transportation improvement, environmental cleanup, infrastructure modifications for people with physical handicaps, housing for low-income residents and the homeless, crime deterrence and law enforcement, and neighborhood development and renewal.[4] By framing arena and stadium funding as a form of redevelopment, governmental entities try to justify spending funds from the public redevelopment budget. Even so, there are many other city projects that could use the $250 million to $375 million that is required to construct a typical sports facility.

In many cases—to avoid public dissent—city, county, and state governments advance money for sports facilities from funds that do not require direct public approval. These funds go toward tasks such as site preparation, transportation improvements, and land acquisition. For example, June 2000 marked the middle of the construction of the "privately funded" Nationwide Arena in Columbus. At that time the city government had spent a total of $29.7 million for street widening, sewer relocation, and increased labor costs.[5]

However, without voter approval for bonds, loans, subsidies, or other financial instruments, local governments are unlikely to appropriate the hundreds of millions of dollars required for the construction of typical arenas, stadiums, and ballparks. Once a sports facility project becomes dependent on voter approval, the usual processes of political contention come into play.[6]

The public funding of sport facilities is an issue in every major city in the United States and in many second-tier cities as well.[7] Many citizens groups simply are not willing to watch politicians spend their tax dollars on the construction of arenas, stadiums, and ballparks for privately owned professional teams—especially when those same dollars could fund projects with greater priority. Often the opposition groups couch their arguments in terms of opposition to "corporate welfare." Increasingly, a large segment of voters has shown its opposition to this concept. At its most basic level, the pro-development groups and the opposition groups have the same goal: mobilizing voters to support their side of the issue.

One City's Battle over Public Funding

These two sides fought such a sport facility battle in Columbus. Pro-development supporters wanted the public to pay an increased sales tax to fund two projects: an arena to house a new major league, hockey expansion franchise *and* a stadium to house a relatively new major league soccer franchise. However, the results of the Columbus battle became a turning point in the national debate over public funding. The pro-development group argued that the franchise investors needed a tax increase for their arena and stadium for two reasons: to win the competition among cities for the hockey franchise, and to prevent the Columbus soccer franchise from relocating to another city. In contrast, the opposition group argued that the public was being asked to underwrite the local elites' ego trip. In the end, the pro-development group lost the vote when 56.3 percent to 43.7 percent of the voters rejected its demand for a new tax that would support construction of both the arena and stadium.

Within days of its defeat at the ballot box, the group of hockey team investors secured private funding from a major corporation to build an arena. In addition, within months, the soccer team's investors provided the private funding for their stadium by cutting a deal for property with a state agency. The speed with which these two groups of sport entrepreneurs gained private funding completely undercut their original claim that the *only* profitable way to have these sports in Columbus was to force the county's residents to pay increased taxes.

Opposition groups in other cities took note of the Columbus owners' about-face and used it to illustrate the potential duplicity of sport owners who demand public financing. Indeed, some have suggested that the victory of the opposition in Columbus will deter future sport entrepreneurs from gaining public funding that requires voter approval. If team owners go to the public too often, voters may be likely to lose trust and confidence in them and question their intentions, motives, and promises. Furthermore, voters might be more likely to accuse them of using the public to bear the costs and risks that owners could and should bear themselves.

The Columbus arena and stadium issue is a story of a major community conflict that includes several pursuits: local pro-growth decision makers and their dream of sport entrepreneurship, big time professional sports owners seeking wider markets for their product, and local politicians and developers grasping at opportunities to turn a brownfield into a profitable, urban redevelopment showplace.[8] This is also an account of social class, race, gender, and not-in-my-backyard (NIMBY) politics.[9] It covers unexpected but strategic oppositional alliances, backroom deals, disputes among elites, public vilifications, lawsuits, and the tainting of trust for subsequent public-funding issues.

Nor is that all, for community issues do not occur in a vacuum. Rather, they take place in a snapshot of time that is but a part of a longer stream of time. What happens in that snapshot affects a city's current set of issues, and the outcomes of these issues affect matters that will follow. In addition, specific issues and actions themselves become embedded in the overall social tapestry of a community's structure. Thus, important local events are best understood by the role of the event in that area's specific tapestry. This perspective helps explain the outcome of events that come after Columbus's hockey arena and soccer stadium conflict.

Furthermore, aspects of the Columbus story can be generalized to other cities. After all, community issues mirror societal issues—such as poverty, unemployment, crime, welfare, education, housing, resources, energy, and finances—that are all salient both at the national and local levels. Yet these matters filter through a community's particular social, economic, and political system in ways that often make similar concerns unfold differently in other communities. So it is with stadium, arena, and ballpark issues, and understanding their resolution requires a consideration of both outside actors, opportunities, and action triggers, as well as a consideration of local history, social organization, and personalities. In other words, one must understand three crucial factors: the urban connection, the importance of place, and the convergence of trends.

The Urban Connection

Unlike a century ago, contemporary American cities are integrally tied into national and global hierarchical networks of communities. These networks encompass flows of commerce, people, information, opportunities, influence, issues, power, and culture. Local communities are nodes in a grand network of places, both large and small. Some are more powerful than others, and they control and mediate what happens in their network segment.[10] Severe economic, social, environmental, or political problems in these powerful nodes can disrupt the normal functioning of the entire network. For example, when the economy declines in Chicago, communities throughout the Midwest experience the shock. Conversely, positive advances in important cities can enhance the quality of network flows and thereby improve the well-being of community network members. When conditions are positive in Chicago, conditions tend to be positive throughout Chicago's Midwestern sphere of influence.

Cities at the apex of the global system, such as New York, London, and Tokyo, serve as headquarters to the organizations that control the global economy.[11] These leading cities are also home to the key financial and specialized-service firms that have replaced manufacturing as the most important sector of the economy. It is no accident that the headquarters and home offices of the major professional sports leagues are in these cities, along with the headquarters of the media networks that transmit games to communities across the country. By headquartering in these leading cities, the big time sports entities have become integrated with the worlds of mass media, advertising and marketing, corporate and contract law, and information services. The influence of sports flows down the hierarchy of cities, as does that of other commodities, information, and social control. The decisions about stadium specifications that are made in New York by major-league baseball (MLB) can have a bearing on whether towns such as Waterloo, Iowa, will have professional minor-league baseball teams in them. Such less powerful cities sit further down the urban hierarchy and are on the receiving end of the effects from more important cities. These second- and third-tier cities understandably exert less influence on cities above them. Life in Waterloo is greatly shaped by decisions made in Chicago, but life in Chicago is *rarely* shaped by decisions made in Waterloo.

As the sheer scale of American society has increased, so too has the local community's permeability. More than ever before, the local community has become open to issues and trends from afar.[12] Teenagers in Beaufort, South Carolina, now copy the dress, attitudes, and lingo of teens in Los Angeles, as transmitted by the media, often to the consternation of their more traditional, coastal "low country" parents. Indeed, in most ways, Beaufort teens, given especially the influence of the Internet and TV, are more like teens of similar social class in Los Angeles than they are like their hometown parents.

Another example of the local connection to the larger society is the case of the "art cows." Beaufort residents were treated to public art from Chicago with the "Cows on Parade" fiberglass sculpture installation in the Windy City in spring of 2000. In this instance, several cows from the Chicago display during the summer of 1999 turned up in Beaufort and were called "Cows on Vacation." As a result, the art world of Chicago shaped the discourse of the low-country's art world for a significant portion of that year.[13]

In sum, the urban connection means that an almost endless variety of influences enters the community every day—people, commodities, information, opportunities, and triggers for change. The degree to which communities are exposed to these outside stimuli has much to do with the niche in which they are located in the network of cities. Some locations are more central than others. Cities in the most central network locations have the greatest range of influence on other cities.

The Importance of Place

Place also matters in how national trends become local issues.[14] Although impulses for change enter the local community through a variety of avenues, they still filter through the social system of the community that influences their expression. Ultimately, life is lived at the local level and not at the national level.[15] In the local community people obtain food, shelter, and clothing; children are born, socialized, schooled, age, become sick, and die. It is also at the local level that people organize for mutual support, protection, and coordination; allocate performance rewards and punishments; join together to explore the greater meanings of existence, purpose, and self-expression; and develop a history, traditions, and conventional ways of treating each other. Because of all of these activities, a local culture develops that sets one community apart from others. To be sure, trends, issues, and events emanating from the outside world influence local culture, but local culture is rooted in local history, tradition, and custom.

Local cultural differences among communities are observable. Life in Salt Lake City differs from that in Chicago, and life in Chicago is not the same as that in Little Rock. Likewise, Broken Arrow, Oklahoma, and Johnstown, Pennsylvania, are about the same size but display different social worlds in many important ways. In addition to the effect of isolation from each other—they are twelve hundred miles apart—their distinctiveness stems from long-standing differences in economy, region, ethnic mix, and history.[16] The outside world sends impulses for change to both Broken Arrow and Johnstown, but each place interprets the impulses differently and responds in ways that are consistent with the local sociocultural system. Just because matters play out in a particular way in Cleveland, there is no guarantee that they will manifest themselves in the same way in Cincinnati.

The Convergence of Trends

Finally, recent sports-facility battles in cities result from the convergence of three important societal trends. The first of these is the growth of professional sports as a powerful institution. Big time sport institutions control billions of dollars, attract tens of millions of fans, and employ hundreds of thousands of workers. They successfully lobby Congress for legislation to secure their economic position in society. These sports enter nearly everyone's home every day through newspapers, television, radio, magazines, and the Internet—even the homes of those that have no interest in sports at all. They have become socially ubiquitous and culturally anointed as a teacher of life lessons. Their games and demands on participants have become cultural metaphors for how human affairs should run and how people should live their lives. They have provided an avenue of economic and social mobility for members of marginalized, racial and ethnic minorities that possess athletic prowess. For many people, big time sports function as a civil religion with beliefs, codes of conduct, regularized rituals, appeals to the transcendental, and opportunities for emotional catharsis.

The sports-facilities craze also draws momentum from the decline of the inner city and the desperate attempt of local leaders to redevelop the urban core with projects that are beneficial to both the city and the local leadership.[17] Over the past fifty years, there has been an out-migration of people, jobs, shopping, and entertainment from the downtown core of America's older cities to the growing metropolitan fringe. Suburbs of various kinds have prospered while the old urban core has declined. In fact, the social and economic distress in large cities has increased greatly since the 1970s.[18] The core's infrastructure has fallen on hard times as well. Old and deteriorating buildings, outmoded water and sewer systems, inadequate public transportation, and an increasingly precarious fiscal position have severely challenged the city's downtown interests. Adding to these problems are air, water, and transportation concerns. The latter is especially true in large and sprawling metropolitan centers that have few alternatives to cars.[19]

Federal involvement in solving city problems has also tapered off. This decline has been so steep that local governments and private sector developers must find and fund solutions to the growing problems in the urban core. Some cities have been successful at this. In fact, so much rebuilding has gone on in Chicago's core that some have suggested that the construction crane should become the city's logo. This redevelopment has spilled beyond Chicago's Loop into adjacent inner-city neighborhoods. Because other cities have not done so well, they are willing to grasp at even the most limited of projects.

Pro-development interests in most cities have tried several strategies to reinvigorate the core. These include the construction of new office complexes and upscale shopping malls and the conversion of warehouses and other older buildings into residential loft-style dwellings. In addition, pro-development interests have attempted to replace brownfields with complexes that combine shopping, entertainment, and residences. Also, downtown interests have become involved in attracting new stadiums, arenas, and ballparks or in rebuilding the old ones. They argue that these venues serve as magnets for entertainment dollars that will spill over into the city center's restaurants, bars, and hotels. They also claim this will help downtowns become new entertainment centers for the metropolitan area. For that same reason, developers have refurbished old theaters, built convention centers, and encouraged the emergence of weekend festival activities that take advantage of attractive downtown sites, such as river and lake fronts and large municipal parks. As one expert on core city change put it, "[W]hat we're seeing now is a major shift in the idea of what a downtown should be. It's a more holistic point of view that a downtown is not just a collection of office buildings, but a place where people live and work and play, as well."[20]

As successful as some of the Chicago type of redevelopment has been, it has done little for the major problems facing the city, such as unemployment, crime, health care, and poverty. The greatest benefit has gone to the professional, managerial, and middle-class people of Chicago. They are the ones that have the time and resources to take advantage of such changes.

The third major trend that is converging with the others in contemporary American cities is the emergence of a populist, oppositional social movement. This movement aims to stop the public funding of projects that benefit mainly the private sector. Their cry is "stop corporate welfare." This sentiment resonates with the beliefs of many people who think that today's political economy ignores the problems of average people, while advancing and supporting the causes of the economic elite and big business. This is especially true in the era of the Enron debacle.

Populist opposition activists are educated, articulate, and knowledgeable about the way the urban system functions, who makes decisions, and how they make them. They know how to use the media and how to reach sympathetic city officials. They know the law and how far they can carry their objections. They know how to organize rapidly when there is an issue that runs counter to their ideology. They know how to mobilize voters to action. In fact, many of these leaders were schooled in campus protests of the late 1960s and early 1970s, and they often link their urban development concerns to broader issues of the environment, women's liberation, and racial equity.

These opposition leaders come from a variety of political ideologies ranging from the far left to the far right, and they willingly set aside major ideological differences to focus on a single issue on which they all agree. They lack power and massive resources, however. In these areas, they cannot match the elites and pro-development coalitions who push redevelopment projects. The opposition leadership is *most likely* to have a chance of winning if it can force an issue onto the street and set the stage so that "elite-advanced" projects require voter approval. The opposition leaders are great street fighters, but once the decision makers retreat behind closed doors, opposition groups are at a major disadvantage. The challenge for the opposition is to force public issues to the ballot; the challenge for the pro-development coalitions is to secure public funding from sources that do not require voter approval.

What does the convergence of the growth of big time sports, inner-city decline, and populist opposition mean for sports facility issues? It means that most large cities have become sites for the expansion of the big time sports empire. Local elites are eager to get on board because sport facilities contribute to the elites' redevelopment strategies. In some cities, big time sports provide the opportunity for local elites to become players in the pro-fessional-sports ownership game. However, redevelopment through sport is often fractious. Increasingly, citizens' groups oppose the spending of public funds for facilities that they think benefit sport franchise owners dispropor-tionately. To them, public money for sports facilities means that less public money is available for other community projects.

Taxpayer wrangles with local politicians and owners of sport franchises is part of a nationwide competition. Given that (1) professional sports leagues want profitable markets for their product, (2) the number of avail-able franchises is finite, and (3) many cities seek professional sports fran-chises, a highly competitive game has emerged as to where to locate these franchises. This game focuses on the availability of new and potentially profitable venues—stadiums, arenas, and ballparks. Cities that provide such venues are "rewarded" by receiving a franchise or retaining one they have had for a long time. Cities that do not are "punished" by either not receiv-ing a franchise or having an existing one moved to another city. This game is played not only by the established professional sports of baseball, foot-ball, and basketball, but also by the more recently emerging professional sports of ice hockey and soccer. We call this the "stadium game," and we take it up in the next chapter.

2

The Stadium Game

The pride and the presence of a professional football team is far more important than thirty libraries.

—Art Modell, former owner of the Cleveland Browns and the Baltimore Ravens

CURRENTLY, EVERY major metropolitan area has at least one major league sports franchise, and most have three or four. Professional sports are city based and city relevant, and sport facilities are an important, and often imposing, feature of the urban environment. This is so because cities are the obvious places that meet the needs of big time sports—they have the labor force, the consumer market, the media, the capital, and the powerful people willing to make it all happen.

Even so-called secondary cities are linked to the national network of big cities through the hosting of minor league affiliates. For example, the state of Virginia, which is not home to a major league baseball team, nonetheless has several professional minor league teams that are smaller-town agents for their major league, big-city affiliates. These are as follows (by town, team name, and major league affiliate): Woodbridge Potomac Cannons (St. Louis Cardinals), Norfolk Tides (New York Mets), Richmond Braves (Atlanta Braves), Lynchburg Hillcats (Pittsburgh Pirates), Salem Avalanche (Colorado Rockies), Danville Braves (Atlanta Braves), Martinsville Astros (Houston Astros), Pulaski Rangers (Texas Rangers), and Bristol White Sox (Chicago White Sox).

Also, just across the state line into West Virginia, which also does not have a major league team, are the Princeton Devil Rays (Tampa Bay Devil Rays), the Bluefield Orioles (Baltimore Orioles), and the Charlestown Alley Cats (Kansas City Royals).[1] These minor league teams involve the exchange of communications, resources, people, and power between themselves and their major league affiliates. So, even cities without major league teams of their own usually have a direct connection to the big time through their hometown teams.

Besides professional sports, amateur sports have emerged into the big time. They now involve thousands of participants, billions of dollars, and hundreds of organizations.[2] The oldest, largest, and most comprehensive amateur sports organization is the International Olympic Committee (IOC). The IOC moves the summer and winter Olympic games regularly from country to country and from city to city. The competition is fierce among cities that vie with each other to host the games.

Three major incentives motivate cities to compete for Olympic host status, and the same ones come into play for lesser sport events such as the World Series in baseball and the Superbowl in football. The first is the prestige that comes with being a host city. For example, many Australians believed that Sydney's hosting of the 2000 summer games validated its claim of being a global city that occupies an important niche in world trade. Indeed, there is evidence for the veracity of this claim. In anticipation of the Olympics in Sydney, many international firms initiated operations there. By the time the Olympics were held, two-thirds of the international organizations doing business in Australia had located their headquarters in Sydney.

The stimulation of local business is the second reason for hosting the games. Economic analysts in Sydney estimated that even before the games began, the Olympics had drawn twenty million visitors to the city who contributed greatly to Sydney's tourist industry. This figure was multiplied many times over during and after the games.

The third reason for hosting the games is the opportunity they provide for major urban-redevelopment projects. The Sydney games were centered in a formerly run-down, tidal wetlands section of the city called Homebush Bay. Before the Olympics, the area had become an industrial wasteland. Former activities in the area included a rubbish dump, a slaughterhouse, a racetrack, a brickworks, and the navy's arms depot. More than $2 billion was spent in turning the area into an Olympic park with first-class sport venues. In addition, another $3.6 billion spent in general construction across the city added twenty new hotels and numerous office and apartment buildings.[3]

Downtown as Festival and Sports Central

If a city's downtown is declining physically, economically, and culturally, how does one turn it around? For the last thirty years, many city leaders across the country have asked this question. One answer has been to make the urban core a "fun" place; that is, leaders situate in downtown those entertainment activities that would attract people to the core. Presumably, while in the city, people will dine, shop, and sample other city attractions. Urban areas with lakes or riverfronts have been especially active. When cleared of rundown buildings and spruced up with parks, amphitheaters, malls, and gardens, these waterfronts offer pleasant expanses for arts and book fairs, music fests, ethnic celebrations, and the like.

For many years downtowns have been home to main branches of public libraries, museums, galleries, jazz clubs, theaters, and symphonic halls. With suburbanization of the population and retail shopping and the growing popularity of television, DVDs, VCRs, cable TV, and the Internet, families now cocoon more. Add this to the physical and socioeconomic decline of the old urban core, and it becomes difficult for traditional urban attractions to draw people downtown.

Over the last thirty years, it has become clear that most metropolitan areas have a growing, centrally located market for entertainment and cultural activities. This market reflects several patterns. One is the overall increase in the population's level of education. Between 1960 and 1998 the percentage of persons 25 years and older who completed college grew from 7.7 to 24.4 percent. Over the same period, the percentage who graduated from high school went from 41.1 to 82.8. With increased education, interest in theater, symphony, museums, and dance also increases and translates into greater attendance at cultural events. For example, between 1985 and 1997 the total annual attendance at local professional theaters went from 14.2 million to 17.2 million; attendance at Broadway road shows jumped from 8.2 million to 18 million; and attendance at professional opera rose from 6.7 million to 6.9 million.

Another factor in the burgeoning city entertainment market is the increased affluence of the middle and upper-middle classes, whose discretionary income is often spent on entertainment. In 1997 people spent $782 million on tickets for touring Broadway shows, $350 million on local theater performances, and $391 million on local symphony performances.[4] In addition, in 1997 more than 122 million people attended professional major league sports contests, most of which were played in urban ballparks, stadiums, and arenas.

The third factor contributing to the growth of downtowns as festival and entertainment centers is the willingness of civic leaders and developers to invest in the construction and renovation of sites for these cultural activities and to aggressively seek events to occupy them. Chicago is an example of a city that, over the last thirty years, has not only rebuilt the downtown in shopping, offices, housing, and civic works, but also made it a center of festival entertainment, attracting millions of attendees every year. The Chicago mayor's office actively organizes large-scale events and regularly produces a city calendar full of weekend attractions.

Chicago has a major advantage that many cities do not: Grant Park. Just to the east of Chicago's Loop, or central business district, Grant Park occupies a large tract of the Lake Michigan shoreline. Grant Park consists of 319 acres, which include large open areas for outdoor concerts and picnicking, ball fields, flower gardens, and music shells. Grant Park is also home to many cultural institutions and civic sites, including the Art Institute, Buckingham Fountain, the Field Museum of Natural History, and the Adler Planetarium. Nearby are the Shedd Aquarium, the Museum of Science and Industry, and Soldier Field. Over the course of a summer, weekend events in Grant Park attract not only people from the city and the suburbs, but also tourists from afar. Often the park is the site of ethnic festivals such as the Irish Fest. It is also the site of major concert events devoted to gospel music, blues, jazz, country music, and Latin music.

Some of the festivals are so large that they spill out of Grant Park into other in-town venues. An example of such a mega-event is the World Music Festival Chicago 2000, hosted by the city government. Music groups from around the world played at this ten-day happening. Grant Park and the Field Museum were the center of the action, but music performances were also held at the Daley Center, the Museum of Broadcast Communications, Wells Park, the American Indian Center in the Newberry Library, the Old Town School of Folk Music, the Spirit of Music Garden, the Museum of Contemporary Art, the Chicago Cultural Center, the Chicago Symphony Center, the Chopin Theatre, and a host of Chicago music clubs, pubs, and bars. Chicago's success in making the downtown a thriving festival and entertainment center has been repeated in many other cities. In fact, it is now common for community leaders to build festival and entertainment events into their strategies for reinvigorating their downtown.

For many Americans, big time sports is their favorite form of public entertainment. So it is no wonder that the downtown, pro-growth coalitions would add sports venues to their wish list of desired redevelopments.[5]

The Local Drive for Civic Pride and Community Redevelopment

Federal funds for urban redevelopment have declined since the late 1980s, and city leaders have had to look elsewhere for such funds. The reasons for the decline of federal subsidies are too complex to describe in detail here.[6] The economic point is clear, however. The decline in federal redevelopment resources has led to serious situations in many cities. Urban problems that are not attacked through federal funding often become the burdens of state and local governments.

Without development funds—either public or private—modern downtowns would be essentially dead. Stated more positively, a Columbus, Ohio, economic-development manager said succinctly, "If you redevelop property, that means more money for the schools, to the city in tax dollars, and to businesses."[7] The downtown elite have a vested interest in attracting money, but so do the business community, the local politicians, the labor leaders, the redevelopers, the mass media, and the denizens of the inner-city neighborhoods. Attracting redevelopment funding is a matter of economics and politics, but it also is a matter of *community pride.*

Every city has an image, and community pride is a reflection of that identity. New York, among other things, is the "Big Apple." Chicago is the "City of Big Shoulders." Los Angeles is "fantasy land," and Hollywood is "Tinsel Town." Milwaukee's image is forever linked to beer and brats. St. Louis's is wedded to its arch; New Orleans's is tied to Mardi Gras and Bourbon Street. Philadelphia is home to the Liberty Bell. Pasadena *is* the Rose Parade. Amplifying the importance of image, a famous sociologist wrote many years ago: "The entire complex of urban life can be thought of as a person rather than as a distinctive place, and the city may be endowed with a personality—or, to use common parlance—a character of its own. Like a person, the city acquires a biography and a reputation."[8]

Cities without a connection to a notable team or some other identifying feature sometimes go to great lengths to attract a professional sport franchise, no matter what the sport. Lesser sports such as hockey and soccer will suffice if baseball, football, or basketball are not possibilities. Local pro-development groups are often willing to make all kinds of concessions. These include tax abatements and financial inducements, such as building a state-of-the-art facility to the specifications of the sports league to attract a team that may be moving from another city or to attract an expansion franchise.

Why do these local pro-development groups chase professional teams? It will be good for business, they always argue. They also contend that attracting a franchise will make the city "major league." If it makes the city "major league," then it makes the leadership of the city "major league" as well. Many people have their own self-image tied up with that of their community. In other words, they see themselves as the kind of people that live in that kind of city. If my town's a tank town, then "I" am a tank towner, they think. If my town's a big-league city, then "I" am a big leaguer.[9]

Building stadiums, arenas, and ballparks permits cities to hope that, by enhancing the entertainment content of downtown activities with sports, a trickle-down effect will result that will energize other businesses and shopping. Civic leaders also hope that new sports facilities will be a catalyst for further downtown-redevelopment projects in housing, offices, shopping, and entertainment. In addition to the potential direct economic benefits of sports-facility construction—and probably more important in the long run—civic leaders and a large segment of a city's population believe that attracting new professional franchises to their town or maintaining teams they already have will ensure the city's image as big league. As such, the city is then a player in the national network of places that "count." Being a leader or simply a resident of such a city means that, in some intangible way, its individual citizens count, too. After all, they are the kind of people that live in that kind of city.[10]

Given the powerful set of motivations at play on the part of cities to acquire sport facilities, what are the motives of the owners of sport teams to accommodate cities by expanding franchises or moving teams to those new stadiums and arenas?

The Stadium Game

The earliest big time sports to organize themselves into successful cartels—baseball and football—were also the first to build stadiums. These stadiums are now among the oldest in professional sports. The owners of these teams often viewed sports as a family business or a community trust and took pride in their involvement in the community. For instance, the Haas family, heir to the Levi Strauss fortune, purchased the Oakland A's in 1980 and operated it for fifteen years as a civic philanthropy. As the salaries for baseball players escalated in the 1990s, however, the team began losing money, causing the Haas family to sell the team to two local real estate developers.[11]

The number of teams as a family-owned business continues to shrink as the older sport families sell out to owners with more diverse interests. Rupert Murdock, for instance, represents the newly emerging pattern. His fortune is derived from a vast media conglomerate, and he has invested heavily in franchises such as the Los Angeles Dodgers baseball team, the

New York Knicks basketball team, and the New York Rangers hockey team. Murdock hopes that through pay-per-view programming for major sporting events, he will be able to generate vast profits for his already successful conglomerate.[12]

When a conglomerate owns a sports franchise, the ties to the local community are weakened, and whether a team stays in its "hometown" is no longer a matter of family pride. It becomes merely another business, admittedly a romantic one, whose purpose is to generate profits. Moreover, the motive for owning a stadium also changes from civic pride to producing a viable revenue stream. Old stadiums, however much local fans revere them, do not generate the kinds of revenue streams that new stadiums do. This is especially true for older, multipurpose stadiums whose revenues are shared by two teams.

If owners can avoid much of the cost of stadium construction, they may benefit even more from the income the stadium generates. These revenues come from different sources—souvenir shops, club seating, personal seat licenses, restaurants, commissions on food and beverages, advertising signage, naming rights, parking fees, and a portion of the gate sales from other promotional events held in the stadium or arena. In some cases, owners may purchase land surrounding the stadium and then benefit from the increased value of the land when the facility is built.

In effect, owners whose teams occupy older stadiums are at a competitive disadvantage with those with new facilities. This puts financial pressure on the owners of teams playing in older stadiums to relocate to new facilities. In many cases, the newer facilities are replacing the older, multipurpose facilities. Now owners of baseball and football teams, once satisfied with sharing a facility, each seek their own sport-specific venues now (see, for example, Chapter 8). Similarly, hockey and basketball teams can easily share the same arena, but the owners find their potential revenues reduced unless the same person or corporation owns both teams.

While owners claim a financial necessity for the competitive position of their teams to play in single-sport stadiums, there is also the possibility of a great personal windfall for those owners who manage to move their teams into new facilities with enhanced profits.

Consider the case of Art Modell. As the owner of the Cleveland Browns football team, he was nonetheless an important figure in Cleveland from 1961 to 1995. When Modell purchased the Browns in 1961, his team played in Cleveland's municipal stadium. Built in 1931, the stadium was part of a downtown development project that included several large, attractive structures. Municipal Stadium was not, however, particularly well designed for football. Among other things, its locker rooms were too small to hold an entire team, and posts and pillars blocked many fans' view of the field.

Modell obtained a twenty-five-year lease on the stadium in 1973, and his major tenants were his own team and the Cleveland Indians baseball team. Things changed in 1986, when David and Richard Jacobs purchased the Indians. The Jacobs brothers, experienced land developers and tough negotiators, threatened to move their recently acquired baseball franchise in 1990 unless the Indians received a new facility. This threat helped persuade voters to approve a "sin tax" on alcohol and cigarettes that went toward the construction of the Gateway Complex, a vast urban-redevelopment project in the center of Cleveland, just a few blocks from Municipal Stadium. Once the new stadium—named Jacobs Field—was built, the team prospered both on and off the field. Soon the Indians, not the Browns, ranked as Cleveland's favorite team.

Modell now wanted a new football stadium, but the costs of the Gateway Complex spiraled so far beyond estimations at the same time that the city of Cleveland found itself in serious financial straits. Consequently, Cleveland was unable to promise Modell a new facility but agreed to support a public referendum on a $175-million deal to refurbish Municipal Stadium. Modell was not an owner with deep pockets, and he feared that he would be unable to pay for the many unanticipated expenses that he would incur should the referendum pass. Instead of selling his team or borrowing more money, he chose to move his team to Baltimore.

Baltimore offered Modell a new $200-million stadium rent free for thirty years, along with generous allotments of cash to move his team, a guarantee on sell-outs for ten years, and a promise of virtually all revenues generated by the stadium.[13] Modell moved in 1995 amidst a storm of protest. The media vilified him, and he quickly became an outcast to his former friends and political allies.

While Art Modell's move to Baltimore ruined his reputation as a civic booster in Cleveland, it produced a real payoff for his family's finances. The move greatly enhanced the value of the franchise, and the team's worth easily surpassed $500 million in 2001. Modell's original investment in the Browns (now named the Ravens) in 1961 was $3.9 million, and most of that was borrowed money.[14]

When Modell moved his team, he demonstrated that no city was immune to the loss of their team. The Browns had been successful in Cleveland and had enjoyed a strong fan base for many years. Other owners of professional football teams realized that they too could move, or at least threaten to move, to get better facilities. According to one analyst, the Browns' relocation contributed to the building of new football stadiums for at least eight teams: the Ravens, the Redskins, the Bengals, the Browns, the Buccaneers, the Lions, the Forty-Niners, and the Seahawks.[15]

The important point here is that the stadium game is irresistible for big time sport owners. If they are successful in getting cities to build them new facilities, they increase revenues, which may help their teams recruit better players and market themselves more effectively, and they enhance the value of their franchises for their own personal gains when their teams are sold. Thus, an irresistible force, the desire of many cities to acquire a major professional sport, is meeting a "moveable" object, the professional sport franchise. Owners have responded both by threatening to move their teams unless cities build them newer stadiums and by increasing the numbers of available teams—but never to the point where the demand for teams is fully satisfied. The result has been a boom in stadium and arena construction in recent years, as Figure 1 illustrates.

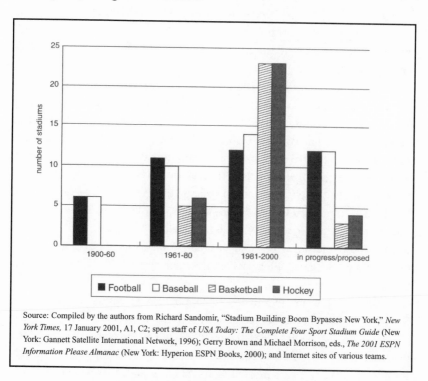

Source: Compiled by the authors from Richard Sandomir, "Stadium Building Boom Bypasses New York," *New York Times,* 17 January 2001, A1, C2; sport staff of *USA Today: The Complete Four Sport Stadium Guide* (New York: Gannett Satellite International Network, 1996); Gerry Brown and Michael Morrison, eds., *The 2001 ESPN Information Please Almanac* (New York: Hyperion ESPN Books, 2000); and Internet sites of various teams.

Figure 1. When Were the Stadiums Built?

Emerging Sports of Hockey and Soccer

Professional hockey has a long history in North America, but only recently has it made a full commitment to becoming a national sport in the United States. Put another way, the early history of hockey is similar to that of the larger, professional sport organizations of baseball, football, and basketball. Franchises were unstable, many teams struggled, and many moved from city to city or folded.[16] Competing leagues developed and some failed, while stronger teams within those leagues then merged with surviving organizations. The current prospects for professional hockey look better than they did a few decades ago because of the increasing value of professional sports to commercial television.

Professional hockey originated in 1917 in Canada, when four teams formed the National Hockey League (NHL). Only two of those teams, the Montreal Canadiens and the Toronto Maple Leafs, have survived. Of the numerous teams that attempted to join the league over the next decade, only four remain: the New York Rangers, the Boston Bruins, the Detroit Red Wings, and the Chicago Blackhawks (originally Black Hawks). These six teams, known as the "Original Six," formed the NHL before World War II, and more than four decades would elapse before the NHL added franchises in other cities.[17]

At the start of the 1967–1968 season, the league doubled in size and became a coast-to-coast sport. The six new teams included franchises in Minnesota, Philadelphia, Pittsburgh, and St. Louis. On the West Coast, Los Angeles and Oakland were also added. The league had sixteen teams by the start of the 1972–1973 season and suddenly found itself in a struggle with a rival league, the World Hockey Association (WHA). The struggle ended in 1979, when the NHL absorbed four of the WHA clubs—the Quebec Nordiques, Edmonton Oilers, Winnipeg Jets, and Hartford Whalers. More franchises were added to the NHL during the late 1980s and throughout the 1990s. These additions included the San Jose Sharks, Tampa Bay Lightning, Ottawa Senators, Florida Panthers, and the Mighty Ducks of Anaheim.

Remarkably, from 1993 to 1999, there have been almost as many NHL franchise shifts to new cities as there were in the preceding seventy-six-year history of the league. By 2000, the NHL had added the Nashville Predators, the Atlanta Thrashers, the Minnesota Wild, and the Columbus Blue Jackets for a total of thirty teams located in sixteen U.S. states, as well as the District of Columbia and four Canadian provinces.[18]

Such rapid growth, combined with the closing of some of the older, beloved hockey arenas—Boston Gardens and Chicago Stadium in 1995, the Montreal Forum in 1996, and Toronto's Maple Leaf Garden in 1999—has left some hockey fans wondering whether hockey will take root and thrive in some of the new franchises.[19] Along with its strength in U.S. areas where hockey has traditionally been a popular sport—along the eastern seaboard and in the Northeast and the Midwest—the NHL now has franchises in areas where hockey is not played as frequently, such as North Carolina, Tennessee, Georgia, Texas, Florida, and Arizona.[20] For its part, the NHL is confident it can revive natural rivalries through conference realignments. The league voted to expand from four to six divisions for the 1998–1999 season. It also hopes to promote a "hockey culture" that spans North America and provides encouragement and support to young people's hockey clubs.[21]

Social and economic forces have forced the league to become more market oriented. The Players' Association was formed in hockey in 1957 but did not become a strong force until a collective-bargaining agreement was achieved in 1975. The financial instability of the league during the late 1970s and 1980s prevented much union activity. In 1991, however, the union replaced its executive director and became much more combative about salaries, which were comparatively low for professional athletes. In 1991 hockey players received less than one-third of the salary of baseball players and only half the salary of football players.[22] Since then, the union has succeeded in raising players' salaries despite the owners' resistance. The union organized a players' strike during the 1994–1995 season over the issue of salaries and sharing revenues from photographs of players. As a result, hockey nearly became the first major professional sport to lose an entire season because of a labor conflict. However, an agreement was reached in time to finish out at least part of the season.

The contract expires in 2004. Meanwhile, professional hockey has become a millionaires' club. According to one source, the NHL has 268 millionaires. In comparison, the NFL has 514, MLB has 382, and the NBL has 268.[23] To put it even more succinctly, on average, hockey players currently earn $285 per minute of play.

Given the high salaries, the owners of Canadian hockey teams face two major difficulties in trying to field competitive teams against their colleagues in the United States. First, Canada has prohibited the practice of the government's underwriting of sports arenas for privately held teams. This means that hockey teams in Canada must pay more of their revenues toward the rent of stadiums or else underwrite the cost for building arenas.[24] Second, in recent years the Canadian dollar has been valued at less than the U.S. dollar. Therefore, Canadian teams have to pay relatively more to match the salaries offered to U.S. players. To illustrate, the Calgary Flames traded its star player, Theo Fleury, to the Colorado Avalanche. The entire Calgary payroll is about $20 million (U.S.), and Fleury could command $8 million (U.S.) on the open market. To explain his decision to let Fleury go, the Flames' general manager said the team just could not generate enough revenue because it sold tickets in Canadian dollars.[25] The owner of the Ottawa Senators said that his team will be forced to move to the United States if there is no relief. Teams that have already moved include the Quebec Nordiques in 1995, the Winnipeg Jets in 1996, and the Vancouver Grizzlies in 2001. Some believe that if the Canadian government does not intercede, Toronto will eventually be the only Canadian team to remain in the NHL.

As the economics of professional hockey have changed, new sources of funding have also become important. The league discovered that one easy way to increase its revenues is to raise the franchise fee. In 1993 the fee was $50 million, and it is now $80 million. This increase is passed on to the new owners, who must absorb not only the increased costs of player salaries, but also the franchise fee and other start-up costs.

Revenues from gate receipts, concessions, sponsorship, and advertising in the arena are not likely to be sufficient to meet the escalating demands of player salaries and other administrative hockey costs. It seems unlikely that ticket prices can be raised much further because the average price of seats for a family of four for an NHL game in 1997 was $228.39, an average that excludes luxury boxes or club seats and still represents about 30 percent of the average household's weekly earnings.[26] Despite its rowdy, working-class image, hockey draws its fans from upper-income groups. Even so, those fans must compete with corporations for the best seats. Furthermore, because teams build luxury suites in the choice locations, the cheaper seats sold to fans on game day are farther and farther from the action. Resentment among the average fans is building because of the combination of high prices and poorer seat position.[27]

Yet the league still needs to find new sources of revenues, most likely from national and local cable television. By adding new franchises in cities with potentially large viewing audiences and by creating or moving franchises to help create a national audience for hockey, the NHL has positioned itself to generate revenues from both national and local television audiences. An important event occurred in August 1998, when the league signed a new, five-year contract with ABC and ESPN. The deal, granting exclusive American television rights to the two networks beginning with the 1999–2000 season, is worth an estimated $600 million. This figure is more than three times the league's previous $155 million contract with Fox sports that began in the 1994–1995 season.[28]

Fox did not have an exclusive arrangement with the NHL and often had to compete with local TV outlets. Even so, Fox introduced numerous innovations to hockey coverage in an effort to broaden the game's appeal. These included electronically enhancing the visibility of the hockey puck, so viewers could more easily follow its course on the ice. In addition, Fox placed microphones an inch under the ice to capture the sounds made during the All-Star Game.[29] While initially more viewers were attracted to hockey than ever before, the audience actually declined in the 1997–1998 season. Fox, along with CBS, TSN, and ESPN, announced slides from five to twenty-five percent in the hockey audience.[30]

By obtaining an exclusive monopoly with the NHL, Disney now hopes to promote hockey more effectively than Fox. It also plans to promote the sport through its various outlets on TV, radio, the Internet, and paper publications. Disney hopes that the growing interest in youth hockey and the 2002 Olympic hockey games will boost the appeal of watching hockey on television.[31]

The puck is now on Disney's ice, so to speak. This will show whether national ratings can be increased to justify its $600 million in expenditures. Disney's prime-time ESPN ratings for hockey have included around one percent of U.S. television-watching households for the last decade, and Disney realizes that it will have to generate some of the same excitement that live hockey does if it is to succeed.[32]

Major League Soccer

Major League Soccer (MLS) aims to become the fifth major professional sport in the United States, following the NFL, the NHL, the NBA, and MLB. Major League Soccer also wants to produce players and teams that are competitive on an international level. While the other leagues are trying to export their sports to other nations and to develop a global fan base for American sports, Major League Soccer seeks to import an international sport to the American scene and develop a North American fan base for a sport whose fans are traditionally European and South American.

Alan I. Rothberg, chairman and CEO of Major League Soccer, announced its formation on December 17, 1993. The new league had little difficulty in attracting formal bids for franchises from twenty-two cities. Corporate sponsorships and financial investments helped teams sign many top U.S. and international stars for the 1995 inaugural season. The enthusiasm for professional soccer seemed somewhat surprising to some observers since previous attempts to form a professional soccer league in the United States had not been successful. For instance, following the success of the World Cup in England in 1966, a group of businessmen tried to establish a soccer league in the United States. The two leagues were named the United States Soccer Association (USSA) and the National Professional Soccer League (NPSL). These leagues competed with one another and then merged in 1968 to become the North American Soccer League (NASL). The second year of the NASL was a financial disaster, with only five of the original seventeen teams surviving to a third year. The league struggled along until 1984, when a lack of revenue forced it to shut down.[33]

Newfound optimism arrived after the 1994 World Cup, which was held in the United States. Attendance for the matches (3.5 million) exceeded many people's expectations. Some of the large soccer crowds gathered at the Cotton Bowl in Texas (67,600) and the Foxboro Stadium in Massachusetts (53,100), places where one might not expect to find a huge number of soccer fans. More importantly, television ratings ran much higher than anticipated, and the viewing audience for the World Cup games exceeded that for baseball on ESPN.[34] Much of the excitement was generated in the first round of play, when the U.S. team pulled off an upset, a 2–1 win over highly favored Colombia. Suddenly, soccer was receiving a vast amount of attention, and soon U.S. players, who had labored in obscurity for years, were invited to be guests on *Good Morning America* the next day.[35] Windfall profits from the World Cup, estimated at $40 million, went to fund the MLS, which gave the fledgling league sufficient financial resources to get underway. The U.S. team did even better in the World Cup in 2002. They got to the quarterfinals but lost there to Germany, the eventual champions, by a 1–0 score.

Further interest in soccer was a result of the growth and success of American women's amateur soccer. Interest in the women's game actually increased attendance at men's games. It also positioned women's soccer to advance to professional standing.

Another reason for optimism may be the niche that soccer entrepreneurs saw developing at the lower-priced end of the professional sports market.

Ticket prices for football, baseball, and hockey have risen to the point where middle-class families must budget carefully if they hope to attend any games. MLS believed it could attract families with children who play and support soccer through its competitive ticket prices and family-oriented promotional days at the stadium. With a 1997 average ticket price of $13.38, MLS believed it could carve a niche in the professional sports market by targeting families who could not afford the more expensive sports ticket prices.[36]

The MLS presented soccer to potential investors and corporate sponsors as the sport of the future in the United States. As the U.S. soccer team's attorney explains, soccer is the sport that much of America's youth learns before any other, and the United States has a large ethnic population that grew up on soccer.[37] The game is attracting new fans and more players each year and may eventually become the sport of choice for school districts weary of injuries and other problems generated by football. It is already the most prominent international sport. According to one recent poll, approximately 1.2 billion people play soccer daily. Each week nearly one-third of the world's population watches soccer on television.[38] In an effort to develop an international following and to promote the development of home-grown soccer players, the MLS allows each team the option of carrying five international players on its twenty-player roster. The league believes that through such melding of international and U.S. players, the MLS will soon be competitive on an international level.

As a way to control expenses, MLS adopted a unique ownership and operating structure. While the other professional sports leagues are a relatively loosely organized confederation of individual franchise owners, MLS was structured as a single, limited-liability company (single entity). As such, the league owns all of the player contracts, and each team operator owns a financial stake in the league as a whole, not just in their individual teams. The single-entity design is also supposed to limit the disparity between large- and small-market teams, which have created enormous inequalities in the ability to meet a payroll in professional baseball. MLS offers an "integrated sponsorship and licensing program" that is calculated to appeal to commercial affiliates while decreasing the opportunity for commercial sponsors to play one team against another. The single-entity structure was also designed to prevent the establishment of a group of superstars who are paid much more than their teammates.[39]

Whether the single-entity concept works out as planned remains to be seen. A number of questions still burden the league. For instance, will owners have the incentive to compete against each other for players when the league ultimately controls player salaries and contracts? For that matter, how will owners who own multiple teams allocate their resources among those teams? Will the more successful teams resist sharing the wealth with the less successful teams? When the league makes decisions that affect their starting lineups, will coaches abide by those decisions? Will owners accept decisions made in the league's best interests if those decisions also have a negative effect on their team?

Like other professional sports, MLS is aware of the importance of television exposure for generating revenues and increasing its share of the professional sports market. MLS arranged for a comprehensive television package for its 1998 season along with an agreement with ESPN to show a minimum of 12 regular-season and playoff games on ABC and 35 games on ESPN and ESPN2.[40] ESPN International also broadcasts MLS games internationally, and MLS owns the over-the-air rights to all of the games of the league worldwide. In addition, MLS games are available on a satellite/cable-operator subscription basis via the MLS/ESPN Shootout. Univision, a Spanish-language television network, will broadcast an additional 25–27 matches on Sundays. These various arrangements result in national or local coverage of ninety percent of all MLS matches.

While a potentially vast international audience is ready to be tapped by MLS, the question remains as to how many international soccer fans will be interested in U.S. soccer. Soccer fans, like fans of other sports, tend to be more interested in watching their own—rather than other—teams play. In addition, within the U.S. audience, soccer must compete with the more established sports. For instance, one observer described the ratings for viewing soccer games in 1998 as "minuscule."[41] However, soccer benefits, as does hockey, from the competition among cable networks for sports programs. Even with low ratings, regular, scheduled, sport programming can fill empty hours at a predictable cost and deliver to a difficult-to-reach audience of 18–45-year-old men.[42]

The dominant professional sports have pioneered the way to generate additional revenues through commercial affiliates. If it is to prosper, MLS must also find commercial affiliates who will pay to have their logos and names associated with the sport. During its first two seasons, MLS generated more than $80 million in long-term deals with major commercial affiliates such as All Sport Body Quencher, AT&T, Bandai, BIC, Budweiser, Fujifilm, Honda, MasterCard, Pepsi, and Snickers. However, potential affiliates remain elusive for soccer because of the great competition among the professional sports in the United States. To ensure its success, soccer must grow quickly.

Columbus plays an important role in the development of MLS. If the Columbus Crew remains a successful franchise, and if attendance at soccer games in Columbus as well as elsewhere in the United States holds steady or increases, then more teams will want their own soccer-specific sports stadiums. They will point to Columbus as an example of a city that has provided U.S. soccer with what it needs to prosper in the future.

No matter what the sport, in Columbus, as well as in other large cities playing the stadium game, the issues of financing, locating, and constructing new sports venues become tangled in local politics over downtown revitalization. Every large city has a high-stakes, locally focused, ongoing redevelopment game. This game ultimately shapes the way the stadium game plays out locally. Redevelopment-game players can assist or block sports entrepreneurs in their attempt to acquire or hold a professional franchise. Sometimes redevelopment-game players themselves become players in the stadium game. We take up sports and the redevelopment game in the next chapter.

3

Sports and the Urban Redevelopment Game

[Mayor Tom Murphy] plans to sweep through the shabby heart of downtown [Pittsburgh] with a wrecking ball. He wants to demolish more than 60 buildings in a six-block area of the compact downtown business district known as the Golden Triangle and build Main Street-style buildings for suburban-mall types of retailers. . . .

—Haya El Nasser, USA Today

THE PRECEDING epigraph reports an ambitious urban redevelopment plan proposed by Tom Murphy, mayor of Pittsburgh since 1994. What Mayor Murphy did not anticipate is that his latest plan would launch a national debate over the "do's and don'ts" of smart urban planning. The influential National Trust for Historic Preservation dubbed Murphy's goal as "one of the most wrongheaded revitalization proposals to appear anywhere in this country in the last 30 years. Urban experts are bemoaning it as a return to 'urban renewal,' the post-1950s demolition craze in cities that were desperate to wipe out urban blight and revive ailing neighborhoods."[1]

Clearly, the process of urban redevelopment is extremely contentious. Redevelopment proposals usually attract a wide variety of disparate economic and political groups, including big time sports. Each group has its own image of the city and is willing to fight to see that it becomes the template for evaluating specific proposals. Conflict among the contending groups often turns rancorous, and things often get said in public that make eventual cooperation and compromise difficult to achieve. City planners frequently get caught in the crossfire among the quarrelsome contenders and beat a hasty retreat into the politically safer background of statistical analyses, alternative-scenario creation, and technical consultation. As one young city planner told us, "They didn't teach us in planning school how to deal with these nuts."

The hassle in Pittsburgh over the future of the Golden Triangle is representative of similar conflicts in many cities. Just as in Pittsburgh, mayors and supporters have one image of the city, the local merchants who would be displaced have another view, and the taxpayers have yet another. The ultimate outcome of a redevelopment scuffle usually reflects the contenders' ability to translate their image of the city into action. To be successful, they need to gather and exercise power, marshal resources, form strategic alliances, and enlist the public's support. In a sense, they will be playing a game. This is not a lighthearted, frivolous contest, but a deadly serious game in which fortunes will be made and lost, political clout redistributed, lives changed, and the future of the city shaped.

The Urban Redevelopment Game

Very few people grow up without playing games. In fact, game playing is a cultural universal; that is, all human cultures have games, although some games are more serious than others.[2] To understand the redevelopment game, one must know the elements that form the game, the players, and the ways that so-called rational urban planning fits into the picture.[3]

Community Games

From our perspective, whatever else a city is, it is a complex network of games in which the players of the different games make use of each other.[4] There are four important items to know about these community games: (1) Games are pervasive, interconnected, and share a similar structure; (2) ultimate success comes from controlling the game itself; (3) game players may be either individuals or organizations led by point persons; and (4) personal career success is affected by success or failure in playing community games.

In the banking game, for example, the bankers use newspaper reporters, business owners, redevelopers, and others to further the bankers' success in the game. The redevelopers, in turn, make use of the banker, the reporter, the labor leader, and others to further the redevelopers' success in the redevelopment game. People may play in more than one game although one game is usually more important to them than the others. Big-business magnate George Steinbrenner, for instance, has played in both the shipbuilding game and the baseball-ownership game, and he has achieved a high level of success in both. Within baseball, he is considered one of the most influential, powerful owners in the major leagues. Not only does he control the fate of his own team (the New York Yankees), but he also disproportionately influences the entire U.S. professional baseball operation.

The many games played in the local community include a redevelopment game, a political game, a contracting game, a civic organization game, an ecclesiastical game, an education game, a real estate game and many others. All community games share basic characteristics. Games have (1) two or more players whose goal is both to "win" and to receive the approbation of knowing onlookers; (2) well-established goals that must be achieved to indicate the success of the players; (3) clearly defined players' social roles that make participants' behavior predictable and subject to external evaluation; (4) shared strategies and tactics among new and old players that are learned through experience and subject to improvement; (5) an elite, insider public whose members can reward winners and sanction losers; and (6) a general public composed of members who appreciate the players' standing and who sometimes emerge as players themselves.

The ultimate criterion for winning or losing a game is the achievement of a player's goals. Depending on the specific game, these goals include a mix of power, profit, and prestige. Players win in the redevelopment game if their development is constructed, their profit objectives are met, they receive acclaim from both insider and general publics, and they increase their influence and control over both local and nonlocal, future redevelopment issues. The redevelopment player loses the game if the opposition delays, blocks, or kills the project outright. Project failure translates into potential loss of power, profit, and prestige. Redevelopment players often compete with other redevelopment players for clients, contracts, funding, staff, and public recognition.

While success in a community game comes from achieving one's goals, the highest level of success a player can achieve is the ultimate control of the game itself. A player who designs the game's rules, dictates the criteria of winning and losing, and determines who can play is "king of the hill," "numero uno," "the Man," or some such approbation. Struggles for overall control of the game tend to be extended episodes that stretch across several projects and operate as the subtext to contemporary games.

Additionally, control of an important game and continued success in game playing confer superstar status on a player and admit the player into the tight circle of the power elite. Admission into the elite status group places the player in a social circle of game winners who regularly interact, intermarry, and undertake common forays into the world of regional or national leadership.[5] For instance, baseball's George Steinbrenner received an honorary doctorate degree from Ohio State University at spring commencement in 2002, partly in recognition of his many contributions to the university and community. He shared the platform with the president of the United States, George W. Bush, who also received an honorary degree. In his opening remarks, President Bush made complimentary remarks about Steinbrenner, which increased Steinbrenner's status even further and signaled his acceptance into a powerful social circle.

Control of the urban redevelopment game has been a major point of struggle among its players. For fifty years the federal government, state governments, and city governments have vied with each other as well as with private-sector real estate interests and entrepreneurial capitalists for control of the urban redevelopment game. In the 1950s and 1960s, the federal players controlled redevelopment funding and the game itself. In the 1970s and 1980s the states and cities gained control as the federal government altered its role in redevelopment. In the 1990s private sector developers and their compatriots in state and local governments have come to the fore as federal urban policy declined and eventually hit a low point.

Importantly, game players may be either organizations or individuals. Organizational players are led by point persons who are embedded in the organizational system and draw their goals, strategy, and support from within the organization. Increasingly in modern society, however, the fundamental societal building blocks are large-scale organizations, bureaucracies, and corporations.[6] When the organization itself is the game player, it acts through the point person, who is seen as the front-stage actor.

In reality, that front-stage actor is supported by and connected to a back stage of other individuals who provide logistical, moral, and directive support to the front-stage game player. People understand that Andrew Cuomo, the U.S. Secretary of Housing and Urban Development during President Bill Clinton's administration, expressed not only his own views but also those of the Clinton administration when he said, "In some ways, housing discrimination is even more insidious today than it was 30 years ago. . . . We must take steps to combat it because any kind of discrimination slams the door of opportunity to minorities, persons with disabilities, and families with children."[7] Observers also understood that Secretary Cuomo was backed by an office support staff who pulled together data, organized operations, and even drafted many of the secretary's pronouncements.

The point person in the urban redevelopment game also occupies a potentially favorable niche in a community game. A point person who accumulates wins can move up the game's status hierarchy to lead in a variety of local campaigns, projects, and events. Successes in mundane events such as organizing parades and community picnics can lead to bigger and more prestigious jobs such as heading community charity fund drives. A strong, long track record in these tasks may result in the admission of the young executive into the lower rung of top community decision makers. It may also contribute to the young executive's movement up the corporate hierarchy. A poor community track record results in the young executive's being frozen out of further decision-making opportunities and may even result in being overlooked or pushed aside in job advancement.

Back-stage actors often wield such great power that they can make or break a point person. Indeed, one of the worst things that can happen to a front-stage actor is being "fragged" or "hung out to dry" by back-stage colleagues who willfully cut off the support and assistance that only the staff can render. On the other hand, back-stage actors, by skill and determination, can make a critical contribution to a front-stage actor's success. Some back-stage organizational people become well known in the game for their prowess at back-stage action and receive rewards, prestige, and advancement for this skill.

The Land-Market Playing Field

The urban redevelopment game is played on the field of the urban land market, which is both the context and the location of the redevelopment game. The land market is the set of interacting institutions, organizations, and activities that engage in the buying, selling, renting, developing, and building of the community's land and that are responsible for the overall spatial form and built environment of the community. Several sets of groups are involved in land-market activities.[8] The first group consists of the real estate, construction, and land-development organizations and entrepreneurs, who are central in the buying, selling, and developing processes. They are the "big money makers" who frequently profit from high rates of return on their investments. However, they are also risk takers who are willing to undertake high up-front costs without assurance of success. These actors are aggressive entrepreneurs not only for the redevelopment of the old but also for the development of the new.[9]

The second land-market group consists of large industries, businesses, and utilities that purchase the largest and most strategic parcels of land. Their local decisions are "priming actions" in land development and redevelopment that trigger waves of activity by Realtors, builders, developers, bankers, and investors. Priming actions affect the future location of other businesses, churches, schools, and various residential populations. Developers pushing for the construction of an arena, stadium, or ballpark claim that their construction will trigger the building of new eateries and drinking establishments, hotels, movie theatres, office complexes, and upscale apartments.

The third land-market group consists of the individual landowners and other small consumers of land. They are unorganized for the most part, although they are the potential supporters or opponents of specific redevelopment proposals. As such, they become the focus of those redevelopment game players who attempt to enlist public support for their side of the issue.

The fourth group operating in the land market consists of the government and public agencies that deal with land matters. School districts, fire and police administrations, zoning boards, and planning commissions are all involved at one time or another. Some of these public organizations are large land consumers themselves. Other public bodies regulate land use, construction, and land transactions. Often these public groups work at cross-purposes, which further complicates the whole operation of the land market.

In short, the redevelopment game is played in the context of the land-market maze. Players who, because of their redevelopment projects, amass profit, prestige, and power that may extend beyond the land market to other realms of life, win the game. Just as in any game there are solid winners, clear losers, superstars, also-rans, has-beens, and up-and-coming new faces in the redevelopment game.[10]

The Players by Position

Redevelopment is a team game with seven player positions that differ from each other in their roles.

The first position is the *redeveloper,* the visionary and field general who identifies a specific project and puts together a team to carry out the project. Later in this monograph we will encounter several redevelopers who identified the projects of a new hockey arena and soccer stadium, assembled teams, and fought to have these structures built.

The second position on the redevelopment team is the *investor* and/or several "money people" who advance the funds required for the project's execution. They may be private-sector capitalists and financial institutions or public-sector government agencies. They may advance the money from their own pockets, use corporate resources, or raise funds from others; in the case of the public sector, they may levy taxes, assign use charges, or issue bonds or other financial instruments.

The *concept people* make up the third position on the redevelopment team. They take the redeveloper's vague concept and translate it into an architectural concept, a working design, and an actual set of blueprints. They often marry the architect's preference in the competing paradigms of architecture with the clients' concern for an attractive, functional, and profitable development. The drawings they submit as their ideas develop are often used to generate community support for the project.

The concept people are in close contact with the fourth position—the *operations people.* The operations people include the contractors, builders, engineers, plumbers, masonry workers, and others doing the hands-on work of land clearing, site preparation, construction, finishing, and decorating. Frequently the operations people are the strongest advocates for the project since they will benefit directly from its construction.

The *legal agents* are the fifth position on the redevelopment team. Their job is to guide the project through the morass of laws, regulations, and contracts that attend any significant project action. They also work closely with the urban regime, the group of politicians, public administrators, and local elite who support and encourage development. Members of the regime may fill positions on the development team themselves, or they may remain in the background and provide assistance and encouragement to redevelopment projects. They act similarly to boxing "cornermen," who stay out of the ring but patch up, strategize with, and encourage a boxer as the fight progresses.

Accountants and their computer record keepers are the sixth team position. They keep the books, deal with tax matters, collect and make payments, make and analyze financial projections, and in general keep the financial lifeblood of the organization flowing. They keep a low public profile, but they often have a final say on a project's direction.

The seventh position on the redevelopment team is the *contact agent.* The contact agent is the project's interface with the public by dealing with the media and representing the developer at public hearings and community forums. The contact agent is the "go to" person when questions arise from outside the team and makes whatever cases have to be made in whatever form is necessary to push the project along.

Politicians who are also potentially active players in the redevelopment game deserve a special word. They will often tie their political fate to one or more projects in the hope of attracting votes, establishing a reputation that is negotiable for future offices, and leaving the community a better place than they found it. Since public funding is often sought for redevelopment projects, their participation is often required. Politicians frequently form alliances with successful developers and thereby, in effect, become de facto members of the team.

All-Star Players and Super Teams

Winning redevelopers work hard to put together teams of capable players much in the same manner that a professional sports franchise does. They may sign a "star" accounting firm or an architect for a single project just as a sports team may sign a big time player for a single season. Alternatively, the redeveloper may work out long-term contracts with successful players just as do the professional sport owners with their best players. In doing so, the redeveloper brings the talented player into a more permanent, redeveloper-run organization.

Winning redevelopers are ruthless in dismissing position players that do not measure up to the redeveloper's performance standards. Likewise, winning redevelopers regularly scout for bright, capable, and up-and-coming architects, lawyers, accountants, public relations people, and other promising minor players. They also steal all-star position players from other redevelopment teams in the same way that professional teams bid free-agent players away from other teams.

Position players get rated for the work they do in the game by both their professional peers and the public. A player's overall success reflects both the success of the redevelopment team as a whole and the quality of the player's individual performance. The greatest rewards for a player usually come from the player's peers. Take, for example, architect Rem Koolhaas, whose projects include the concert hall in Porto, Portugal; the Seattle Public Library; the student center at the Illinois Institute of Technology; three Prada stores in the United States; and the Dutch Embassy in Berlin. Many of his peers acclaim him as the world's greatest architect. Indeed, he has won architecture's highest honor, the Pritzker Prize. Frank Gehry, another of the world's leading architects, has said that Koolhaas is "capable of challenging everything" and ranks as "one of the greatest thinkers of our time."[11] Just as with any super star, Koolhass and his firm are in high demand for a wide assortment of projects. His prestige flows not so much from the general urban public but rather from the acclaim of the insider public of the architecture social world.

In redevelopment as in baseball, some players are better than their teams. For example, outfielder Sammy Sosa of the Chicago Cubs was rated by baseball observers as one of the best players in major league baseball in the late 1900s and early 2000s—yet his team was a perpetual loser. Similarly, redevelopment team players may accrue professional respect, prestige, and success even when they are on unsuccessful teams. In the case of our Columbus soccer stadium/hockey arena controversy, Doug Kridler served as the point person for the unsuccessful tax initiative team, yet went on to achieve considerable professional success and recognition.

Urban Planners and the Redevelopment Game

There are many different images of what planning should be, who should do it, how much of it should be reserved for the planning professional and how much for the average citizen, and which schools of architecture and/or planning offer the most creative planning concept. The ideal in urban planning and redevelopment, however, holds that *professional planners* possess both the vision and the skills to do great things. Planners, the reasoning goes, are trained to have both a comprehensive vision of the city, its needs and prospects, and the knowledge to develop and execute comprehensive community plans that will guide the city toward a sound, attractive future. In the middle of the twentieth century it seemed certain that the city planners would be central actors in the urban development and redevelopment processes.

Federal funders of urban redevelopment in the 1950s and 1960s underwrote this assumption by demanding a quid pro quo of each city—the development of a comprehensive city plan in return for federal dollars. This plan was to make explicit the community's redevelopment needs and to supply the vision of the city's future that would serve as a blueprint for future development. In reality, some cities followed their plans more closely than others, whereas some cities simply shelved them and let the land market play out as it would.

During comprehensive plan implementation and revision, however, many planning offices resemble only moderately controlled chaos at best. It seems that in many cities plan implementation or revision *follows* developer actions rather than leading them. One observer, an urban sociologist and Chicago planning committee member, describes this state of affairs as follows: "City planning, then, was a way of aggregating together a lot of independent projects so as to give them an appearance of unity in purpose and public acceptance. . . ."[12]

In light of this observation, planners seem to be a very pragmatic lot. But that is not the whole story. American city planners vary along a practical-visionary continuum anchored at one end by "the irreverently practical" and at the other by "the unworldly utopian."[13] Most planners are near the middle of the continuum. Even those who are pragmatic have a streak of visionary in them and those who are the most visionary have a streak of practicality. As a result the planning imagery of the American city reflects both characteristics. This planner duality means that in the redevelopment game, planners pressure the players to add elements of vision to their pragmatic proposals. In return, developers insist that planners approve their plans with minimal challenge, and members of the public who oppose a particular redevelopment project insist on being heard. In addition, leaders of local governments who want the planners to smooth the path for developers lean on the planners to cooperate with them. On top of all these outside demands, planners pressure themselves to push for a utopian component in even the most mundane of situations.

In the urban redevelopment game, then, planning is a wild card. Planners can be assets to the redevelopers, or they can be impediments to achieving a redevelopment goal. More often than not, their actions will be consistent with the views of the local political leaders. Nevertheless, redevelopers can ill afford to take planners for granted.

The Urban Crisis and Redevelopment

Redevelopment attacks the problems of the city's physical environment. Projects such as stadiums, arenas, ballparks, office buildings, convention centers, residential towers, museums, pedestrian malls, memorials, and shopping malls reshape urban space and function in startling ways. They attract attention. They are capable of evoking emotions of awe, pride, and joy in onlookers. They can refashion the city's overall image. Buckingham Fountain in Chicago, the United Nations building in New York, the Ghetty Museum in Los Angeles, and River Walk in San Antonio are but a few examples of high-image-impact projects of the built environment.

Many times, though, redevelopment projects must do more than just enhance the urbanscape. They are expected to create jobs, stimulate business, attract new investment to the downtown area, make the city more lively and user friendly, and enhance the fiscal health of the city government.

In short, redevelopment projects are sometimes expected to go a long way in solving the nagging problems of the urban core. This means that the urban redevelopment game is played for very high stakes that go far beyond the simple won-lost record of any individual redevelopment team.

Are such high-powered expectations for redevelopment reasonable? To answer this we need to understand several more points. Next we describe the urban crisis and the conditions that prevent easy solutions. If you will, these are the critical conditions of the game—how a project is defined by these conditions may determine whether it is perceived as a success or a failure when the game is concluded.

The Urban Crisis

Most cities have big problems. All cities, to some extent, have decaying and deteriorating physical environments, and, to some extent, populations that are plagued by serious social and economic conditions—including crime, drug addiction, inadequate housing, unemployment and poverty—inhabit these dilapidated environments. In addition, city institutions including the school, the criminal justice, and health-care delivery systems often fail to perform at an acceptable level. On top of all of this, many cities are fiscally stressed, which means that they do not have the financial resources to make the large improvements necessary to enhance the local quality of life.

Some see this gloomy picture of today's cities as a crisis, and they demand immediate solutions to some of the many problems. If the solutions are not forthcoming, they make dire predictions for the city's future. Los Angeles, for instance, had a severe smog problem in the 1970s, and critics claimed that the city was going to become uninhabitable if something were not done to end to the predicament. As a result, strong antipollution laws were enacted. The crisis passed, and the gloomy picture of a city in a smog crisis dissipated.

Because big cities always have problems, some see these not as crises but a more-or-less chronic condition.[14] Observers of American cities have been pointing out poor environmental, social, and economic conditions for more than one hundred years. They claim that, in response, many social actions have emerged to improve city life, including muckraker journalism, the settlement-house movement, reform politics, federal programs, and antismog regulations.[15]

In other words, those who see the contemporary city as chronically in trouble argue that this gloomy picture is an overstatement. In fact, we can make a case for an "urban revival," as evidenced by numerous redevelopment projects, that may easily go unnoticed.[16] According to this view, most of the older cities have aimed to improve their downtowns, renovate core neighborhoods, and attract new shopping, convention, and entertainment complexes. These actions have contributed to a "city renaissance," they say, that will make the city a more attractive place. It may even improve working, living, and playing conditions for both the affluent whites and minority residents.

We find ourselves somewhere between the urban crisis and urban revival positions. However, we believe that the way in which the problems of the city are defined is very important. If the problems are defined as *crises,* then we expect that a redevelopment project or two can be successful only if it somehow solves massive unemployment, poverty, physical decline, and fiscal shortfall. If the problems are regarded as *chronic,* a redevelopment project will be deemed successful if it makes even a small dent in the scale of the city's most serious problems.

Suburbanization and City Decline

The second point we must understand to assess the rationality of having high expectations for urban redevelopment is the simple fact that the loss of people, jobs, shopping, and recreation to the suburbs makes the task of core redevelopment extremely difficult. Redeveloping the city's core is greatly complicated by the very morphology of urban expansion. Put another way—as people move to the suburbs, a number of social processes are set in motion, some of which are difficult to reverse. Suburban political independence from the old central city means that suburbanites are free to pursue their own goals and to develop their local agendas often at a great variance from and in conflict with those of the city. The city is no longer their home but has become a very large competitor for scarce resources, requiring constant and close scrutiny.

Moving to the suburbs—*decentralization*—also hurts core city redevelopment efforts to secure federal and state government help in ameliorating the urban crisis. With the shift of America's metropolitan population from the central cities to the suburbs, the plight of the inner city—the inner part of the core cities of metro areas—has become less of a concern to the voters and to those who are elected to state and federal political offices than was the case fifty years ago. Numerically, the votes are in the suburbs, the campaign contributions come from there, and the high rate of voter turnout is there as well.

Thus, contemporary political power is increasingly found in the suburbs and not in the central city. Concerns for the city's redevelopment are left largely to the downtown business interests, the old neighborhood groups, new residents of old neighborhoods, human service institutions (schools, hospitals, and religious congregations), and the local political administration. These local actors are almost on their own when it comes to dealing with the urban crisis. State and federal urban policy has become anemic and consequently has not provided enough resources to help matters rebound in the cities.

Gentrification and Redevelopment

The next thing we need to keep in mind when we think of the possibility of core urban redevelopment is the importance of attracting affluent populations back to the city. With the out migration of people, jobs, and shopping, the local economic and political elites and neighborhood groups concerned with downtown survival have searched for alternatives to reinvigorate the city's core.

One alternative popular since the 1960s is *gentrification*—the conversion of low-income areas of the city to middle-class residential enclaves.[17] What distinguishes gentrification from government redevelopment programs is that gentrification is a private-market action. People invest their own or borrowed capital into old and sometimes rundown but architecturally appealing houses in the city's older downtown neighborhoods. The investors select houses for both their own residential use as well as for long-term financial gain.

Beyond finances, however, gentrifying neighborhoods represent a prospective lifestyle that resonates with gentrifiers' cultural values and self-image. The movement of young, middle- and professional-class couples into gentrifying areas can cause a wave of reinvestment in nearby properties by longtime residents who see the wisdom of upgrading their own property as the gentrifiers pursue and attain neighborhood improvement. The upgraders often do this to make their dwellings more marketable to the incoming gentrifiers.[18]

This may work well for the old-time property owners, but not all pre-gentrification residents fare well in the process. Most vulnerable to this process are low-income renters who have few other places in the city where they can find affordable housing. As their landlords make their rentals available for purchase by the gentrifiers or convert rentals into condominiums, thus pricing them out of the reach of their former, poorer tenants, these people become the displaced.

From the standpoint of the downtown elite, gentrification is a good thing. It brings people with money into the urban core who will do most of their shopping and recreating in the city center. Gentrification enhances the city's tax base as housing is upgraded and taxed accordingly. It also attracts people who are more stable, orderly, and civically active than previous residents. However, gentrifiers also make demands on the city to improve neighborhood infrastructure, safety, and traffic flow. All of these enhancements cost real dollars. The city administration may see these demands either as an investment to upgrading the city's core or as a drain on resources already overstretched. Nevertheless, gentrifiers represent a critical mass of support for urban redevelopment as they seek to upgrade the segment of the city they call home.

The Special Problems of the Disadvantaged

The final point we need to understand when we think of the possibility of redevelopment in the core is that there are no bigger potential supporters of the promise of urban redevelopment than the disadvantaged urban core dwellers. They form a critical mass of people who recognize the need for economic improvement and redevelopment. Development projects offer the possibility of improving their lives through job creation, better services, and advancement opportunities.

Yet, the disadvantaged are skeptical of what any single project can do for them and justifiably so. They have been told in the past that if they supported proposed projects, jobs for them would result. They have seen these promises fail to materialize. Indeed, in the case of the building of a new downtown arena, one member of this population opined that she might be able to get a job scrubbing toilets in the new arena, but for sure that job would not pay enough for her and her children to attend a game.

At the heart of the problem is the fact that the poor are concentrated and isolated mainly in racially and economically homogeneous neighborhoods that are excluded from the city's mainstream economic and political life. The physical environment of such areas is deteriorated and unhealthy. It poses a risk to the lives of both children and adults from fire, toxic chemical residues, uncollected waste, aggressive and uncontrolled rodents and other pests, building abandonment, vandalism, broken windows, disrepair, and heavy traffic.[19]

People living in such neighborhoods are also likely to be victims of crimes and major incivilities. They see many of the neighborhood children inducted into gangs and street life. And they see many of the children becoming engaged in drug trafficking and the drug war. Indeed, it is not unusual in many of these neighborhoods for a high percentage of the young men from eighteen through twenty-five years of age to either have served time in the past or currently be serving time for a variety of serious offenses. Moreover, it is not unusual for such neighborhoods to have a high violent-death rate for their teenage children because they become caught in the pervasive local culture of violence.

Residents of poor neighborhoods also experience poorer quality schools, inadequate and overpriced shopping opportunities, restricted mass transit, high unemployment, and minimal health care, even though they require more in the way of government services than do residents of other sections of the city. Unfortunately, the cost of such services at the level required in the poor neighborhoods is prohibitive for city administrations without the taxes of people who are better off. Thus, the problems in poor neighborhoods inevitably worsen.

Given these limiting conditions, we are not optimistic about the success of urban redevelopment projects that claim to change a city core overnight. Certainly, however, there are opportunities to improve the quality of life in the core city by selecting projects that will make a difference in a neighborhood and, when repeated in additional neighborhoods, will make a difference to the city as a whole.

Columbus had not escaped the urban crisis. Downtown sorely needed help to redevelop. The redevelopment game players thought that a new stadium, a new arena, and a new professional sports franchise were just the tickets to jumpstart the comeback. In the next chapter we discuss who the game players were, how they saw the downtown as ripe for redevelopment, and how sports was their logical choice for the focus of redevelopment.

4

Columbus: Facts, Image, Games, and Players

It's a great city, but nobody knew about it. . . . When you said you were from Columbus, you had to say "Columbus, Ohio." The one thing missing was major league athletics.

—John McConnell, founder of Worthington Industries

COLUMBUS IS the largest city in Ohio—larger than Cleveland, Cincinnati, Toledo, and Dayton.[1] Yet, in comparison to these other cities, Columbus has been far less well known, both nationally and regionally. Outsiders, if familiar at all with the city, tend to think of it as a state capital, a college town, and perhaps a home to a few corporations such as Nationwide Insurance. At best, Columbus is to many people strictly a minor league city— not at all in the same class with Pittsburgh, Detroit, Atlanta, Milwaukee, and other cities that are represented on the national stage by major league sports franchises.

Columbus's sleepy, bucolic image has masked the facts of the city's last thirty years. Columbus has been the most rapidly growing and dynamic city of the old industrial Rustbelt. Its economy is a well-balanced mix of manufacturing, services, and trade. As Ohio's state capital, Columbus looks to public employment as a major factor in the community's economic stability. It is also home to The Ohio State University (OSU), one of the largest state universities in the world. It annually teaches more than 50,000 students on its main campus and employs more than 18,000 university and medical staff. When the old steel towns of the region suffered major economic setbacks in the late 1970s and 1980s, Columbus plowed ahead with economic and population growth.

Some Columbus residents have been miffed that the city does not get the national respect that they feel it deserves. This has been especially true of the core of the Columbus elite. They are the winners of the myriad community games played in the city—banking, media, manufacturing, politics, education, retail, health care, and the like. Many of them think that their significant accomplishments are somehow diminished by Columbus's image as strictly minor league. They are winners, but winners in the minors, not the majors. They would like to play on a more significant and respected stage. In their opinion, one way to do this is for Columbus to become a major league sports town.

Columbus: Fact and Image

To gain an understanding of Columbus we must know about several of its dimensions: the city's economy and the ongoing redevelopment game; the people and the places in which they live; the political scene and the role played by a group of businesspeople who dominate political life; the importance of sports in the city; and OSU's exceptional and historic position in the community.

The Economy and the Redevelopment Game

Columbus is located in the middle of the state, a location significant in its becoming the state capital in 1812. State capitals usually have a heavy concentration of insurance, real estate, and financial corporations among their local industry, and Columbus is no exception. Nationwide Insurance, Allstate, CIGNA, Farmer's, State Auto, and others have regional or national headquarters there. Other corporate headquarters and major employers are Borden's, Abbot Laboratories, Aetna, Federal Express, Ford, General Electric, General Motors, Honeywell, ITT, The Limited, Bank One, State Savings, CompuServe, Battelle Memorial Institute, Micro Center, Wendy's, and Chemical Abstracts.[2]

As the largest city in central Ohio, Columbus is the center of transportation and trade. This area has specialized in corn production, meat products, sheep and wool, orchard fruits, clay and glass products, and coal mining. Numerous businesses in Columbus have serviced these industries through manufacturing, processing, and transportation. Even though Columbus was never a manufacturing center on the scale of Cleveland, it did have a viable manufacturing sector that included firms specializing in meat packing, manufacturing of fabricated metals (structural steel, tools, and implements), heating and cooling equipment, metal stamping, glass and glass products, roller bearings, testing devices, and footwear.

The city's public employment, together with this variety of economic activities, prevented Columbus from experiencing the severe economic decline that the cities of northern and northeastern Ohio did when the steel industry all but collapsed in the 1970s. Consequently, the city weathered that economic downturn effectively. That fact has given the city an economic advantage over other Ohio cities in attracting new economic activities. With the structural reorganization of America's economy, the manufacturing employment in Columbus, as in many cities, has been declining and is being replaced by employment in services, trade, and communications.

Indeed, the heavy concentration of executives, administrators, and professionals in the local labor force gives Columbus a distinctly white-collar-professional culture that is linked with a relatively large amount of discretionary income that it uses for recreation and entertainment. This combination of white-collar culture and income makes Columbus attractive as a site for professional sports franchises.

In the 1950s downtown Columbus was the dominant employment and shopping center of the metropolitan community. State government employment was large, but so, too, was retailing with major department stores such as F. & R. Lazarus, which anchored the south side of the central business district, and the Union, which anchored the north side. Between the two stood a wide range of specialty shops, many of which were targeted to an upscale, professional clientele. Other stores catered to middle- and working-class tastes and budgets, including Woolworth's and Montgomery Ward. Downtown hotels served tourists, business travelers, and out-of-towners doing business with state government. A large number of dining, entertainment, and recreation establishments gave the urban core an attractive vitality.

Old, well-established residential neighborhoods ringed the downtown and, as they have aged, they have become the core areas for the gentrification that has taken place since the 1970s. When combined, the population of these neighborhoods was forty thousand in 1960. Having so many people living next to the downtown provided a solid market for retailing and professional services. It also contributed to the lively ambiance of downtown, especially in the evening. German Village, located on the south border of the central business district, was one of the first gentrified neighborhoods in the United States.[3] Gentrification in German Village began in the 1960s and continues to this day.

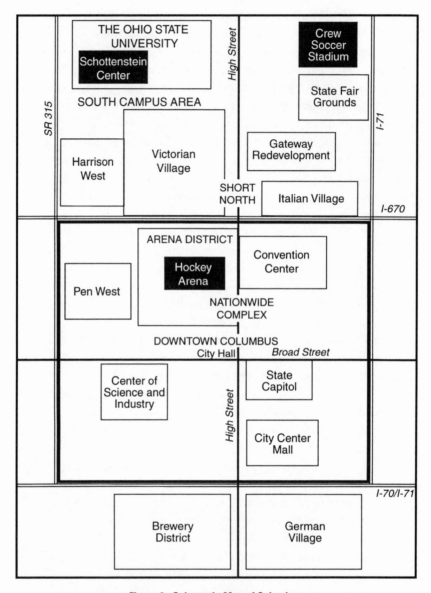

Figure 2. Schematic Map of Columbus

German Village maintained its vitality throughout the 1970s and early 1980s, a period in which the rest of the core was sliding. It became a beacon of hope for the city leadership and early redevelopers and showed that downtown was still valuable and worth saving. It also demonstrated that it was a viable market for gentrification in the city and served as a model for the city's second gentrified neighborhood—Victorian Village—located to the north of the central business district and just south of OSU (see Figure 2).

Downtown Falls on Hard Times

The number of downtown residents in Columbus dwindled from 40,000 in 1960 to 7,200 in 1990. In addition, the socioeconomic position of this population had slipped and could no longer support the economy that it once had. Also, physical decay was evident in many inner-city neighborhood areas, thereby making them unnerving, scary areas at night. The downtown was no longer the first choice for recreating and relaxing. Indeed, downtown Columbus seemed like a ghost town at night. It was this decline that eventually led to the push for downtown urban redevelopment and ultimately to the arena issue we discuss in this book.

Two major events contributed to the downtown economic slide. The first was the suburbanization of shopping that kept pace with the suburbanization of the population. In 1960 shoppers had to go downtown to make most of their significant purchases. However, in the 1960s the first ring of peripheral shopping centers was either started or completed; these included Town and Country, Graceland, Great Western, Northern Lights, Great Eastern, and Great Southern. As the population further suburbanized, another ring of distant malls was constructed, including Northland, Westland, and Eastland malls. In recent years new suburban malls have been eclipsed by or included in the city's dynamic, peripheral cities.[4] With the rush of the population to the suburbs and the migration of large downtown stores to the fringe to become anchor stores for the new malls, the downtown has experienced a significant decline in shopping and business. In 1960 downtown Columbus had 659 retail stores, but by the 1980s only 150 remained.

The second factor in the decline of downtown was the completion of the metropolitan freeway system that linked Columbus to Cincinnati on the south, to Cleveland on the north, to Wheeling-Pittsburgh on the east, and to Indianapolis on the west. These north-south and east-west interstate axes interchanged in the heart of downtown and provided an excellent escape route for downtown workers fleeing to their suburban homes. Next, a circumferential freeway that skirted the outer suburbs and linked them to one another was completed, making it unnecessary to enter the downtown to travel from one suburb to another.

Suburbanization and edge city development, as it is today, would have been impossible without this freeway system. These freeways made it

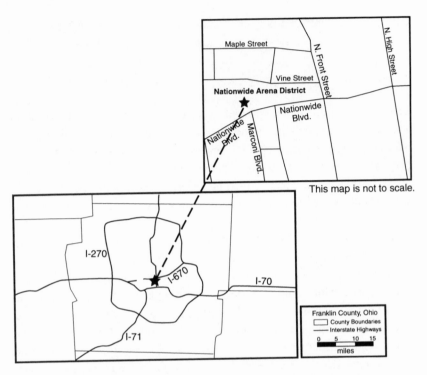

Figure 3. Freeway System and Location of Nationwide Arena District

possible for even more population, employment, and businesses to be drawn from the core to the periphery. By the 1980s decentralization was clearly reshaping Columbus.

The freeway system also sliced the city into several distinct segments, which heightened racial and social class segregation and created serious barriers to the easy flow of people from one neighborhood to another. Particularly important to our study is the 270 outerbelt. Suburban growth is rapid on both sides of this freeway, increasing the distance of Columbus residents from their suburban neighbors.

Downtown Turns Around

From the mid-1980s through the mid-1990s, however, downtown Columbus experienced a turnaround. An energized pro-growth coalition created several successful redevelopment projects. Parts of the city core made a strong comeback in new businesses, offices, and hotels. Among the most significant redevelopment projects were the construction of a major convention center, the City Center shopping mall, several new high-rise office buildings for both private businesses and state government offices, new hotels (and the upgrading of older ones), and expensive, high-rise housing and low-rise loft conversions as well as the refurbishing of several old but elaborate theaters—the State, the Palace, and the Southern. Gentrification has spread to other inner-city neighborhoods including Goodale Park, Italian Village, the Brewery District, and Old Town East. The hockey arena issue our study describes was considered by the power wielders as critical for the next stage of downtown reinvigoration. Nevertheless, economic and demographic forces were at work in the city's core to slow and even threaten the progress of this era.

The Redevelopment Game

The Columbus downtown redevelopment game has been played cautiously and successfully with relatively few false starts or bad investments. The steady but slow pace of redevelopment fits well with three aspects of local culture: the conservative political climate, the preference of the economic actors for substantial public subsidies in support of their capital investments, and a general but subtle suspicion of outside investors and developers.

At the core of Columbus's downtown redevelopment project has been an ongoing dialogue among the city's economic leaders; the city, county, and state public officials; the business community as embodied in civic organizations; and the developer/contractors and related professionals who actually take the field as various projects are proposed and undertaken.

As long as these players' goals have meshed, redevelopment has largely avoided public fights, squabbles, and fractious debates. Of course, the public has not supported all of the redevelopers' proposed projects. Programs for mass transit, downtown outdoor amphitheaters, and arenas and stadiums have regularly taken a beating at the ballot box. A populist, tax-oppositional coalition has sometimes frustrated the redevelopers. Nevertheless, redevelopers have proceeded with a combination of private funds, redevelopment bonds, and state and local public funds that do not require voter approval. Success has been on their side most of the time.

The People of Columbus and Where They Live

An important feature of city politics is that Columbus is less suburban than most other large metropolitan areas. In 2000 there were 1.6 million people in the Columbus metropolitan area. Forty-five percent of these people lived in the city of Columbus, and the other 55 percent resided in the suburbs.[5] For example, in Cleveland 78 percent of the metropolitan population lives in the suburbs, and in Cincinnati 77 percent of the metropolitan population lives in the suburbs. For other Rustbelt metropolitan areas, the pattern is the same—in Detroit 77 percent reside in the suburbs; for Buffalo, the suburban percentage is 77 percent; and for Pittsburgh, 85 percent.

The extent to which the city of Columbus has held on to and expanded its population in large measure reflects the bipartisan annexation activities of its mayors. In the 1960s Mayor M. E. "Jack" Sensenbrenner vowed that the city would never be strangled by the suburbs.[6] Annexation would be the city's defensive weapon of choice. Since then each political administration, Democratic or Republican, has adhered to this precept. The city administrations have aggressively annexed open space and new fringe residential developments before nearby suburbs could acquire them.

Sometimes the annexation process became brutal. For example, several years ago the city wanted to annex a newly developing neighborhood in the northwest part of its county (Franklin County), but the residents wanted to join a nearby suburb. The mayor of Columbus at the time threatened to withhold water and sewer lines to that development if it voted to join the suburb. Since the city has a monopoly on providing water and sewage treatment in the Columbus metropolitan area, it can reward or punish developments as it sees fit. This form of strong-arming the suburbs and fringe residential developments was common, even though the city and the suburbs publicly presented an image of cordial relations.

Sometimes the argument is less brutal. Columbus and several of its suburbs have developed an education program called Win-Win, which permits parents who live in outlying annexed areas of the city to send their children to the suburban school system (rather than to the Columbus schools) in whose district they lived before annexation.[7] The Win-Win program was very successful. The city was able to retain much of the white population that was fleeing to the suburbs because of fear of both forced busing in the city schools and the declining social and environmental conditions in the city's core. Because of annexation and Win-Win, the city of Columbus has maintained a larger portion of its metropolitan population than have other cities.

The net effect of the annexation activities and Win-Win is that the Columbus city area has stretched to 190.9 square miles. By contrast, Cleveland's area is only 77.0 square miles, and Cincinnati's is just 77.2 square miles. Annexation has resulted in many fringe neighborhoods being encompassed within the political city. If they were at a similar distance from downtown in other metropolitan areas, they would be suburban. This means that the Columbus city administration has concerns not only about downtown redevelopment but also about fringe development not shared by other older cities. The tension between downtown redevelopment and fringe servicing is evident in city political squabbles over a range of issues. In addition, it means that redevelopers, who want tax assistance for their downtown sports and other projects, must convince people to pay for these projects even though many of those people are essentially suburbanites in outlook, shopping habits, and lifestyles.

Sports in the City

Columbus has always been a hotbed of sports enthusiasm, and many Columbus residents have an ongoing interest in the city obtaining a professional sport franchise of some kind. In the meantime, the OSU sports programs attract the interest of students, staff, alumni, and faculty as well as of a large number of enthusiastic, hypercritical fans who have little or no connection to the university. Nonetheless, their views drive a sports subculture that demands not just winning seasons in major sports but championships as a minimum standard of performance. With this constant pressure for championships, it is no wonder that Columbus and OSU are known in collegiate athletic circles as the "graveyard of coaches."[8]

For more than one hundred years, Columbus has been known as a good baseball town, and previous minor league franchises have enjoyed much community support. Today local baseball enthusiasm is manifest in support for the Columbus Clippers, a team that is publicly owned by Franklin County, as is its ballpark, Cooper Stadium. Public ownership of both the team and ballpark is rare in professional sports today. The Clippers are the AAA minor league affiliate of the New York Yankees. As such, many major league stars spend part of their careers either playing for the Clippers or visiting the city as members of other AAA teams. Many locals consider attending Clippers games as the best entertainment deal in the city. For many years the Clippers have drawn half a million fans per season, a gate size that franchises in many other cities envy.

The lack of a big time sports franchise in the city has resulted in the targeting of Columbus by start-up professional leagues. As a result, Columbus has had a string of new franchises that have remained for only a few seasons and then disappeared as their leagues folded. The city has been home to the Quest, a championship women's basketball team. It has been home to the Magic, an early professional soccer team. Columbus also was home to the Glory, a short-lived professional football team, and home to several minor league, ice hockey teams, the latest of which was the Chill. The city used the fact that Columbus residents supported minor league hockey as an argument when it made in its application for an NHL franchise.

In addition to many short-lived franchises, Columbus has been connected to the world of professional wrestling, for which the city served as a major center many years ago. Currently, many older wrestlers live in retirement there. Today local interest in professional wrestling remains high, and when the professional wrestling shows come to town, they regularly play before standing-room-only crowds.

Columbus residents are not just sports spectators. Amateur rates of participation sports are high. In fact, Columbus has greater per-capita sports participation in softball than any other community in the country. National tournaments are often held in Columbus. Also, the city and suburbs maintain a large number of playing diamonds, and there is always pressure for adding more.

With Columbus's recent, rapid growth and with all of the interest in local sports, it is no wonder that the community leadership has also been interested in attracting professional sports to the city. To them, obtaining a major league franchise would help solve the city's "cow-town" image. Consequently, the issue of sports has always been on the city's agenda, but it has always been blocked by one major fact—the city simply did not have the kind of facilities that would be acceptable for a big time professional sports franchise.

Players in the Redevelopment Game

Who runs Columbus? Although some people seem more influential than others in the public eye, the fact is that no single person and no single set of persons calls the shots for everything that occurs in the metropolitan area. The city is too big, the things going on are too many and too diverse, and the citizens' interests are too varied. In fact, the city serves as the playing field for a large number of games—in banking, manufacturing, retail, communications, welfare, education, health care, redevelopment, and so on.

Some are more important than others; as a result, the winners of those games have better shots at playing in the more important events.

The most important games are those that involve the greatest financial resources, affect the largest number of people, and have the most valued rewards for success. In each game the winners amass prestige, material rewards, power, and influence. Some players participate in more than one game and thereby reinforce the winnings from their other events.

The winners may go on to the ultimate game in the city, the civic game. The public often thinks that these players are those who run the city. Players score points in this game by taking the lead on projects that have clear public benefit, by publicly endorsing and supporting charitable drives and events, such as the United Way campaign, and by working to minimize community conflicts. They also score points by contributing positively to the ongoing public dialogue about the community's future, by working to solve community problems, and by representing the community in national and international venues and events.

The scope and importance of redevelopment activities often attract players from the civic game. These projects often give the civic game players an opportunity to score enough points to consolidate their leadership position. Such projects become high-stakes games just as golf or tennis tournaments that attract the top-rated players. The higher the perceived stakes, the greater the number of civic points that a player may win or lose. Failed projects can adversely affect a player's position in the civic game just as a successful project can positively affect it.

The Titans

As the public sees it, the most powerful people in Columbus are the top players in the civic game and are known locally as "the Titans."[9] Some core members of the Titans come from long-time Columbus families with major controlling interests in banking, manufacturing, and the media. Members of this group control the city's only daily newspaper, the *Columbus Dispatch*. They also hold controlling interests in local radio and television stations. Other members of this select group come from insurance, retail trade, and real estate. With few exceptions, the local business community is aligned with the Titans in their continued pro-growth undertakings for the city. The Titans and their associates control the local Republican Party. They also greatly influence the city and county governments, and, with government officials and the city's business interests, they form an active and decidedly pro-growth regime. From time to time Democrats are elected to high city office, but they tend to share the general pro-growth orientation of the Titans and their supporters.[10]

Titans are not necessarily friends. In fact, there are legendary stories of battles among the Titans over community matters. They strive to keep most disputes out of the general public's eye. They are very successful at forming coalitions that advance their goals as individuals and at compartmentalizing their relationships. There are many examples of Titans engaged in a lawsuit against each other on one matter while drawing up contracts to work together on another matter. In response to the question "Isn't it difficult to be working together on one thing and suing each other on another?" one community influential told us, "Hey, after all, it's just business."

Titan membership changes over time as members age and cease active engagement both in the civic game and in their specific game, such as banking, when they achieve winning status. Sometimes members leave the Titans when business or professional reversals cause them to slip from leadership in the important game they once dominated. Take, for example, John B. McCoy and his father, John G. McCoy, of Bank One. They were top Titan members for many years and excelled because Bank One was a giant not only in Columbus but in the nation as well. The McCoys used their successes to enter into and then excel at the civic game. When John G. retired, John B. took over his family's membership in the Titans. Economic reorganization of Bank One and its merger with First Chicago NBD resulted in John B.'s relocating to Chicago. This took him out of both the local banking game and the civic game. Months later, when McCoy's role in the newly reorganized Chicago-based bank did not work out for him, he left the organization.[11] He returned to Columbus but was no longer the significant player that he once was in the civic game.

New members of the Titans emerge as new people come to the top winner's spots in their basic game. For example, Les Wexner, the driving force of The Limited's retail store empire, did not make the top ten Titan list in 1976 but was ranked as the number one Titan in 2000.[12] In that period, Wexner was able to translate his success in the fashion-retailing game into leadership in the civic game by accomplishing extraordinary charitable and visionary community projects.

The ongoing study of reputational power in Columbus shows that of the top ten Titans in 1976, none made the list in 2000. One family made the list at both times though. In 1976 John W. Wolfe was the top Titan. He held controlling interests in the Dispatch Printing Company, the Ohio Company, and

BancOhio. As one observer puts it, Wolfe was "the city's most powerful and feared man for two decades."[13]

Wolfe died from heart disease in 1994—unlamented in some quarters. As *Columbus Monthly* magazine puts it: "No longer does a Wolfe litter the landscape with the tattered remains of smashed projects and ruined careers as J.W. did by using the *Dispatch* as his blunt instrument."[14] The heir to the Wolfe family's corporate power and civic leadership status was his much more universally liked cousin John F. Wolfe. In 2000 John F. ranked as second only to Les Wexner, the department-store mogul. Wolfe's position among the top group of Titans was solidified by the role he played in the arena and stadium conflicts in 1996.

In that critical year, the Titans consisted of Les Wexner (The Limited), John F. Wolfe (Dispatch Printing Company, newspaper, television, and land development), Dimon McFerson (Nationwide Companies), John B. McCoy (Bank One, insurance and real estate), Frank Wobst (Huntington Bancshares), E. Gordon Gee (president of Ohio State University, big time education and college sports), Ron Pizzuti (Pizzuti Companies, real estate development), Jack Kessler (New Albany Company), Greg Lashutka (mayor of Columbus), and Alex Shumate (Squire, Sanders, and Dempsey).

Not all Titans became players in all civic issues. They used a number of criteria in picking and choosing their concerns. These included their own personal or corporate interests, the costs/benefits/risks of involvement, and their long-term strategy in playing the civic game. In the arena- and stadium-redevelopment issue, the most active Titans were John F. Wolfe, Dimon McFerson, Gordon Gee, Ron Pizzuti, and Mayor Greg Lashutka. Most of these players wanted the taxpayers to publicly fund a new downtown arena and stadium, and several non-Titans joined in this quest, including John H. McConnell and his son John P. McConnell, of Worthington Industries and the Columbus Chamber of Commerce. The success of John H. in bringing professional hockey to Columbus resulted in the listing of both McConnells as top Titans in 2000.

While individuals differ in their motivation for playing any game, the Titans and their associates who played in the arena and stadium issue shared, to differing degrees, mixes of the following motives: (1) the desire to bring professional sports to Columbus (For some, this was an opportunity to become owners of a professional franchise and thereby join the big time sports ownership game. For others it was an opportunity to help move Columbus into the "big time" of American cities.); (2) the desire to advance the downtown's physical and economic redevelopment through the construction of multipurpose arena and stadium facilities; (3) the desire to attract people back to the downtown to live, work, and shop; and (4) the thrill of pulling off a major project.

Another key player was a Columbus outsider, Lamar Hunt from Dallas. Hunt had already been a big time winner in the games of national high finance and big time sports ownership. In the latter world he established and owned both the Kansas City Chiefs football team and the Kansas City Wizards soccer team. By the early 1990s he had identified Columbus as a place ripe for major league sports. In a deal in 1994 he brought to Columbus an expansion major league soccer team, the Crew. During his quest for a new, publicly funded soccer stadium, he added local leaders to the team's ownership in order to cement the new tie between the franchise and the community.

Why would Hunt want to bother with Columbus given his Dallas and Kansas City connections? Insiders told us that among his motivations was advancing the cause of professional soccer in America by expanding the league into solid new markets such as Columbus. He would be able to do so by securing the economic position of his team, the Crew, and by creating a first-rate stadium. He also wanted to enhance his status as a player in the big time sports game, not only via the Columbus Crew but also by joining the Titans in their pursuit of a major league hockey franchise and a new hockey arena.

The Opposition

The Titans and Hunt faced stiff opposition to the soccer stadium and hockey arena scheme, however, for a citizens group fought them every step of the way in their efforts to build this facility at the taxpayers' expense. The opposition's strength stemmed in part from its mixture of people of very different political ideologies, including liberal Democrats, fiscally conservative Republicans, Social Democrats, Libertarians, Green Party members, historic preservationists, and members of neighborhood associations near the proposed site of the arena and stadium.

The core leadership of this oppositional coalition consisted of a small group representing the full spectrum of the members' ideologies. Its most visible spokesman was Richard Sheir, a political liberal, former state employee, and community activist known as the "arena slayer" for his role in defeating pro-growth tax issues in the 1980s. Sheir led the opposition against a 1986 attempt to build a downtown domed stadium and a 1987 attempt by the pro-growth interests to build an arena and convention center. One local weekly newspaper described Sheir as a "47 year old gadfly ... with a perfect track record."[15]

The opposition adopted the name of Voters against the Stadium Tax (VAST). Other members of the VAST leadership were also veterans of other public-interest and political campaigns. Several of them had started honing their political skills as student activists during their college years. They proved to be a formidable opposition.

The Ohio State University: The Colossus of Columbus

Also important in the civic game is the president of The Ohio State University. Whoever occupies that position plays a major role in representing the university in the community. In the past, the downtown leadership has had a major say in what went on at Ohio State, but that was when Columbus was a small town and the university was much smaller and less complex. The downtown leadership and the university president and other chief university administrators now deal with each other on a regular basis and behave like equal power brokers.

The tensions between the downtown and the university come and go and tend to be issue specific rather than generalized. Of course, many of the local leaders have attended OSU, and some have participated on its sport teams and in other campus organizations.[16] Ohio State can be a resource in some of the games played by the downtown leadership, and vice versa. However, neither wants any town-gown disputes to interfere with the larger games they each play. Nevertheless, the university administration is very sensitive to the fact that the downtown leadership is well connected to the state legislature and that the legislature ultimately controls the basic portion of the university's budget. Key state government leaders, however, do not see OSU as a province of Columbus's downtown elite. A statewide institution, OSU draws students and employees from all of Ohio's counties. They see the university as a major asset in the state's total economy and act accordingly by putting the university's interests above those of downtown Columbus.

E. Gordon Gee became president of OSU in 1990. A former president of West Virginia University and the University of Colorado, Gee had supported sports, especially football, because he believed that college sports play a vital part in maintaining school spirit.[17] He continued his support of athletics at OSU and even made appearances in the football team's locker room following a game.

On the surface, OSU's athletic program appeared robust. But Gee soon discovered problems within the athletic department. In 1993 the National Collegiate Athletic Association (NCAA) placed Ohio State on a one-year probation for violations in the men's basketball and men's and women's track and field programs because of a lack of "institutional control." Gee was determined to regain control of the program and to improve the profile and revenues of the athletic department in "a very positive way."[18]

While publicly supporting his coaches and the athletic program, Gee worked furiously behind the scenes to redirect the program to be more in line with his goals. He knew that he needed a new athletic director who could not only take charge of the athletic department but also refurbish and renew the university's aging sport facility infrastructure. Gee also wanted an athletic director who could generate new sources of revenue for the athletic department, while not detracting from the university's other fund-raising programs.

In 1994 Gee recruited Andy Geiger from the University of Maryland as athletic director for OSU. Geiger's reputation had been built on his performance as athletic director at Stanford University. There Geiger had been aggressive in seeking and spending money, and he had seen Stanford teams win twenty-seven national championships during his 1979–1990 term.[19] Although Geiger was in the midst of a rebuilding program at the University of Maryland, he was tempted by the challenge that OSU presented and was encouraged by Gee's enthusiasm in thinking big about the athletic department's future.

Geiger immediately began to revamp OSU's athletic department. After reviewing coaches' salaries and finding that OSU was paying its coaches below the average for like-sized institutions, he increased many of the salaries. He also retired or fired coaches that he thought could not deliver the kind of success he wanted at Ohio State. In addition, he added more staff to the department to improve its marketing and promotional efforts. Starting with a new $3 million baseball stadium, he began an impressive building program and made plans for a new basketball and hockey arena, a new track stadium, and major renovations to the aging football stadium. The cost of those renovations and the building program ultimately increased the indebtedness of the department so much that the university's trustees put a hold on future building plans.[20] Nevertheless, Geiger and Gee both believed that spending money on the sports infrastructure would ultimately bring profits and success to the university. They may have been correct. During Geiger's administration, the revenues of the athletic department increased

from $30 million to more than $70 million—the highest of all college athletics. Increased revenues poured in to the university. Football alone showed
a profit of $14.8 million in 1999. The board of trustees showed its appreci-
ation and raised Geiger's salary in 1999 to $250,000—nearly double the
$130,000 that he was offered in 1994.

Ohio State and Columbus Redevelopment: Campus Partners

As Andy Geiger began building athletic facilities on the west side of campus, Gee turned his attention to another important initiative—improvements
in the areas south and east of the campus. From 1900 through the 1960s, the
university area was a pocket of upper-middle-class housing. Beautiful Victorian homes lined Neil Avenue, which connects the south entrance of campus to the downtown business district. Since the 1970s, however, the
condition of housing in the campus area had deteriorated, especially south
of campus. Most of the single-family homes that once surrounded the university had been either converted to rooming houses or torn down and
replaced with high-density, low-rise apartment buildings. This happened
not only because of the housing needs of the growing student body, but also
because the city changed its zoning code to permit the development of
intensive rental structures for nonstudents near the university. The original
quality of many of these homes was well demonstrated by the fact that in
one portion of the area south of campus, a successful gentrifying neighborhood called Victorian Village slowly took shape.[21]

In 1971, recognizing the beginning of blight in the area, the city government, the university, and other area institutions established the University District Organization (UDO) as a planning agency for the university area.
The UDO developed plans to improve the local environment. Unfortunately, these plans were not followed by action, and the major neighborhood
shopping and entertainment sites for students became a seedy-looking area
of run-down buildings and rowdy bars.

Gordon Gee's inaugural tour as president included this unsightly area.
Concluding that this neighborhood had the potential to become a "very
grave problem," Gee determined to do something about it.[22] In 1992 he
appointed a task force to improve housing in the area and two years later
enlarged the scope of the initiative with another task force. Shortly after the
appointment of that second task force, an Ohio State student living in the
area was abducted and murdered. Revulsion over the murder and widespread disgust among local residents over the declining conditions in the

area enabled Gee to move forward rapidly with a comprehensive revitalization agenda. A new nonprofit organization called Campus Partners for Community Urban Redevelopment was incorporated in 1995. The corporation prepared a comprehensive revitalization plan, discussed the proposal with many citizens and experts, and ultimately won the approval of both the Columbus City Council and the University's board of trustees, which adopted the plan in mid-1997.

Gordon Gee demonstrated the university's commitment to the project by persuading the board of trustees to authorize an investment of up to $28 million in university endowment funds and unrestricted gift money to implement the Campus Partners plan over the next five years. This money allowed Campus Partners to buy property for redevelopment, and the city government began to aggressively enforce both the housing code and the underage drinking ordinances in the area. The Columbus Health Department and the Division of Refuse Collection also began to cooperate in implementing a systematic effort to target south campus.[23]

Campus Partners became a vehicle that enabled the university to interact with the city and with the community at large beyond its historic role as a provider of sports entertainment. Ultimately, the university hoped to magnify and secure the university's investment in the area by attracting many private investment dollars. Plans for a centerpiece project, the Gateway Center, at the 7.5-acre site called for nearly a quarter million square feet of retail and entertainment space, 90,000 square feet of office space, and up to 150 apartments for students and others. An ambitious spending program was envisioned with up to $15 million in public funds for infrastructure plus $50 million worth of land assembled by Campus Partners, as well as $70 million in private investment.[24]

For the Campus Partners' master plan to succeed, the university president had to remain on cordial terms with city officials. Unfortunately, town-gown relations became sorely strained when city officials attempted to locate a civic sports arena in the vicinity of south campus. A civic sports arena was never part of the original Campus Partners plan and did not figure in Andy Geiger's ambitious plans for OSU's athletic facilities. The acrimonious public debate over the civic arena thrust Gordon Gee into the center of the controversy.[25] The debate was costly to Gee. Although it solidified his reputation as a "mover and shaker," it also put him into conflict with some of the Titans and probably figured into his decision to leave OSU for Brown University in 1998.

By the mid-1990s the Titans, the university, and the antitax coalition had stadiums and arenas on their minds. They saw things very differently, though, and their differences came to a head in the fight over Issue 1—a proposed tax increase to fund a new downtown stadium and arena. We describe the development of the fight in the next chapter.

5

Issue 1: To Build an Arena and a Stadium

[This] is a soccer sucker tax.

—Doug Belmont, Columbus resident, before the vote on Issue 1

IN THE LAST decades of the twentieth century, big time sports expanded into many different cities. New sports franchises formed, and new owners joined the world of sports entrepreneurship. Successful local business people found that they could add to their status by becoming owners of professional teams. Meanwhile, fans adjusted to the loss of their favorite players as teams shifted locations or made trades of existing athletes.

New stadiums, arenas, and ballparks spread across the country as taxpayers put up millions of dollars for facilities that might otherwise have gone to pay for improvements in schools, housing, health care, and other human services. All the while, our major cities still faced troubles—spreading physical deterioration, increasing poverty, worsening financial problems, and decreasing investment in the downtowns.

In the face of this downward slide, the urban redevelopment game became much more difficult to play because federal programs assisting the cities provided only a trickle of resources compared to what had been available at midcentury. Through the creative use of available programs, some cities turned the situation around. The idea spread that downtowns could be saved if they connected to places attractive to businesses, shoppers, and residents. Proponents of this view envisioned downtown as a fun place, an entertainment district offering first-class music, drama, dining, and sports activities that appealed to a broad cross-section of the community.

Columbus was no exception to the push for business-district entertainment. As suburbanization drew away people, shopping, and jobs, its down-

62

town sorely needed investment. The Columbus Titans and their friends in the business and government growth coalition worked diligently for at least fifteen years to turn the city around. By the mid-1990s, several major revitalization projects were either completed or underway, including new state and private sector office buildings; a large, new, upscale shopping mall; several new or refurbished hotels; a new county criminal-justice center; a new center of science and industry; several new or restored theaters; a world-class convention center; an upgraded farm market; and high-rise luxury condominiums. Public parks and spaces were created or upgraded. In addition, gentrification spread into several of the neighborhoods near downtown. And inner-city neighborhood associations became increasingly feisty and vociferous and demanded that city government pay more attention to their problems.

In addition, people enjoyed summer festivals—arts, jazz, ethnic, blues—along the improved banks of the Scioto riverfront in the heart of the central business district. Nearby businesses prospered along High Street, the main north-south street passing through the heart of downtown, a thoroughfare lined with all manner of art galleries, boutiques, hostelries, and eateries. This redevelopment stretched from the northern tip of downtown to just south of Ohio State's campus area, a lively stretch known as the "Short North" bounded by gentrifying neighborhoods to the west and east (see Figure 2 in Chapter 4).

Yet downtown was still in trouble. The northwest corner of the central business district was particularly in need of a facelift. It was the site of the former Ohio Penitentiary (Old Pen), a complex of a dozen or so buildings collapsing from neglect. It had become a safety hazard to passersby, and much of it had to be razed. The state of Ohio eventually passed ownership of the Old Pen site to the city, a problem that remained unsolved through the administrations of several mayors.

How could downtown redevelopment be moved ahead? To the Titans, what could be better than to link a new professional sports franchise for the city with a new hockey arena and soccer stadium located on the Pen site? Such a project could enhance the operation of the nearby convention center and stimulate a business comeback of the northwest sector of the downtown. Several of the Titans, known locally as the "Dream Team" because of their collective social and business prominence, had a good shot at obtaining a National Hockey League franchise. There was a catch, however: The Dream Team needed an arena, and they wanted the taxpayers to pay for it.

The winter and spring seasons of 1997 in Columbus were marked by a heated battle over a ballot issue known as Issue 1, which asked voters to support a three-year sales-tax increase to construct both an arena and a stadium that would house professional sports and other entertainment events. Issue 1 was played for very high stakes, and its passage would result in some very desirable outcomes.

Taxpayers would provide the money for the construction of a hockey arena, and the hockey arena would secure the Dream Team's entrée into the world of big time sports entrepreneurship. Taxpayers would also pay for the construction of a soccer stadium, and that would ensure that Lamar Hunt's professional team, the Crew, would remain in Columbus. In addition, the construction of the soccer stadium and hockey arena on the site of the old, decrepit Ohio Penitentiary would be a major catalyst for the revitalization of the rundown northwest section of downtown. The hockey arena, given its proposed location, would provide a much-needed expansion of the convention center's meeting space and would thus help attract the largest conventions to Columbus.

For the populist opposition group, the defeat of Issue 1 would be a major political victory. In their view it would be a significant step forward in their continuing battle against the top-down, local government's and business community's support of corporate welfare, the waste of public funds, and taxpayer exploitation. The opposition had beaten the Titans earlier on arena-tax issues, but this time the stakes were higher. To overcome the resources that the Titans would pour into the campaign against them, the opposition leadership would have to use their most persuasive skills because this was their only weapon. They had virtually no finances to bring to the fray.

Issue 1 Background

Several separate matters became intertwined and tangled at the time of the Issue 1 sales tax battle.

- There was active planning of two arenas. OSU and the downtown pro-growth coalition each planned to build an arena. These arenas would only be two and one-half miles apart. Indeed, they would be in sight of each other.

- The Titans kept up their ongoing efforts to bring major league sports to Columbus.

- The Franklin County Convention Facilities Authority (FCCFA) planned to undertake a major expansion of the convention center that would include a major arena/convention center on the Pen site.

- The sense grew among people in Columbus as well as across the country that the big time sports entrepreneurs who demanded public funding for their new stadiums and arenas were exploiting taxpayers.

Dueling Arenas?

Andy Geiger, Ohio State's athletic director in the 1990s, pursued a major upgrading and expansion of the university's athletic facilities (see Chapter 4). Building a new arena *on campus* was the centerpiece of his plans, and it was to be home to university basketball and ice hockey. It would also host other entertainment and university functions.

Yet OSU was not the only Columbus organization planning for a new arena. The Franklin County Convention Facilities Authority, an independent public authority, but an important and powerful arm of the local pro-growth regime, also wanted an arena. The FCCFA managed the convention center, which was funded by a local hotel-motel bed tax, and it wanted an arena so it could book shows and sports events and thereby attract more visitors. The center was located on the north end of the central business district.

The state of Ohio had granted the FCCFA, as a public authority, the right of eminent domain, the authority to take private property for market-value price for use in the authority's activities. The Titans could use the FCCFA to further their ambitions for downtown by acquiring property near the Old Pen site—an arena added to the convention center would revitalize the north part of town *and* solve the problem of the Old Pen eyesore.

This seemed reasonable because convention business had been good. Between 1993 and 1996 the number of conventions the center hosted rose from 446 to 702. Attendance grew from 686,165 to 825,955. The local economic impact went from $402.8 million in 1993 to $512.0 million in 1996.[1] Yet the FCCFA believed the center could do even better with more assembly space and improved facilities. This looked like an attainable goal and one well worth pursuing. It made sense to the downtown leadership that an arena should be adjacent to or part of the convention-center complex. It would help the center expand its available convention dates and offerings and generate revenue from nonconvention activities. Furthermore, it would provide a venue that professional sports would find attractive.

Both the downtown interests and OSU wanted state money to help with their arena plans. The state of Ohio's 120th general assembly appropriated $15 million for OSU's arena but attached serious strings to the offer. Most importantly for our story, the state's capital-improvement budget legislation required the university to consult with the city of Columbus about "specific site, use, and operations" for the OSU arena.

The legislature's requirements were a response to three concerns. First, many of those inside and outside the legislature felt that Columbus could not support two new arenas in proximity—one downtown and one on campus. Second, the state could get stuck financially with an unsuccessful hockey arena venture. Third, several local elites wanted to make OSU a partner in the downtown project as long as OSU would pay a good share of the construction costs. The elites had floated the idea that, as a good neighbor of the downtown development interests, OSU should move its home games in basketball, hockey, and other sports to a downtown civic arena. The university as usual strongly opposed such an arrangement. It contended that OSU activities must stay on campus, and it eventually consulted with the city, but only because the legislature demanded it.

On June 6, 1994, OSU's President Gordon Gee and Columbus Mayor Greg Lashutka appointed a two-person team to conduct a conversation between the university and downtown. An important Titan, developer, and sportsman, Ron Pizzuti, represented the mayor. OSU trustee George Skestos represented Gee. During their discussions they considered but dropped a proposal to construct a facility located midway between downtown and campus. That option was not acceptable to the university. It also was not the best alternative for the downtown interests because it did not contribute to the convention center's upgrading. In its report to President Gee and Mayor Lashutka on September 13, 1994, the committee concluded that "no single arena could serve the needs of OSU and the community."[2]

The committee provided several reasons for this conclusion. First, Ohio State's scheduling needs for sports, commencements, convocations, and other university-related activities simply did not provide enough open dates for community events and professional sports. Second, OSU planned to use tax-free bonds to fund the arena. For this type of funding, federal tax laws limited the extent of use that private profit-making entities could make of such a facility to only ten percent of all dates. Clearly, professional sports franchises and other profit-making ventures would not have been able to obtain enough dates under this law. Third, conference rules prohibited university-owned arenas from housing professional sports franchises. Fourth, an arena that complemented the downtown convention center would best serve the downtown redevelopment interests.

Although the committee concluded that "joint use of this facility is not practical," it did not give OSU a free hand. The committee approved the university's preferred on-campus site, adjacent to its new baseball stadium and close to its famous "horseshoe" football stadium. However, the committee said that OSU's arena use of nonuniversity event dates should complement rather than compete with a downtown civic arena. The committee also mandated that the OSU arena not contain skyboxes, club seating, or other amenities of the sort associated with professional sports arenas, an especially bitter pill for the university since these facilities have proven to be big moneymakers in other places.

That was not the only bitter pill to emerge from the committee's work, however. The committee's support for the OSU project meant that the state of Ohio would furnish $15 million to the university for planning and building its twenty-one-thousand-seat arena. At the same time, the state rejected the city's request for $1 million for planning for a downtown arena. Instead, the state passed legislation saying that any further state help for the city's arena project would depend on the local voters' willingness to pass a sales-tax increase. OSU's victory and Columbus's loss in the legislature intensified the tension between the university and downtown. Now it was clear that Mayor Lashutka and President Gee were rivals and not pals.

The town-gown friction was further exacerbated when OSU launched a commercial campaign to attract seat-license investors to its new arena. Radio ads promised seat-license buyers that they would qualify for priority tickets for events in addition to OSU sports. The ad promised that "when the circus comes to town, when big time wrestling takes center stage or when the rodeo gallops into Columbus," seat-license holders will have the first choice of tickets.[3]

This ad enraged the downtown interests, who thought that the parting of ways of the two arenas would give the downtown arena first claim to general entertainment events. Mayor Lashukta said that OSU's arena use "flies in the face of the commitment made back in 1994. . . . There was a clear indication that the university was pursuing its arena for gender equity in its sports program and as a convocation center and that [it] would not be pursuing activities in conflict with what would be offered at the arena being pursued Downtown."[4] The shock and anger the mayor expressed were also felt by many members of the downtown elite. They had been absolutely convinced that the OSU arena would not compete with a downtown stadium. Some of them felt they had been misled or tricked by OSU.

Given the intensity of the downtown reaction, Ohio State's Andy Geiger had the commercial pulled from the air. He said that the ads "caused confrontational feelings in this community that were not intended. . . . We intend to manage the building wisely and aggressively but not confrontationally."[5] Geiger went on to say, however, that a campus community of many thousands of students and employees needed a wide variety of entertainment events, and those interests should be reflected in the university arena's schedule. He also pointed out that the university arena would be in operation two years before the downtown arena. "We aren't going to sit here and have our arena dark in the meantime," he added.[6] OSU started a direct-mail campaign carrying essentially the same message. Clearly the arena race was on and OSU was ahead.

Soccer, Hockey, and the Dream Team

While Gordon Gee and Andy Geiger had focused on enhancements to the campus athletic and entertainment infrastructure, Titan Ron Pizzuti had taken the lead for many years in the city's attempt to bring major league sports to Columbus. He was a primary catalyst in the community leadership's development of a pro–major league sports stance. In 1994, when a major, professional soccer league was becoming a reality, Ron Pizzuti attracted sports entrepreneur Lamar Hunt's interest in Columbus as a potential site for an MLS franchise. Hunt regarded Columbus as ripe for such a franchise, but Pizzuti and other local investors refused to take on majority ownership. So Hunt, who was based in Dallas, bought sixty-three percent of the franchise and became the majority operating partner. The Columbus team was named the Crew.

OSU responded to the arrival of professional soccer in Columbus by striking a deal with the Crew that leased Ohio Stadium to the soccer team for home games and gave OSU game concessions and parking money. This deal was acceptable for the short run, but the Crew wanted to control its own facility and keep all of the revenues generated by attendance. So early on, it was clear that something had to be done about a stadium for the Crew. Hunt, when asked by a reporter if he were willing to come up with the cash for a stadium, said, "We are certainly desirous of being helpful in that respect. The Crew will be a prime tenant in the stadium, and we are certainly knowledgeable about what it takes to put a stadium together. We want to be part of the process."[7] Most observers took this to be a "no" to the prospect of Hunt's funding the stadium. In the long run, however, Hunt did much more than just contribute to the "process."

At this time it was becoming clear that the National Hockey League was preparing to expand and was looking for cities that would be profitable for the NHL. Ron Pizzuti and the other Titans believed that Columbus would be competitive as a location for an expansion team. The Dream Team seeking the franchise initially included Ron Pizzuti, John F. Wolfe, John McConnell, and Horn Chen, owner of the popular minor league Columbus hockey team, the Chill.[8] Pizzuti persuaded Lamar Hunt to join the group, after which Ameritech joined the others. As the Dream Team organized itself in October 1996, it took the name Columbus Hockey Limited Partners. Hunt would emerge as the managing partner if the franchise were awarded, a smart move, many observers thought, because Hunt had connections, a good reputation, and experience with the old American Football League (AFL), the Kansas City Chiefs of the current National Football League (NFL), and the Chicago Bulls of the National Basketball Association (NBA).

The NHL required a significant down payment from expansion-franchise applicants. The Dream Team paid a nonrefundable $100,000 for the application fee. If the franchise were awarded, the Dream Team would then have to raise another $75 million in addition to the operating money required to stock and run a team. To receive a franchise, the Dream Team would also have to have an arena that met professional standards, and they would have to sell a large number of season tickets ahead of time.

In the winter and early spring of 1997, there was serious movement in the quest for a hockey franchise. The Dream Team's presentation to the NHL's expansion committee in January was very well received, and it was clear to all that Columbus would be one of the cities on the final list for an expansion team. Later, when NHL Commissioner Gary Bettman and the league's expansion committee made its official visit to the city, they were treated to a rousing pep rally of Columbus fans who were demonstrating their support for the Dream Team's franchise application. The visit of NHL officials made it clear that Columbus was under serious consideration for a franchise. The NHL expansion committee was scheduled to meet on Friday, May 9, to award the franchise. By then the Dream Team had to have a firm commitment for an arena if it were to be awarded a franchise.

Realizing that the arena had to be committed by May 1997 and wanting to avoid paying for it themselves, the Dream Team collaborated with the Franklin County Convention Facilities Authority in an attempt to obtain public support for an arena. The FCCFA was glad to have the Dream Team on board. It now appeared likely that a potential NHL franchise would clinch taxpayer support for the proposed hockey arena.

The Convention Center

Serious planning for downtown sport facilities got underway in 1995.[9] The FCCFA began to think about building an indoor arena near the existing convention center site as well as an outdoor stadium a few blocks away that would be home to Lamar Hunt's Columbus Crew team. In March the Franklin County Commissioners, the mayor of Columbus, and the Greater Columbus Chamber of Commerce appointed a ten-member work group to develop soccer stadium plans under the auspices of the FCCFA. This group's members were a solid representation of the core of the downtown interests and included the city auditor, the county finance director, the president of the Columbus Association of the Performing Arts, the president of the Columbus Chill (minor league hockey team and potential arena tenant), the executive director of the Development Committee of Central Ohio (who also was senior vice president of the Greater Columbus Chamber of Commerce), the executive director of the FCCFA, the finance director of the city of Columbus, the vice president of marketing for the Greater Columbus Chamber of Commerce, the community relations director of the FCCFA, and the deputy county administrator.

The work group held its first meeting on April 3, 1995, and met over the next eight months more than fifty times. By June the FCCFA had decided it needed an economic-impact study to contribute to its plan development. For the study, the proposed stadium was originally described as a multipurpose outdoor facility with a total seating capacity of 30,000–35,000 people. The proposed arena was envisioned as a multipurpose indoor facility with a seating capacity of 19,000–23,000 people. It would host professional sporting events, concerts, family shows, and high school basketball games (at that time the plans were vague as to which professional sports team would use the indoor arena).

The competitively bid contract for the study was awarded to the California firm of Deloitte and Touche, LLP, which reported its results to the FCCFA late in the fall of 1995. The study's results were considered favorable for the pro-growth interests. Over a construction period of 2.5 years the project was estimated to generate $197 million in total citywide economic output, support 2,555 full-time equivalent jobs, and yield $1.8 million in new tax revenue. The study forecast additional tax revenues of

$767 million for Franklin County and $7.5 million for the state of Ohio. The annual operation was estimated to produce $100.4 million for the city, support 1,443 full-time-equivalent jobs, and generate $1.15 million in total municipal tax revenue. Additional tax revenue was estimated at $539,000 for the county and $3.8 million for the state.[10]

The Deloitte and Touche report was based on the optimistic assumption that professional sports would use the facilities and that most of the other available dates would be booked. Not factored in was the inevitable competition between these facilities and OSU's new arena, named the Value City Arena in the Schottenstein Center. Nevertheless, the downtown arena interests adopted the attitude that "if you build it, they will come."

On November 30, 1995, the work group met for a final review of the report. The report's favorable tone was taken as a green light by the pro-growth forces. Within a month the work group issued its own report to the community.[11] The report recommended the construction of a 21,000-seat arena at a total cost of $163.9 million and a 30,000-seat expandable stadium with a total cost of $112.9 million. The arena site would be at Nationwide Boulevard and Front Street, adjacent to the convention center. The stadium site would be just west of the arena on the land of the former Ohio Penitentiary.

To finance this massive construction project, the report recommended placing two separate ballot issues on the November 1996 ballot, one for the construction of the arena and the other for the construction of the stadium. The report stated that private interests should pledge 22 percent of the project costs (excluding parking and land) before the issue was placed on the county ballot. The report assumed that state involvement would provide grants totaling 12 percent of costs with another 3 percent in loans. It recommended that local public financing of the project would take the form of a half-percent countywide sales tax for three years. This was to be voted on in a countywide vote.

Clearly, much work needed to be accomplished in a short time for any of these plans to come to fruition. To get the ball rolling, the county commissioners decided to require that twenty percent of the construction costs ($43 million) had to be raised from the private sector before they would give their approval for placing a countywide sales tax on the ballot.

The Heart of the Issue 1 Battle

The Titans and other backers of Issue 1 faced two challenges. First was the challenge of raising private sector funds to get on the countywide ballot. Second, once the issue was on the ballot, they needed a campaign to get the voters to pass the proposed tax increase to build the hockey arena and soccer stadium.

The task of crafting a ballot issue and raising the private sector funds was assigned to Doug Kridler, executive director of the Columbus Association for Performing Arts. After months of hard work, Kridler, in his capacity as president of the Community Development Council, was able to raise the required private sector funds. Titan Dimon McFerson's Nationwide Insurance pledged $17.5 million, John McConnell's Worthington Industries pledged $5 million, and Titan John McCoy's Bank One pledged $35 million for the naming rights for the project.

In addition to the private funding, William Jennison, executive director of the FCCFA, figured that the proposed sales tax would raise $193 million, the state of Ohio would provide $41.5 million in grants, investment earnings would produce $5.2 million, and the resale of mixed-use land would bring in $5.2 million. All of this would materialize only if the commissioners approved a ballot issue for the tax and the voters passed the levy. Kridler's group planned to ask the county commissioners at their upcoming February 18, 1997, meeting to place the issue on the ballot. If the vote passed, the complex design work for the project would be completed in 1997, start-up construction would begin in 1998 and heavy construction in 1999, and arena move-in would take place in the fall of 2000. The stadium move-in would be in the spring of 2000.

In addition to asking the commissioners to place the issue on the ballot was the matter of the timing of the vote. It could be in either May or November. The arena proponents were divided about which date would be better. If May, there would be only about ten weeks in which to persuade the voters to support the issue—maybe too short a time to mount a convincing campaign. If November, the arena tax might come up against a raft of tax-increase proposals for schools, libraries, and mental-health issues—maybe a bad time for an entertainment issue.

Another matter that lurked in the background and lent urgency to the Issue 1 proponents was the timetable for the National Hockey League to make its decision about expansion. That decision was to be made at the NHL's May meeting, and that would be only three days after the potential May ballot. A firm commitment to arena construction had to be made by then. Given all of these considerations, it seemed that the vote, if there was to be one, had to be held in May. Even so, several of the Titans had reservations about the May ballot, and they worried that it would have less of a chance of success than if it were on the fall ballot. They called another meeting to rehash the decision about the ballot date a week before the commissioner's meeting, but the outcome was the same—they would go for May. The issue had momentum now, and further delays might weaken the enthusiasm.[12]

The first head-to-head skirmish between pro and oppositional interests took place at an open hearing conducted by the commissioners on February 18, 1997. At the hearing, eighteen people spoke in favor of placing the issue on the May ballot and eleven against.[13] The speakers supporting May used both pro-growth logic and passion. Missing from the meeting, however, were presentations by the core elite involved in the quest for professional hockey—Crew owner Lamar Hunt, developer Ron Pizzuti, Worthington Industries' John McConnell, and newspaper publisher John Wolfe. They trusted their lieutenants to carry the day, and carry the day they did. Some observers interpreted the absence of the Titans from the meeting as the Titans' awareness of image problems and their reluctance to have the issue viewed as "toys for rich boys."

The opposition was much more individualistic and populist in argumentation. While it covered the full political spectrum from very conservative to very liberal, the opposition united behind one sentiment: no tax money for the hockey arena and soccer stadium construction and no ballot in May. At this point, the best way for the opposition to win was to convince the commissioners to refuse to place the issue on the ballot. The opponents argued their case well, and it became very clear that there was to be no middle ground on this matter and no room for compromise.

At the end of the meeting, the commissioners voted unanimously to put the proposed tax on the May ballot—all in one package: Issue 1. For good or ill, Issue 1 linked the fates of the hockey arena and soccer stadium. The issue called for a three-year, half-percent, countywide sales tax for the hockey arena–soccer stadium project. If the proposal passed, the county sales tax would be raised from 5.75 percent to 6.25 percent. Proponents estimated that the tax would raise $192 million of the $277 million needed for the project. Several members of the opposition thought the commissioners' vote was a "done deal" from the start, given their ties to the city's political regime. Regardless of the accuracy of that claim, the hearing gave both sides an opportunity to articulate their positions.

The Issue 1 Campaign Heats Up

The county commission meeting adjourned after scheduling the vote on

Issue 1 for the May election. This signaled the start of the campaign in earnest. One local paper's headlines screamed in large, bold print, "THE THRILL OF VICTORY" to describe the county commissioners' support of the arena backers. The paper went on to say that Richard Sheir, "the leader of the anti-arena movement, had just been dealt a serious blow. The first official engagement of the arena battle had gone, decisively, to the other side."[14]

Sheir did not agree. He knew that, at best, this was only a minor skirmish in a much longer war. In response he said, "This is exciting, a really exciting time for this city. . . . People from the left and right, all different kinds of people coming together, finding common ground."[15] In contrast, the Wolfe-owned *Columbus Dispatch* described Sheir's allies as a rag-tag coalition dedicated to killing the issue.

The opposition was far from rag-tag, however. Active in the defeat of previous arena issues, Richard Sheir (see Chapter 4) had been dubbed the "Arena Slayer" by one local paper, a nickname that stuck and conferred on Sheir celebrity cachet.[16] Over the course of the campaign, he ably translated this reputation into media access in which he surpassed the media attention given to the downtown interests. Sheir was experienced in community conflict, savvy about power and politics, articulate without being offensive, and adept in putting together a working oppositional coalition. The only criticism of Sheir by his anti-arena associates was, as one put it, that he could be "a loose cannon and obsessive. Things were fine as long as Richard could be kept on message." The members of his coalition all agreed, however, that he had the fire, the experience, and the energy needed for a powerless and underfunded group of citizens to take on the powerful downtown interests and have a chance of winning. He was the right person at the right time and place for this campaign.

Indeed, Richard Sheir began his oppositional campaign before the commissioners' meeting. The week before that event, Sheir captured the limelight at a news conference held in the lobby of the Franklin County Courthouse. There he decried the proponents' attempt as part of the arena plan to have the taxpayers pay for a $21-million garage that was expected to generate $2.4 million in annual revenue. Sheir argued that it would be better for local taxpayers if the garage's construction were financed through revenue bonds that would be repaid from parking revenues. He also criticized the plan's call to set aside $14.75 million of the proposed sales tax to cover operating expenses. This amounts to "excessive taxation," Sheir argued, and provided an "operational subsidy for the whole project."[17]

The arena proponents reacted quickly to Sheir because the parking revenues were targeted to be the reserve funds for keeping the project afloat. Bill Jennison, the convention center's executive director, said, "Whether it's parking revenues or operating reserves, Richard Sheir seems to want to strip from the project the layers of protection [that] the work group included for the taxpayer."[18]

Sheir's message expressed the view of many community members, however. One resident asked a telling question in a letter to the editor. "Haven't we already said 'no' and on four separate occasions?" he wrote. "How is it under these circumstances you bring this project back before us? We have given you our will: we will not pay for this foolish rich man's folly with our tax dollars." Going further, the resident called Issue 1 "an insult, a travesty of your duty to us and a complete violation of our public trust in you that borders on political and fiduciary malfeasance in office."[19]

The downtown interests dismissed this reaction as a fringe response that was not representative of the general public. They assumed that the public would support the project. As matters played out, the downtown interests were wrong. This person's views were mainstream for the voters.

Sheir's group gained strength from its diversity because several able community members who were experienced in local political battles joined him. They included Libertarians, Greens, Democratic Socialists, Democrats, and Republicans. In addition, neighborhood Not In My Back Yard (NIMBY) activists in the Short North and Victorian Village joined the anti–Issue 1 coalition on the grounds that the additional traffic and noise generated by stadium and arena events would contribute to a declining quality of life in their areas. Some historic preservationists joined the opposition, too; they were especially disturbed by the plans to complete the leveling of the historic Ohio Penitentiary that was part of the preparation of the arena and stadium site.

As varied as these components of the coalition were in general political philosophy, they agreed on one overarching position—that the arena tax issue had to be killed. Heather M. Loughley, a member of the local Libertarian executive committee and Voters against the Stadium Tax (VAST) cochair, said, "We may have different reasons for opposing the tax, but we do oppose it."[20] VAST cochair Mark Higdon, a classic low-tax Republican and one-time member of the Franklin County Republican Central Committee, said that there "is always an issue that will bring political enemies together in a common cause and this is one of those issues."[21] Third cochair of VAST, Dennis Knepley, a treasurer for the Central Ohio Green Party, argued that stadiums and arenas should be located on the outskirts of the city and not downtown, which should be embellished with parks and open greenbelt areas. George Boas, cochair of the Democratic Socialists of Central Ohio, spoke for most of the opposition when he called Issue 1 pure and simple "corporate welfare!"[22]

During the campaign Richard Sheir of VAST and Doug Kridler of Citizens for a Downtown Future and president of the Community Development Council roamed the county making their cases daily. They attended citizens' gatherings of all types—morning coffees, luncheon meetings, neighborhood interest-group sessions, and community-service organizations meetings. They became hot items for the local media, both print and electronic.

Other members of both the pro–Issue 1 group and the oppositional coalition made public appearances as well. They went to places as varied as suburban newspaper offices and inner-city African American churches. Both the opposition and the pro-arena groups developed Internet web sites to express their positions. This was a new and particularly good strategy in a white-collar, professional town that served as a corporate home to computer-information businesses. Many observers argued that the opposition's web site was better at presenting its case than the pro–Issue 1 site.

Hunt Steps Up

All through the short campaign, the opposition attacked Hunt as an outsider who could easily move the Crew to another city at any time he wanted. Essentially, the argument was that he simply could not be trusted. To counter this, Hunt made a long-term commitment to Columbus sports and entertainment. In a letter of intent to the Franklin County Convention Facilities Authority signed 25 days before the vote, Hunt and the Hunt Sports Group agreed that Hunt would share some of the operating *profits* with the community as well as provide a number of other tangible benefits in exchange for the exclusive right to control and manage the soccer stadium and hockey arena and the related parking facilities and to collect *all* revenues from the use of the facilities. These included a set of 25-year leases for each facility, payment of rent to FCCFA of $3 million per year for the duration of the leases, and a guaranteed profit payment to the FCCFA of $200,000 per year for 25 years.

Hunt was also willing to provide Franklin County residents with priority ticket-purchase opportunities and to operate the facilities in such a manner as to secure prime tenants including Major League Soccer and NHL hockey. He promised to work with the FCCFA to keep design and construction within the established budget and cover all of the operating costs, thereby relieving the city of Columbus, Franklin County, and the FCCFA of fiscal responsibility for revenue shortfalls.

Richard Sheir reacted swiftly to Hunt's offer. He said that this deal between Hunt and the FCCFA was a giant-sized, unbid contract between a public agency and a private organization. He asked, "How are we to know Hunt Sports is the best bidder for the project when it isn't a public bid?" Sheir also pointed out that cost-containment measures applied to operation and not to construction overruns. He argued that the cleanup of the Old Pen site portion of the project might reveal that the site was contaminated and would require a very expensive cleanup. This was not reflected in the proposed budget. Who, Sheir wanted to know, would pay for that?

Responding to Sheir, convention facilities executive director William Jennison said that he believed the Hunt deal "guarantees a profit" and protected against losses and that nobody but Hunt can do that."[23] Other Issue 1 proponents were no better at replying to VAST's criticism. They could only promise that the FCCFA would simply work to contain costs.

Gordon Gee Steps Up

In addition to Lamar Hunt, OSU's President Gordon Gee played a prominent public role as a supporter of Issue 1. In many ways his participation was very curious and certainly did not seem to advance the chances for Issue 1's passage. Even though relations between Ohio State and downtown were strained over the potential competition between OSU's new Value City Arena and the proposed downtown hockey arena and soccer stadium, the downtown interests had named Gordon Gee as a cochair of the pro–Issue 1 campaign. Social pressure on Gee was high. How could Ohio State's top man risk his reputation as a good community citizen and not get on board? Campus insiders figured that Gee was just going through the motions in order to ease tensions with the Lashutka administration. Serious opponents of Issue 1 also viewed it as a public-relations move. Everyone knew that the campus arena project was Gee's real priority and that he would do anything to protect OSU interests.

Gee made appearances supporting the issue, gave interviews, and even appeared in television and radio commercials. However, the commercials proved to be disastrous for the pro–Issue 1 supporters. Gee, normally a highly energetic, ebullient, and intelligent communicator, displayed none of those characteristics in the commercials. Many observers thought that he looked dour, strained, and sounded unenthusiastic—not at all like his normal self. The ad was pulled after a few days, but by then the damage was done, and the message was clear that Ohio State's interests were first, last, and always Ohio State. To make matters even worse for Issue 1, President's Gee's wife, Constance, wrote a letter to the editor of a local paper that seemed to speak out *against* the issue.

In this chapter we saw how a number of separate matters became intertwined in Columbus at the time of the Issue 1 sales-tax initiative. The Titans worked on attracting professional sports teams to Columbus. The FCCFA included both an indoor arena and an outdoor stadium in its plans for an expansion of the convention center. OSU made plans to build its own indoor arena, which would compete with a downtown facility. Meanwhile, people in Columbus, as well as elsewhere in the country, were becoming sensitive to the fact that big time sports entrepreneurs were exploiting taxpayers through demands for public funding for their new stadiums and arenas. In the next chapter we see how these matters are fought out when we observe the final weeks of the campaign and the vote on the Issue 1.

6

From Win-Lose to Win-Win

I said time and time again during the Issue 1 campaign that if we stop this tax in its tracks, it will create the opportunity for a private plan.

—Mark Higdon, Cochair of VAST—the organized opposition to Issue 1

THROUGHOUT THE winter and early spring of 1997, the Issue 1 campaign was fought rough and tumble all over the county—in public forums, on radio and television, and in the newspapers. Issue 1 proponents told the Columbus and Franklin County voters that the community really needed the arena and stadium—now called by the proponents the Downtown Family and Sport Entertainment District. It would make downtown a center for family entertainment, they said. It would bring an NHL hockey team to town. It would encourage further economic rejuvenation of downtown. Most importantly—it would put Columbus on the map. The proponents thought that by framing the issue this way, they could get the support of the majority of voters.

They thought they could persuade women voters with the "family" part of the concept, and they thought they could win the young male voters who would want to see big-league, professional sports. They hoped they could get the concertgoers who regularly drove to Cleveland, Cincinnati and Indianapolis for the big shows to vote for an arena downtown. They thought they could gain support from the suburban soccer parents who drove their kids all over the metropolitan area for games, and they thought they could win the Black voters with the lure of more downtown jobs. They also thought they could get the independent business class who regularly lined up behind the chamber of commerce issues.

All through winter and early spring, however, the opposition stayed on their message and framed their anti–Issue 1 stance in terms of corporate welfare. The dissenters knew from past experience that Columbus voters were not inclined to support tax increases unless there was a demonstrable payoff, such as mental health services, a library, and improvements in children's welfare.[1] The opposition was careful to say they were not against the building of a soccer stadium and hockey arena per se; what they were against was asking the public to fund what the corporations should fund themselves.

Win-Lose

Paying the Price

The tough campaign took its toll on the participants. Doug Kridler, point man for the Issue 1 proponents, and Richard Sheir, point man of the opposition, grew weary from their nonstop campaigning.[2] As draining as the campaign was for those two, it was Mayor Greg Lashutka who paid the biggest physical price for Issue 1.

The mayor's fifty-third birthday on March 28, 1997, had to be one of his least happy celebrations.[3] He held his weekly cabinet meeting that morning and was treated to a birthday muffin decorated with the appropriate candle. After blowing out the candle, he headed to the emergency room at OSU's hospitals to have a persistent chest pain examined. He was admitted immediately and fortunately survived a heart attack in reasonably good condition. After days of intensive observation he was released with the admonition: no more sixteen-hour days, no more fast food, and regular heart-rehab exercise. The mayor counted himself lucky. After returning to work, he said that his illness made him clearly see that his family was what really mattered the most. In fact, in the flurry of TV commercials shortly before the vote on Issue 1, Mayor Lashutka told viewers that his heart attack helped him focus on what really mattered in life—his family and his community—and that was why he supported the Downtown Family and Sports Entertainment District.[4]

April Surprises

By the middle of April the Issue 1 campaign had saturated the news. By then, Columbus residents pretty well knew what was at stake and the arguments on both sides. The poll results made it look doubtful that Issue 1 would pass. The *Columbus Dispatch* poll, considered by many polling experts as one of the most accurate in the country on electoral issues, had Issue 1 going down by 55 to 38 percent.

By this time the opposition became emboldened as they sensed victory. In fact, Richard Sheir gave his opposition leadership colleagues a major surprise as well as "the fits" when on his own, he called a highly placed Franklin County administrator and told him that he, Sheir, would support the arena if the county would yank it from the forthcoming ballot, drop the soccer stadium, and finance it the way Sheir wanted them to finance it— without a tax. Sheir, in effect, was offering the proponents a draw, but no one saw it that way.[5] The proponents said that Sheir was just grandstanding. With Hunt's need for a stadium, there was simply no way for Sheir to be taken seriously. Moreover, Sheir's colleagues in the opposition were shocked that he would go so far off message when victory was so close. They wanted Sheir just to cool it and stay on message—too much was at stake.

Peter Karmanos Jr., Detroit businessman and the owner of the NHL's Hartford Whalers, initiated a second April surprise in the Columbus community. Karmanos was planning to relocate his franchise from Hartford to a city that had a higher potential for successfully supporting a big-league hockey team. Columbus was at the top of his list. Karmanos saw the lack of an arena as only a temporary problem. In fact, he considered as a short-term solution the possibility of remodeling an unused hangar at the city's main airport. He said this would work until the city built an arena for his team. The Issue 1 proponents were quite upset with Karmanos. They saw all their hard work in getting Issue 1 on the ballot, building support for hockey and soccer, raising funds to campaign, and carrying the issue to the community coming to naught. They viewed Karmanos as a usurper who would ruin things for the downtown elite by stealing away their opportunity to become big time sports owners. They saw him as playing off Columbus against other cities in a bid to get the best possible deal for his team. They also regarded Karmanos as confusing the voters at a crucial, make-or-break time in the Issue 1 campaign. Ultimately, Karmanos decided to take his franchise elsewhere. He left few friends in Columbus. Indeed, many downtown elite blamed Karmanos for the defeat of Issue 1.

John McConnell, a former investor in the Pittsburgh Pirates, a successful industrialist and principal of Worthington Industries, and a Columbus civic leader, gave the third April surprise to the National Hockey League

commissioner Gary Bettman. A month before the vote on Issue 1 Bettman
and about a dozen NHL owners and executives visited Columbus. It was the
league's official tour of the city as a possible site for an expansion franchise.
During the visit the Bettman group met with the Dream Team. In that session Bettman asked Hunt whether he was prepared to go forward with the
franchise and the project if the voters turned down Issue 1. Hunt told
Bettman that he would not go forward if that happened. Essentially this
meant that Columbus would be out of the running if Issue 1 failed. The
NHL group was not pleased by Hunt's response since it had identified
Columbus as a very desirable place for a franchise. As the meeting was
coming to a close, John McConnell, who had been sitting in, pulled
Bettman aside and told him, "Listen, we're going to make this work. If the
referendum fails, we'll figure out another way to build a building."[6]

The Voters Decide

As the Issue 1 campaign moved along, endorsements poured forth. Most
suburban mayors supported Issue 1—including those in Dublin, Upper
Arlington, Bexley, Grandview Heights, Gahanna, New Rome, Hilliard, Val-
leyview, Harrisburg, Groveport, Marble Cliff, Obetz, Urban Crest, Worthington, and Riverlea. This was great news for the Dream Team. The
suburban soccer parents were a group of voters especially targeted by their
campaign. Others gave their endorsement as well. Michael Coleman, a
Democrat, the president of city council, future Columbus mayor, and a
leader in the local African American community, gave his support to Issue
1. The Columbus Educational Association and the Columbus Public School
teachers' union, some five thousand members strong, also supported the
cause, saying that the increased job base generated by Issue 1 would be
good for local education. Many other civic bodies and prominent players in
the community also got on board.

City council president Coleman's backing was especially prized because
two other minority-community leaders—state senate minority leader Ben
Espy and state representative Charleta Tavares—opposed Issue 1. Among
their reasons for opposition was that the tax money that Issue 1 raised might
be needed for education since the state was reexamining the whole issue of
how Ohio schools were funded. They also stated that Issue 1 would hurt
poor people because they paid a larger share of their income in sales taxes
than more affluent citizens. Espy and Tavares pointed out Columbus's long
history of taxpayers' bailing out projects organized by the local business

leaders. They raised the question of the need for a downtown arena considering the availability of the new Ohio State arena. The opposition was most pleased to have these two state officials on their side because they were highly respected in both the minority community and the wider community.

While the pro-development group won the endorsement war, the weekend before the election it was clear to those following the polls that they would lose the Issue 1 election. The pro-growth group was incredulous. How could the voters not see the wisdom of the proposal? It would cost the average family only another $70 a year in sales tax. Was it not worth it?

The voters said "No." On election day, despite spending $1.2 million on its campaign compared to only a few thousand by the opposition, the pro-development group lost, 56.3 percent to 43.7 percent. Issue 1 lost in 60 of the city's 74 wards—especially those that were predominantly Black, working class, and lower-middle class. Issue 1 also lost in 9 of 14 suburbs and in 25 of the 26 outlying townships. The daily paper summed it up when a reporter wrote, "many saw the issue only in terms of taxpayers building a venue for wealthy owners."[7]

Reactions

In its final form, the passing of Issue 1 would have raised $203.5 million in increased sales taxes over three years. This would have paid two-thirds of the costs of the arena and stadium construction. An additional $57.5 million was to come from private sources, and it was expected that the state of Ohio would contribute $41.5 million more to the project. The city of Columbus would pick up the infrastructure costs required to locate these facilities in the old penitentiary site. To the elite, this sounded like a great deal. Voters did not agree. In fact, it was not a particularly good deal compared to projects in other cities. The average public/private split for other cities was 51 percent/49 percent. The bottom-line split of public/private funding for the Columbus project would run about 85 percent/15 percent.[8]

The Dream Team and the rest of the Titans saw the failure of Issue 1 as much more than just the defeat of a good construction deal. They considered it also to be a loss of a big time sports franchise, a loss of face for the city, and a loss of a major opportunity to reinvigorate downtown. Lamar Hunt said, "This will make it impossible for the National Hockey League to come to Columbus. I'll say again, we were at the 99.9% level as far as certainty of getting a franchise if the issue had passed."[9]

Others expressed their disappointment as well. "Columbus," said a *Dispatch* editorial, "will continue to miss many top-draw concerts and shows that other major cities enjoy. In the competition to provide an attractive civic environment, Columbus will remain behind places like Cincinnati, Indianapolis and Nashville, Tenn., which invest in this type of civic infrastructure."[10] Mayor Greg Lashutka simply said, "It's a huge lost opportunity."[11] And Columbus developer and Titan Ron Pizzuti complained that "folks think that it's a fat-cat enterprise, they should know that only eight (NHL) hockey teams made money last year. I think seven made money the year before. This was about the future of downtown and the region."[12]

The opposition did not gloat but made feisty statements at their victory party. "It's a credit to the good sense of the Franklin County voters," noted Mark Higdon, "that they have rejected another bad idea, as they have three or four times before,"[13] VAST cochair Heather Loughley said the results were "a tremendous victory for the people of Franklin County. Once again, the Republican and Democratic politicians of this city joined forces in an effort to raise our taxes. As a Libertarian, I am personally thrilled that the people had the courage to say 'no' to their ruthless campaign of bribes and threats. It's a mandate against corporate welfare. If the politicians come back with some other tax for this purpose, it will be an affront to the voters."[14]

Clearly, the tax opposition won on Issue 1, and the Dream Team and their downtown pro-growth allies lost. But was the game over? Many local people thought that a "plan B" was waiting in the wings. By that they meant that the Dream Team had planned all along to pay for the construction of their arena and stadium if the public rejected Issue 1. Pro-development insiders maintained that there was no plan B. Members of the opposition leadership said that if there was not already a plan B, then one would very likely emerge.

Win-Win

Word of the defeat of Issue 1 spread quickly to the New York offices of the National Hockey League. Commissioner Gary Bettman called Mayor Greg Lashutka and expressed his disappointment. He asked Lashutka whether there was another way that an arena could be funded. Bettman made it clear—no arena, no franchise, and this was "decision week" for the NHL.[15] A meeting was scheduled in New York for Friday, at which the NHL was to award the expansion franchises. Time was running out fast for the Dream

Team. The NHL committee met on May 9, three days after the Issue 1 defeat, and the members decided to delay any action on the applications for new franchises to give Columbus time to put something together. The next meeting of the NHL's decision-making group was scheduled for June 25. The Dream Team had a little over a month to find an alternative way to get the hockey franchise.

Dimon McFerson and Nationwide Step Up

On the morning after the defeat of Issue 1 the locals were discussing what should or would be done now. Nationwide Insurance CEO and Columbus Titan Dimon McFerson looked down from his office window on the thirty-seventh floor of the Nationwide tower on the degraded Old Pen area that would have been the site for the arena and stadium. When recounting those moments, McFerson said that he thought there had to be another way. He was mindful that an NHL franchise was there for the taking: "We are the largest top-50 city in America without a downtown arena. We need it for the vitality of downtown. We need it for work force development. We need it to support so many other things we are trying to do downtown."[16]

McFerson quickly decided to carry the ball himself in order to bring the arena to fruition. It simply was too good an opportunity to miss—both for the city and for Nationwide. After all, an arena would help Nationwide in several ways. It would protect the company's already sizable corporate investment in the north part of downtown. It would provide Nationwide with the Old Pen site, which was ripe for redevelopment. It would enhance Nationwide's position as a key player in urban redevelopment, both in Columbus and other cities.

Nationwide was a venerable Columbus institution.[17] Since its inception, Nationwide had been part of downtown Columbus. Over the years, as the company grew, it moved from one office building to another. Gradually it consolidated its operations into the northwest section of downtown. In 1951 Nationwide tripled the size of the building it had occupied on North High Street since 1936. In 1978, across the street from its North High Street headquarters, the company completed One Nationwide Plaza, a 40-story tower and the largest, single office building in central Ohio. In 1981 Two Nationwide Plaza, an 18-story building with tenant space, was finished. Three Nationwide Plaza, a 27-story building, was added in 1989, and in 2000 Four Nationwide Plaza opened. It is a 9-story building and, together with the others, provided more than 2.6 million square feet of office space.

In addition to building its corporate-office complex, Nationwide contributed to the redevelopment of this area by constructing six of the sixteen major buildings recently added to this part of the city and by partially financing two others. Including the convention center, which is just a couple of blocks north of the Nationwide corporate complex, the recent building construction in the area totaled more than $700 million.

For McFerson's arena plan to work, he needed five things. For starters, he needed an NHL franchise for Columbus and a favorable lease with guaranteed heavy use of a new hockey arena. He also needed access to the Old Pen site and to other properties in the area. He needed a favorable deal with the city for tax and infrastructure matters and an independent tie to the downtown leadership that would contribute to the success of the arena and the redevelopment of its neighborhood, which was soon to be called the Arena District.

In a matter of days McFerson took a trip to New York. He met with Gary Bettman of the NHL and told him of his decision to build the arena in order to keep Columbus in the running for a franchise. McFerson, with the assistance of Mayor Lashutka and others, had to help rally the Dream Team ownership group that was experiencing low morale in the wake of the Issue 1 defeat. According to Bettman, McFerson had to have a signed lease commitment before he could proceed with arena plans. The Dream Team ownership group had to have a lease for the arena for the NHL to keep them in the running.

To set the wheels in motion, McFerson presented a draft of a lease to Dream Team leader Lamar Hunt but received little response. With time running out, McFerson presented the lease draft to John H. McConnell, who then signed on as leader of the re-formed ownership group. Access to the Pen site would come from city council, and with Mayor Lashutka's help this was almost a sure thing. Access to the other properties would come from the Franklin County Convention Facilities Authority with its power of eminent domain.

A favorable tax and infrastructure deal with the city was also a certainty. In Nationwide's past redevelopment activities, the city had been most supportive. For example, in 1975, when Nationwide launched the development of its High Street complex, it made a tax-increment financing (TIF) agreement with the city by which Nationwide would pay its taxes on real estate improvements into a special fund rather than to the schools and other city and county agencies. The city used the special fund to pay for the physical and infrastructural improvements in the blighted area that Nationwide was revitalizing. These funds were essential for the development of the convention center. Without the city's arrangement with Nationwide, it is unlikely that the convention center would have been built at that time.

For the needed local independent tie, McFerson brought John Wolfe of the *Columbus Dispatch* on board for the arena project and the development of the Old Pen site. Nationwide would have a ninety-percent ownership share, and the Dispatch Printing Company would own ten percent. Informed observers saw this as an extremely shrewd move. By securing Wolfe's support for the project, they also guaranteed favorable treatment in the *Dispatch* regardless of any problems that might develop.[18] For many years the *Dispatch* had been active in urban revitalization efforts in downtown, so most locals did not see its involvement in the arena project as unusual. About this John Wolfe said that the Dispatch Printing Company "has unswervingly supported a Downtown arena because of the economic development and quality of life it brings to the city. To be competitive long-term, we need to have these facilities."[19]

The aggressive role the *Dispatch* played in Columbus's revitalization is not surprising. Locally owned newspapers, by their very nature, are place-bound businesses. A newspaper cannot just pick up and move if the local economy suffers a downturn. A newspaper must stick it out and make the best of it. This results in newspapers' tending to be strong civic boosters.[20] The *Dispatch* is an extreme example of such boosterism. It not only supports revitalization efforts, but also actually undertakes them itself.

Nationwide presented its arena plan to the city council on June 2, 1997—less than one month after the defeat of Issue 1. Nationwide and the *Dispatch* proposed to construct a $125 million arena. In return the city council approved for the Nationwide and *Dispatch* developers a favorable package that included a long list of essential items:[21]

- The city would cover the costs of road and other infrastructure improvements needed for the arena's development.

- The city would grant the developers a ten-year lease of the Old Pen site with an option to purchase the site at fair-market value during the seventh year.

- The city council would declare the arena site to be a blighted area so that the Franklin County Convention Facilities Authority could acquire private parcels of land at the site through its use of eminent domain.

- The FCCFA would lease the acquired land to the developers for ninety-nine years.

- The arena site would be exempted from real estate taxes. The developers would set aside a portion of ticket revenues (collected as a surcharge) to pay the Columbus public schools for any property taxes they would have received from the arena site.

- The city would complete an environmental cleanup of the Pen site. Later the site would be paved for parking, and a portion of the parking fees would be paid to the city.

Everyone understood that the deal hinged on the granting of an NHL franchise to Columbus: no team, no city council deal with the developers. The developers hoped to raise $44 million of their $125-million investment from the sale of seat licenses and luxury suites. Nationwide retained the naming rights for the arena. Naming rights are valuable; in the context of Issue 1, Bank One would have paid $35 million for them. However, with the defeat of Issue 1, Bank One unceremoniously withdrew its support from any further arena developments. The Bank One spokesperson said, "The contract was very specific. The money was for naming of the stadium, arena, and plaza in downtown Columbus. It was always understood that if the issue were to lose, . . . the offer is off the table. . . . We operate in twelve states, and we're looking for similar marketing opportunities in all of them. If we don't spend it at Front and Nationwide, we will spend it elsewhere."[22]

Bank One did spend it elsewhere. It bought the naming rights of the newly completed baseball stadium in Phoenix. From this point on, Bank One, formerly a significant player in the Columbus downtown games, was out of the picture. Some insiders said that, had the Columbus McCoy family still controlled Bank One as it had in the past, the company would have continued to support the private funding of the arena.

The Elite Fall Out, and John McConnell Steps Up

The defeat of Issue 1 left the Dream Team in disarray. Lamar Hunt was not interested in a privately funded arena, but John McConnell and others were willing to try it if Nationwide was willing to provide the capital. From all reports, immediately after the election, there was very little communication between Hunt and the others in the ownership group. Hunt, who had led the group during the campaign, returned to Kansas City. Meanwhile in Columbus, Mayor Greg Lashutka, John McConnell, John Wolfe, and the other Titans hurriedly tried to develop a plan to stay in the hunt for a hockey franchise.

With time running out, Nationwide presented the arena lease to Hunt as the leader of the ownership group. However, Hunt had problems with some elements of the lease and did not sign. Meanwhile, he had been talking to community leaders in northern Kentucky, across the Ohio River from Cincinnati. They told Hunt that they would provide him an arena at no charge if he would bring a team there.

Hunt's refusal to act on the lease did not sit well with Nationwide. With time for the lease signing about to expire, Nationwide presented a lease to John McConnell with more favorable terms than those presented to Hunt.[23] Hunt had not told McConnell that Nationwide and Hunt had been discussing a lease. McConnell first heard of the lease when McFerson contacted him. McFerson later said that he turned to McConnell in a last-minute effort to salvage the franchise opportunity. McConnell signed the lease as the leader of a reorganizing ownership group named Columbus Hockey (COLHOC) Limited Partners. With the signed lease, Nationwide approached the city council for its approval.

On June 4, the NHL deadline for Columbus to get its arena plan in place, McConnell had the arena lease in hand and submitted the franchise application under his own name to the NHL. The new ownership group maintained that the door was left open for Hunt to join them as long as Hunt understood that McConnell would be the managing partner. Hunt refused to join the new ownership group. There was some confusion at NHL headquarters as to who spoke for the Columbus application, but the league was pleased by McConnell's application. To the NHL, McConnell seemed to be the right man for the franchise.

On June 17 the NHL expansion committee recommended that Columbus enter the league with a franchise in the 2000–2001 season. Also on June 17 John McConnell and Wolfe Enterprises filed a lawsuit in Franklin County Common Pleas Court against Hunt. They claimed that Hunt had misrepresented the original investors (COLHOC) in his dealings with Nationwide. McConnell and Wolfe claimed that Hunt had breached his agreement with the other members of the ownership group by saying that the lease's terms were unacceptable and allowing the deadline to slide past without even responding to Nationwide. The suit also alleged that, on the day before the expansion committee meeting, Hunt requested that the NHL not award Columbus a franchise until the local ownership situation was clarified. The McConnell and Wolfe suit asked the judge to declare that the locals could acquire a team without Hunt.[24]

Hunt had twenty-eight days to respond to the lawsuit but took only a week. He did so by filing a countersuit. On June 23, two days before the NHL's executive board was to meet and finally award franchises, Hunt filed suit in Franklin County Common Pleas Court. His suit alleged that McConnell and Wolfe had violated their original agreement with him and that McConnell did not have the right to set up the second ownership group. The suit asked that Hunt be awarded the present-day value of the projected profits of the hockey team and arena for the next twenty-five years.

The next day, June 24, Gary Bettman of the NHL met with McConnell and Hunt in an attempt to resolve the ownership dispute between the two, but they produced no resolution. The next day, June 25, the NHL board approved both Columbus as a site for an expansion team and John McConnell as the controlling partner of the franchise.

Columbus's pro-growth interests generally were jubilant, as were the Titans and the local sports enthusiasts. A local team-naming contest was held, and the "Blue Jackets" won. Starting in the fall of 2000, then, the Columbus Blue Jackets would be playing their home matches in the Nationwide Arena. John McConnell became both an owner and a local hero.[25]

Not everyone was happy with the outcome, however. The lawsuits between Hunt and McConnell and Wolfe dragged on for two more years. Court decisions, appeals, depositions, and testimony regularly appeared in the local papers. Hunt also filed a suit in New York against Nationwide and the NHL for their roles in helping the McConnell group get the franchise. After both sides argued their cases through late autumn of 1999, exhaustion won out. Both sides agreed to quit and go their own way. Hunt formally concluded things by withdrawing his suit in the New York court.

The net result of all the maneuvering in and out of court was that the Columbus Dream Team Titans got their franchise without any strings to Hunt, and Hunt was squeezed out of the hockey franchise with nothing to show for it except lawyers' fees. The NHL put a franchise into a strong market; Nationwide got its shot at further redeveloping the downtown. And McFerson and McConnell became larger-than-life local heroes.

Figure 4. John H. McConnell, local hero and owner of the Columbus Blue Jackets, shown in his suite at the Nationwide Arena during the first home exhibition game. Source: *Columbus Dispatch*, used with permission.

The Odyssey for the Soccer Stadium

The arena scramble that followed the rejection of Issue 1 did not include any consideration of a soccer stadium for Hunt's team, the Columbus Crew. Hunt and his soccer franchise were now on their own. For the Crew, Columbus was too good a market to leave. A playing facility had to be found in short order, however, because the allowed time for the Crew's playing at Ohio State's stadium was running out fast. Jamey Rootes, the Columbus Crew team president, commented about finding a new home for the Crew, "I think it has now become an appropriate priority. I know it is for us and I think it is for the city too."[26]

The Crew had been playing home games at Ohio Stadium. It was accommodating of the university to open its facilities to the new soccer franchise. However, for several reasons it would not be particularly good for the Crew to stay there in the long run. The stadium floor was not the right size for soccer; the stadium's huge seating capacity worked against the right ambiance for soccer—in a venue that seats 90,000 people, a soccer crowd of 15,000 seems minuscule. For Crew night games, temporary lights had to be rented, trucked in, and set up at cost to the Crew of $20,000 per game.

Parking and concessions income, normally significant moneymakers for teams, went to the university. Furthermore, as a student athletic facility, the stadium did not sell alcoholic beverages, also a significant moneymaker for most stadium operators.

On top of all this was the fact that the stadium was scheduled to undergo a major overhaul and expansion that would necessitate the Crew's playing elsewhere for a couple of seasons. However, Ohio State's athletic director, Andy Geiger, and its president, E. Gordon Gee, facing heavy costs for the expansion and other construction projects, wanted to continue the connection with the Crew for financial reasons. The university suggested that the Crew's concerns about the stadium plant be incorporated into the remodeling plans. The university also suggested that, as an alternative, it could expand its new track and soccer stadium to twenty thousand seats to meet the Crew's attendance expectations.[27]

Something had to happen soon on the new soccer stadium front because the Crew had only one season left to play in Ohio Stadium. With the defeat of Issue 1, the team began a series of informal conversations with officials of suburban communities along the metropolitan area's interstate beltway, I-270. This arc of communities was called the "soccer belt" because of the rapid growth of youth soccer programs there and the increasing popularity of scholastic soccer for both boys and girls. These communities had supported Issue 1 and were home to the stereotypical "soccer moms and dads." One of these suburbs now had a chance to become home to the Crew. Early on, the affluent suburb of Dublin emerged as a leading contender. No stranger to professional sports, Dublin was the setting of Jack Nicklaus's Muirfield Village Golf Club and the site of the Professional Golf Association's annual Memorial Tournament.

By the end of September 1997 the Dublin city staff had briefed the city council on their talks with the Hunt group. Hunt signed a letter of intent to build a 30,000–35,000-seat stadium in the community. He envisioned the stadium as being expandable to 60,000 seats. The suggested 180-acre site was just west of the city, and Dublin proposed to buy it and annex it to the city. Annexation was possible if the county government would approve the transfer of the land, and that was likely to happen. The land would then be leased to the Hunt Sports Group, which would build and operate the stadium. Hunt would lease the land for $10 per year. The initial lease would be for 25 years and renewable for another 25. When the 50-year lease expired, the stadium would become city property.

The question that Dublin residents most frequently asked about this proposition was, "Who would pay for all of this?" The purchase of the 180 acres would be Dublin's responsibility and would cost the city $30 million. The city would use its right of eminent domain to acquire the land and would then lease it to the Crew. The Hunt Group would construct a no-frills stadium for $26.5 million. The annual debt service would be $1.9 million on a 25–30 year mortgage. To finance the construction, a nonprofit sports-development corporation would be formed, and they would sell taxable public bonds. Hunt would be the guarantor of the bonds. The City of Dublin would cover the infrastructure costs—constructing roads and extending water and sewer service. This would cost the city $10.6 million. The road construction would be paid for by property taxes generated by the stadium. Water and sewer lines would be financed through the city's current budget. Dublin would also have to provide off-site traffic control for at least twenty soccer events per year at a cost of $90,000. The city would pay Hunt another $62,500 per year to hold up to ten community events in the stadium.

Dublin's city council held a public hearing over the proposal, and six hundred residents attended. They seemed to be split pro and con. The arguments that night and in the ensuing months resembled those of the Issue 1 campaign of the preceding spring. Dublin residents were worried about traffic, noise, area flooding because of overdevelopment, alcohol sales, the possibility of the MSL folding or the Crew moving, the effect of spin-off development of hotels, bars, restaurants, and the like on city congestion and infrastructure and were also concerned about how the city's share of the costs would be covered without raising taxes in the future. The Dublin schools were concerned about the diversion of property-tax money from the stadium development into the provision for road servicing.

The city council had every intention of deciding the issue, apparently in favor. However, a group of citizens opposed to the plan drafted a petition and obtained enough signatures by November 11, 1997, to bring the matter to a public vote in February 1998. The pro-stadium forces organized a polit-ical-action committee to support their cause and were largely funded by the Crew and Major League Soccer. The opposition had fewer funds, but it well understood the mindset of the Dublin residents. As the pro- and anti-stadium groups contended with each other, the city of Dublin set about acquiring land for the stadium.

This venture was to come to naught, however. On February 10, the Dublin voters turned down the Hunt stadium deal 59 percent to 41 percent. Hunt now had to decide what to do next—the Crew needed the stadium in a little more than a year. The city of Dublin now had to decide what to do with the land it had acquired.

The next suburb to come forward was Gahanna. It too is located on the I-270 soccer belt. Gahanna was situated next to the metropolitan area's principal airport—Port Columbus. The land that Gahanna officials would have liked to develop for the stadium was adjacent to the airport. The airport authority caught wind of Gahanna's plan, however, and moved quickly to squash the community's hopes. The authority used its right of eminent domain to take the 122 acres of land, explaining that those acres were too close to the airport's landing and takeoff paths to be used for other purposes. The authority did not want a large structure and stadium lights creating a hazard for its air operations. It also knew that, sooner or later, the stadium managers and fans would complain about the takeoff and landing noise generated by the scheduled air traffic. Those complaints would put the authority in the middle of a noise conflict that could drag on for quite a long time.

Whatever was to happen next would have to be done without a public vote on a stadium. With the Dublin defeat and the earlier Issue 1 loss, the Hunt group was 0 for 2 in stadium referenda. Hunt's people met with the state of Ohio's economic development officials late in March. They suggested that the Hunt group look at the state fairgrounds (Ohio Expo Center) as a possible site and sent them to see officials at the Ohio Exposition Commission who controlled the fairgrounds. The north side of the fairgrounds had large parking lots and plenty of room for development. To be sure, the Ohio Historical Society's museum was located there as was Ohio Village, the society's reconstruction of a small Ohio village of the 1800s. The Historical Society's board of trustees had planned to build a warehouse and a service facility in the area, but there was ample space for location flexibility on the property.

The Expo Center land was a good choice. Interstate highway I-71 runs just by the east border of the center. It connects Columbus to Cleveland to the north and Cincinnati to the south. Interstate entrance and exit ramps lead directly to the fairgrounds entrance. The heart of downtown is only ten minutes to the south on I-71, and OSU is only about six blocks to the west. The Expo Center is surrounded by old working-class neighborhoods, but with the configuration of the freeway and the fairgrounds, those areas would be separated from the stadium. Tim Connolly, president of Hunt Sports Group, said, "there is 'no down side' to this site. It is in the heart of Columbus. It is in the city limits of Columbus. Mayor Lashutka wants to keep it in Columbus. When you are six or eight blocks from Ohio State, you're in the middle of things."[28] Others disagreed, however. The site sat too far from downtown to be a part of the city center's renewal. The construction of a stadium there would fall outside the domain of the downtown redevelopment game. Hunt would be free to do whatever he wanted in developing the soccer stadium as long as it was within the limits the Exposition Commission set.

Discussions between the Hunt group and the Expo Center representatives went well. The proposed deal was that the Expo commission would lease to the Crew 12–14 acres in the north parking lot of the fairgrounds for 25 years at a cost of $50,000 annually, plus about 25 percent of the parking income, which would amount to about $120,000 per year. The lease would be renewable for another 25 years and would give the Crew the right to construct and operate the stadium. Soon Hunt would construct a 22,500-seat stadium that could be used not only for soccer but also for concerts, high school football, and other sports such as lacrosse and field hockey. The construction cost would be $15 million–$17 million. Hunt would sign a guarantee to cover all of the construction costs. If the Crew should leave town or if Major League Soccer should fold, then the stadium corporation would be allowed to find another major tenant. If that failed or if the Crew was unable to pay the annual lease fee, the Expo Center would have the right to take ownership of the stadium or to demand that it be torn down and the site returned to its previous state. Also, the Crew would minimize events at the stadium during the two weeks the state fair was held. This way, the traffic congestion that soccer games generated would not be detrimental to the free flow of fair attendees.

This type of lease was new to the commission, so the members undertook a study of stadium leases. This was during the period of the lawsuits between Hunt and the Dream Team over the hockey franchise. In Columbus, while support for the Crew and its young, personable president and general manager, Jamey Rootes, held firm, people were beginning to see Hunt as a sports entrepreneur pure and simple. They feared he had little commitment to the city or to the well-being of downtown. In fact, one commission member said that "Lamar Hunt has a history of being litigious. Lamar Hunt sued some of the city's patriarchs." He added that Hunt's "Texas lease negotiator was arrogant and pugnacious. These wealthy owners get wealthy because they get such good leases. I feel we've sold our birthright for a bowl of porridge."[29]

Nonetheless, the consultants reported favorably on the proposed lease and on May 15, 1998 the Ohio Exposition Commission voted 6 to 2 for entering into the lease with the Hunt group. With the specific site firmed up by agreement with Historical Society and the lease approved, the state's Administrative Services and the Governor, as required by law, signed approval of the deal. Ground breaking was held in August and the stadium was ready for play May 13, 1999. Hunt and the Crew had their stadium and Hunt's Columbus odyssey had come to an end.

Aftermath

The events following the Issue 1 battle may be characterized as a "win-win" situation because the key players got all or most of what they wanted. The Dream Team got its hockey franchise. The tax-opposition group continued its string of victories by defeating yet another arena tax. Nationwide built a nationally acclaimed arena and acquired the rights to further redevelop its corner of downtown. By the fall of 1991, the Arena District was moving ahead. It had the arena. It had added bars, restaurants, and office buildings, and housing was coming down the line. The district also boasted a beautiful greenspace mall. It had a green light from the Columbus Downtown Commission to build a multiscreen movie theater with 1,800 seats. This would be the only movie theater downtown, and it included appealing features such as leather seats in the balcony and the most sophisticated sound system in town. The older theaters had been renovated and were now sites for plays, musicals, and concerts.

With the development of the Old Pen site on Neil Avenue, the street dividing the Arena District from the area to its immediate west had become known as Pen West. Here a $5.5-million entertainment venue was constructed that would hold events whose audiences would be too small for the Nationwide arena or that required an intimate performance space—2,500 for indoor concerts and 4,000 for outdoor. In addition, developers were in the early stages of floating plans for replacing the aged industrial structures in Pen West with new housing and office construction.

The Franklin County Convention Facilities Authority had backed an arena since its inception. With the Nationwide arena's fruition, the FCCFA proceeded with an $81-million major expansion of the convention center that increased its size from 1 million square feet to 1.275 million. The convention center is just up the street from the Nationwide office complex and the arena. Its expansion would further contribute to the redevelopment of the northern part of downtown. As a result of the increased convention space, more hotel rooms, more restaurant meals, more drinks, more parking fees, more tickets to downtown performances, and more bed-tax income would all enhance the downtown economy.

Also, with the defeat of Issue 1, OSU felt free to develop its arena without constraints. During the campaign, in a spirit of cooperation with the downtown elite, the university's administration had agreed to exclude from its arena luxury boxes that would compete for corporate dollars with the Issue 1 arena. With the defeat of the issue and the apparent evaporation of downtown competition, Ohio State considered all bets to be off. In building the Value City Arena in its new Schottenstein Center, the university included state-of-the-art luxury boxes that were aggressively marketed to the Columbus business community. Seat-licensing arrangements were developed that rivaled the potential profitability of those for new arenas in other cities.

Once Dimon McFerson made his move to build a privately financed arena, the university administration knew that it had only a two-year lead on the likely competition and took advantage of it by bringing in very high-profile concerts and performers. These events, together with OSU basketball and hockey, established the university's arena as a great venue for any type of major performance or event—from Luciano Pavarotti (opera) to Michael Flatley (dance) to Rickey Martin (pop) to giant trucks (good ol' boys). With the success of the university's arena, it became common in Columbus to speak of the possibility of "dueling arenas" when the Nationwide facility came on line.

Time has shown that competition certainly exists between the two arenas. Nevertheless, when important matters arise, the downtown elite still can have a say in university arena matters. Take, for example, the Tim McGraw–Faith Hill concert. These two Nashville performers were on a smash tour in 2000, and both OSU and Nationwide wanted to book them. Indeed, Nationwide wanted them as the headliner act for the arena's opening, so Dimon McFerson called Ohio State's new president, Brit Kirwan, and asked that OSU not sign the act so that the grand opening of Nationwide's arena would not be diminished. Kirwan acquiesced.[30]

Lamar Hunt was a winner in one way, but a loser in another. On the plus side, he built his stadium and secured the future of the Crew in Columbus for many years. Indeed, the stadium was acclaimed to be a soccer gem, as it was the first stadium in major league soccer built especially for that sport. However, Hunt missed out on the hockey-ownership possibility and also lost a lot of local good will. To many in Columbus, he was the adventuresome outsider who failed to play ball with the local Titans in the downtown revitalization game; thus he became relegated to being a perpetual outsider.

Moving On

The downtown redevelopment game had been played for many years before Issue 1 and continues to be played to this day. However, as in all games some players come and go, and some change positions in the game. This is true in Columbus as well. We have mentioned some of these transitions in previous chapters, but it is desirable to summarize them here. In May 2000, Dimon McFerson announced his retirement from Nationwide. At the time he was considered a major winner in the city's civic game, and he said he planned to continue to be involved in civic events. This included his acceptance of an appointment to OSU's board of trustees, where he became one of OSU president Brit Kirwan's bosses.

John McConnell, the businessman who was praised for bringing professional hockey to Columbus, received the highest award possible in the local civic game. In October 1998 he was voted a member of the Columbus Hall of Fame. He joined forty-one other local luminaries including painter George Wesley Bellows; Eddie Rickenbacker, World War I flying ace and airline executive; James Thurber, writer and cartoonist; Howard "Hopalong" Cassady, Heisman trophy winner; Nancy Wilson, singer and entertainer; and R. David ("Dave") Thomas, founder of Wendy's. McConnell is also known locally for his contributions to charity. For example, he donated several million dollars to Grant/Riverside Hospital for the creation of the McConnell Heart Health Center. He also pledged that his profits from the Blue Jackets would go to charity.[31]

Upon completion of his last term of office, Greg Lashutka, the popular mayor of Columbus and tireless worker to bring professional sports to the city, was appointed senior vice president of government and community relations at Nationwide. He also was a member of Nationwide's executive management council.

In January 2000 Titan Ron Pizzuti—Lashutka's partner in chasing professional sports—entered into a major deal with Nationwide Realty Investors, which was designed to create a $1-billion portfolio. Nationwide took a major equity position in Pizzuti Companies. This deal gave Nationwide part ownership in $400-million properties developed by Pizzuti in Orlando, Jacksonville, Chicago, Indianapolis, and Columbus. Nationwide also planned to direct another $600 million through Pizzuti.[32]

In June 1997 Ohio State president Gee resigned his position there and took the presidency of Brown University—a little more than a month after Issue 1 failed. Gee said, "This opportunity at Brown will not come again."[33] After a very short stay at Brown, Gee moved on to the presidency of Vanderbilt University.

In March 2002 Gee's replacement, William "Brit" Kirwan, announced that he would be leaving Ohio State to take up a larger challenge as chancellor of the university system of Maryland. Kirwan cited the added advantage of being close to his grandchildren in Maryland. In April Kirwan was inducted into the American Academy of Arts and Sciences.

OSU's Andy Geiger continued to pursue the expansion of the university's athletic facilities where major cost overruns in the arena's construction and the renovation of Ohio Stadium created budget woes. Nonetheless, he remained popular in the community and served on several blue-ribbon citizens groups.

With the end of the lawsuits between Hunt and the Dream Team and the construction of the Crew's stadium, Lamar Hunt faded far into the background of the Columbus civic scene. Jamey Rootes, the Crew president and general manager who did the heavy lifting in developing the Crew Stadium, moved to Houston, where he became senior vice president and chief sales and marketing officer for the Houston Texans, the NFL's expansion franchise that was scheduled to begin play in the 2002 season. With his efforts, the Texans sold seventy-five percent of the suites and seats in the new 69,000-seat Reliant Energy Stadium.[34] Rootes was well on his way to becoming a major player in the big time sports game.

Richard Sheir, "arena slayer" and leader of the opposition to Issue 1, continued his civic involvement. In 1999 the regional transit authority, COTA, had two issues on the ballot for November, each of which asked for a sales-tax increase that would fund expanded bus service and the development of light rail. Sheir claimed that in the long run this would be a $2-billion deal. He rallied the tax opposition once again and fought a hard battle. The issue, involving a ten-year tax increase, was defeated, essentially scuttling light-rail mass transit in Columbus for the foreseeable future. This was another victory for Sheir, but it was to be his last in Columbus. In June 2001 Richard Sheir announced that he was retiring as a political activist and moving with his wife and daughter to a small town in Vermont, where he could live a quieter life. In parting, he said about the Issue 1 campaign, "the personal reward is driving next to the Arena District and knowing it was built the way it should be. But I'm not waiting for my comp tickets at the window."

Sheir's opponent in the Issue 1 battle, Doug Kridler, was gracious about Sheir's departure. Sheir had, said Kridler, "an eye for opportunity and a flair for the dramatic. If he wasn't always logical or on point, he was always on message—his message."[35] Kridler himself moved on as well. In February 2002 he was appointed CEO of the Columbus Foundation, one of the nation's foremost, city-focused philanthropic organizations. In Columbus, the CEO of the foundation is at the top of the philanthropic game.

As the dust settled from the Issue 1 fight, it became clear that the Arena District had great promise as a redevelopment project. Beyond that, the rest of downtown redevelopment was lagging. It was also clear that the arena was but one successful project and that many more were needed. In the next chapter we describe what was happening downtown beyond the Arena District.

7

Beyond the Arena District: Downtown Columbus (with Benjamin Cornwell)

We have a downtown that's sputtering. . . . If we let it go any further, we'll get to the point where the price to the city becomes severe.

—Bob McLaughlin, City Downtown Development Administrator

SINCE 1994, the arena issue had had center stage in the discussion of downtown redevelopment in Columbus. By autumn 2000 the Nationwide arena had been built, the first puck had been dropped for the Columbus Blue Jackets, and the Nationwide corporation was proceeding full speed ahead with the redevelopment of the Arena District.

By autumn 2001 new restaurants, bars, offices, parks, parking ramps, entertainment venues for live acts, and housing plans dotted the area. As one observer put it, "The Arena District is a happening place!" The Blue Jackets were playing to sellout crowds, and on nongame nights the arena was jammed for a wide variety of acts and events.[1]

Competition with Ohio State's Value City Arena in its new Schottenstein Center was a reality, but both sites seemed to be thriving. Indeed, on the night of January 16, 2002, both the Ohio State Buckeye basketball team and the Columbus Blue Jackets played before sellout crowds in each of their arenas. One local sports commentator, who regularly appears on ESPN college-football coverage, commented that he knew all along that Columbus was a great city that could easily support two facilities and that the fretting over Issue 1 for years was uncalled for. The city's sports fans agreed wholeheartedly.

Clearly the arena and its district were a lively pocket in the northwest corner of old downtown. But what about the rest of the downtown? Did the

Arena District's success spill over to enhance the whole central business district? What did Columbus look like in the winter of 2002? Would downtown decline or flourish? What processes seem to be at work here?

Columbus: A Bird's-Eye View, Winter 2002

During the Issue 1 campaign, proponents of the hockey arena argued that the structure would revitalize the downtown. The authors themselves took a look at the downtown area after the hockey arena was finished in order to decide how much impact the arena was having on revitalization. Let's recount that tour now. We'll start with a bird's-eye view from the north and describe important features of the landscape as we head south (see Figure 2 in Chapter 4).

Looking at downtown Columbus from above, we see that most attractions lie on or near the north-south axis created by High and Front Streets. This makes getting around easy. Most of the city's sports arenas sit north of the downtown core. OSU is situated a few miles north of the downtown area, and central campus is wedged between High Street to the east and the Olentangy River to the west. The renovated Ohio Stadium, on Woody Hayes Drive, is hugged by the Olentangy River and is easily accessed by several bridges. Value City Arena and the Schottenstein Center are on the west side of the river and one block north of the Ohio Stadium, at the intersection of Olentangy River Road and Lane Avenue. Crew Stadium and the state fairgrounds sit along Interstate 71, just two miles east of the university's facilities.

Victorian Village flanks campus to the south, housing many of the university's students and faculty. A redevelopment project called The Gateway is planned for the east side of High Street, across from Victorian Village and just north of an area known as Italian village. Unfortunately for redevelopment, the project largely stalled in the winter of 2002.

The Short North area provides a commercial face to the area just east of Victorian Village, along High Street. These sections of the city tie the university into the downtown area, which is south of Interstate 670. One could walk from a popular bar in the Short North to the convention center in less than five minutes. The convention center, also on High Street, is surrounded by hotels to the east and south, along Nationwide Boulevard, and the North Market on the west side of High Street. These hotels also serve the arena district, which begins just one block west. Next we describe the arena district in greater detail.

High Street also gives passage to the downtown area's oldest attractions. The intersection of High and Broad Streets hosts Rhodes Tower, the tallest building in Columbus, the revitalized Palace Theater (just a block east of City Hall), and the Ohio Statehouse, which takes up the entire face of the block south from Broad Street to State Street. Here we find the gloriously remodeled Ohio Theater, which constitutes a portion of the north face of the Columbus City Center mall, the commercial center of the downtown area. The newly constructed Center of Science and Industry (COSI), one of the city's most popular tourist attractions, sits just three blocks west, across from the Scioto River, between Broad and Town Streets. Finally, the Brewery District (on the west side of High Street) and German Village (on the east side) anchor the city to the south.

All things considered, Columbus's downtown, like many others, contains many amenities in a relatively small space. The distance between Bricker Hall (the office of the president of OSU), on the northern side of OSU's campus, and the Hoster Brewing Company, a popular spot in the Brewery District on the south side of town, is only about four miles. By car, the trip takes about ten minutes. Once in downtown, most of Columbus's attractions are easily accessible on foot.

To the Arena District

In this section we describe the approach to the arena district. This area, not included in the arena district itself, might well be improved through new construction stimulated by the hockey arena. Our route goes down High Street from Lane Avenue, at the northeast corner of OSU's campus. This is a part of town from which many Columbus residents, especially university students and faculty, might begin a trip downtown. High Street is a straight path directly to the downtown area from the university. Since Columbus is so flat, the lights of downtown buildings can be seen clearly straight ahead—even though, at this point, one is a little less than five miles outside of the downtown. Looking ahead to the south, downtown buildings stand in relief against the sky.

One may contrast the scenery to the west with that to the east. To the west are the university grounds, with large trees, well-kept lawns, and collegiate-style classical buildings. OSU does its best to make its campus aesthetically pleasing, so it constitutes a pleasant aspect of the drive. To the east, on the opposite side of the street, is an assortment of shops and restaurants. These places serve a diverse university population and include ethnic restaurants, book and music shops, live-show venues, and bars, among other things. The east side of High Street at this point is mainly functional, so it is not very visually attractive.

A few blocks down the road, the eastern façade of the university ends as we reach its southeast corner near Twelfth Street. Near Tenth Street, commerce becomes more sparse, and we enter perhaps the most neglected portion of High Street. This section hosts several abandoned office and commercial spaces, dilapidated residences, and empty lots. There are a few fast-food restaurants to the west. On the east side of High Street stands a sign that reads "University Gateway Center." The sign promises future development in the area, providing some assurance that the area will eventually be cleaned up and revived.[2]

For the next mile or so, we see only an occasional bar or store until First Avenue, where the scene changes dramatically. At this point we enter an area known as the "Short North," a newly rehabilitated area popular with many Columbus residents. Here one can frequent any one of several art galleries, cafés, clubs, bars, gay/lesbian bookstores, and upscale restaurants. At night, white lights drape small linden trees in front of the trendy shops. Once a month, one can see groups of young people "gallery hopping," but usually the sidewalks are just filled with strolling couples or barhoppers. In many ways this area serves as a front porch to people entering downtown Columbus from the north and foreshadows the arena-district setting. It is an ideal place to spend an hour or two before heading downtown.

Continuing south on High Street, as we approach the northern façade of the downtown area, the surroundings become increasingly developed. To the east, alongside High Street, is the convention center, which stands in front of and is dwarfed by the Hyatt Regency Hotel. In fact, here we immediately encounter some of Columbus's largest buildings. One has to lean over the steering wheel and peer up through the top of the windshield to see the top of One Nationwide Plaza, part of the world headquarters of Nationwide Insurance. The Nationwide complex is a focal point that greets Columbus visitors, with impressive buildings, beautiful landscaping, and, of course, the gateway to the Arena District.

Next we reach the intersection of High Street and Nationwide Boulevard. The latter stretches from east to west across the city and is wedged between the Short North and the City Center mall a few blocks south. The arena is on Nationwide Boulevard, so we turn right at this intersection to find parking. Before a hockey game, this intersection is extremely busy, and it is not unusual to have to wait a minute or so to let a large crowd of people cross the street. In fact, for the remainder of the drive, one is likely get stalled in traffic. This is good news for downtown interests, in that it means that people are returning to the center of downtown at least occasionally. The southeast corner of the arena (the main entrance) can be seen from the next intersection below High Street, which is at Nationwide Boulevard and Front Street.

What can we conclude from our tour so far? Apparently the approach to the district is an assortment of old, dilapidated buildings and newer, elegant structures. Once the Gateway project is completed, the new will outweigh the old, and Columbus will have an attractive entertainment and shopping district that stretches nearly four miles from OSU to the arena district. Even though the construction of the hockey arena did not stimulate the Gateway construction, it serves to anchor one end of it. Interestingly, this area was never planned as an entity but seems to be developing through an amalgamation of many projects, some of which have been "in progress" for three decades.

The Arena District

Moving west on Nationwide Boulevard toward the arena, one is immediately greeted with colorful signs that seem to scream "Arena District!" The arena and main Arena District complex lie on the right side of the street (to the north) when crossing Front Street. The arena itself is constructed of red brick and glass. A seventy-foot-high glass panel makes up most of the front of the building facing both Front Street and any visitors approaching from Nationwide Boulevard. The lower section of this panel houses the main entrance to the arena. Sitting atop this glass panel, in large white letters, are the words "Nationwide Arena." The rounded, glass-enclosed front end of the arena's roof looms above and behind the front entrance.

Passing alongside the building, one notices that Nationwide Boulevard is also constructed of red brick. Since the main Arena District buildings are also of red brick, the downtown environment appears unusually well integrated. Continuing west on Nationwide, we pass the main buildings and enter a vast parking area. The parking complex opens up to a surprisingly undeveloped area to the west, stretching over to Neil Avenue. Only the most observant of Columbus's "old-timers" would realize that this lot sits on what was once the site of the "death house" of the former Ohio Penitentiary. From this portion of the arena's parking complex, one sees that the southwest corner of the arena boasts large red, white, and gray Blue Jackets signs that decorate and advertise the Blue Jackets Bistro Bar. It is a remarkably

**Figure 5. View of the Nationwide Arena inside the Arena District, Main Entrance Area.
Source: *Columbus Dispatch,* used with permission.**

convenient spot for tired travelers to step out of their car, walk across the parking lot, and enter the bar for refreshments. The portico of the building is composed mainly of windows, so one can sit on the second floor and look out over a sea of cars and people while relaxing before a Blue Jackets game.

Even given this welcome to the arena district, one is still surprised at the numerous entertainment options located behind the façade of the arena's southwest corner. The south side of the building does not have a main entrance for fans, so when we approach the arena from the south side and go up the sidewalk from the parking lots, we eventually come to the main stairs to the arena district and main arena entrance. A few reminders of the history and games that contributed to the building of the Arena District flank both sides of this entrance. For instance, to the left, chiseled into the lower part of the building, is the modest identifier: "Nationwide Arena. September 2000." To the right of the entrance, on a short wall, is a plaque that reads: "Ground was broken for the Nationwide Arena on this site May 26, 1998, thanks to the vision and guidance of these Columbus community leaders." Anyone who bothers to explore further will see a series of plain concrete sections of the wall that are dedicated to some of the key figures introduced earlier. These include John P. McConnell, Mayor Michael B. Coleman, Robert J. Woodward Jr. (executive vice president and CFO of Nationwide), John F. Wolfe, Dimon R. McFerson, John H. McConnell (chairman emeritus, Worthington Industries), Ronald A. Pizzutti, Gregory S. Lashutka, and Brian J.

Ellis (president and COO of Nationwide Realty). Each section presents, on a small plaque, the names of these people and their position in the community, and just below it, their names carved (by their own hands) into what was once wet concrete, next to their handprints.

As we walk up the stairs, an entirely different world opens up. We immediately come upon an open brick plaza—the centerpiece of the Arena District. Before hockey games, the plaza is bustling with people, many of them going into the arena's main entrance, which is to the left. To the right are several long rows of black metal benches and trees, a useful place for waiting and resting. Straight ahead, along a large streetlike alley, is a series of places to eat and drink. These include a Starbuck's coffee shop, Buca Di Beppo (an Italian restaurant), and a brewery, among other things. The air is filled with the sounds of people talking, the anticipation of the beginning of the game (or show), and music, which grows louder as we approach the bistro. Walking through the plaza, past several of these places, we happen upon a street sign that stands along a perpendicular alleyway that hosts additional options for visitors. The end of this perpendicular alley opens up to Front Street, along which sits Chipotle (a national chain of Mexican restaurants). If one walks straight through the plaza from the south entrance, one eventually reaches a bridge, just beyond the brewery, that stretches over a set of railroad tracks running along the north side of the Nationwide arena building. People accessing the plaza from a parking area to the north side of the arena use this bridge.

The intimate size of the plaza makes it feel like a miniature city within a city, even though the entire district spans only ninety-five acres. This makes it an interesting and pleasant place to bide time before a hockey game. Happily, the main entrance to the arena is nearby when one finally decides to go inside for the game. Inside the clean and spacious arena, one sees an ice rink, hockey players, vendors, and thousands of screaming fans, like at any other hockey arena. There is little inside that sets this arena apart from others in major cities. In fact, it was based on the design of other successful hockey arenas. After a game, however, many people stay in the Arena District and enjoy its many amenities until late at night. In addition, because there are so many outlets and the highways are so close, exiting the Arena District after a game is not too difficult and takes only 10–15 minutes.

The Arena District in Retrospect

Our tour of the Arena District persuaded us that it is quite an attractive place for sports fans and anyone else who enjoys a night out on the town. Seven restaurants and public houses offer many options for a diverse crowd, and the plaza offers plenty of space for passersby who are simply looking for a place to rest. Some of the restaurants are open even when no events are scheduled, so people saunter in and out of the plaza all the time. Aside from the plaza and the arena itself, the Arena District boasts several other amenities for visitors, including entertainment venues such as the Arena Grand Theatre (which has eight movie screens, a bistro, and balcony seating) as well as the PromoWest Pavilion, an entertainment hall that features an adjustable stage for indoor/outdoor performances. The district also includes a three-acre grass park called McFerson Commons.

Even those who were opposed to Issue 1 concede that the Arena District anchors downtown Columbus very well and lends the city a fresh, welcoming countenance. The district promises to add a great deal to Columbus's image as a tourist-friendly city, as it stands just several blocks from the convention center, downtown hotels, and the city's commercial core. Later, when one hears a commercial on the radio for an event at the Arena District (which happens fairly often in Columbus), it is difficult not to recall a recent visit and the pleasant memories that district events helped create.

It is hard to imagine that a spur-of-the-moment decision was responsible for such a place. It is harder still to believe that such a district and its prize—a professional hockey team playing in a new arena—did not involve vast expenditures of public funds. Moreover, the complicated way in which the district came about involves a spate of sociological topics: the history of professional sports, the competition among cities for professional teams, public bickering among city leaders, and the debate over social priorities. The political battles that preceded the building of Nationwide Arena and the Arena District were fierce and heated. Otherwise calm officials made accusations toward each other, leveled threats, and maneuvered to destroy reputations. Following this political spectacle, the city voted not to build the hockey arena, so the Arena District almost never happened. That it did happen is the result of a long process of public debate followed by decisive action.

The point we want to stress is that the controversy over the arena was ultimately beneficial. The project works because public and private resources were pooled in an intelligent way, and important community leaders put their reputations "on the line" to make it happen. Had this been a project funded mostly by taxpayer dollars, we doubt that the district would have received the same amount of attention from the private sector.

Downtown Revitalization beyond the Arena District

The Slumping Mall

In 2002, the northwest corner of downtown was clearly thriving with the burgeoning Arena District revitalization. But what could be said of the rest of the downtown? Has the arena stimulated construction to the south? Unfortunately, with the exception of the riverfront, where expensive new high-rise condominiums were going in just to the south of COSI, things were getting worse. In fact, the City Center mall that thirteen years earlier had been touted as the showpiece of downtown revitalization had become a retail disaster. The headlines of one local paper shouted, "Downtown's mall will never be the same again."[3]

When the mall opened in 1989, it quickly became ranked as one of the top fifty shopping malls in the country. It regularly had ninety-five-percent retail occupancy of its millions of square feet of space. Next to the mall a major parking ramp was built to allow shoppers to cross directly over a two-level bridge from the ramp right into the three-level mall. The highest-priced stores were originally located on the top level, and the lowest-priced stores were on the lowest, or street, level. In the early 1990s the mall attracted shoppers from all over the county and beyond. Some of its stores were very upscale and found elsewhere only on New York's Fifth Avenue.

Periodically the local mass transit company, the Central Ohio Transit Authority (COTA), even ran a special shuttle over lunch hour through the heart of the business district. This connected points downtown from the convention center on the north and the Short North to the City Center mall and German Village and the Brewery District on the south side of the Columbus business district. The shuttle enabled workers, shoppers, and tourists to efficiently visit several of the points of downtown action.

During the 1990s, while the downtown redevelopment focus was on the arena and hockey matters, developers were building large, classy malls that would eventually become the core of suburbanizing edge cities—areas with not only shopping, employment, and housing, but also areas that serve as magnets to other relocating businesses. Easton on the far northeast side, Polaris on the far north side, and Tuttle Park on the far northwest side plus the new Lennox Town Center just to the immediate west of the Ohio State campus gradually eroded what gains in shopping had been made downtown. The new malls also essentially killed off most of the older malls that were located between the downtown and the outer suburbs.

Gradually the City Center mall lost stores. By winter 2002 its occupancy rate had declined from 95 percent to 80 percent. Most emblematic of the mall's slide was the announcement in January 2002 by Jacobson's, one of the mall's three major anchor stores along with Marshall Field's and Lazarus, that it was closing its doors and filing for Chapter 11 bankruptcy. Commenting on the closing of the 119,000-square-foot Jacobson's, Pete Cooper, the mall's general manager, said that it was not difficult to understand Jacobson's problem given the increased competition from the new suburban malls such as Easton and Polaris.[4]

Although the mall management had hopes of attracting other stores, it had become clear that the mall's whole concept had to be reconstructed. Indeed, this might mean that the mall would undergo a major reconstruction to open it out to the street. The mall had been built in such a way that, from the outside, it resembled a large fortress. Visually it offered only high walls, few windows, and small, uninteresting entryways. Inside, it was splendid, but the outside appearance simply did not coordinate well with the rest of the business district. It offered nothing to casual passersby.

In Need of a Plan

When former Mayor Greg Lashutka left office and moved on to Nationwide, there was a general sense in the community that downtown was on the right track with the new arena and the promise of the developing Arena District. However, to downtown insiders, things seemed different. They were well aware of the erosion of downtown shopping and the out-migration of activities that would previously have been located downtown. The glitz and panache of the increasing downtown nightlife generated by the refurbished Ohio Theater, Southern Theater, and the Palace Theater along with the other new venues built during the 1990s did not obscure the fact that retailing was sliding. What to do?

Mike Coleman followed Greg Lashutka as Columbus mayor. Coleman was the president of city council during the Issue 1 battle and supported the issue's bid for the public financing of the arena and stadium. Coleman, a very popular Democrat, knew what was happening to downtown shopping. Upon taking office, he quickly set about producing a plan for the urban core that would save retailing and jobs. In 2001 Coleman and the Downtown Development Office invested $1.9 million of state of Ohio funds in planning for downtown revitalization. Not only did Coleman involve important downtown interests, but he also met all year with highly placed architects and planners from New York City. Many of these architects and planners had connections to Titan Les Wexner.[5] Ty Marsh, Coleman's chief of staff, said that Coleman "wants to focus on specific areas of downtown where the likelihood of development can occur and needs to occur."[6] The mayor also wanted to reinvigorate inner-city neighborhoods as a way to bring people back into the core and thereby reinvigorate the central city's businesses.

While many people were focused on retailing and the issue of what to do with the mall, anxieties were also building on another front. Downtown bar and restaurant owners were concerned about what would happen to their businesses as an increasing number of eating and drinking places opened in the Arena District. Many of these establishments were within an easy 5–15 minute walk of the new places. The owners were largely resigned to the fact that the people who were coming to the arena and parking in its lots were likely to be patrons of the new places. However, the owners worried that the trendy, new places would also draw away their longtime after-work customers. These owners believed that the number of their potential customers was finite and that once they moved on to the new establishments, new customers would not be available to take their place. The owners felt that any new downtown redevelopment plan would not address their apprehensions.

By January 2002, knowledgeable observers agreed that things were looking bleak for downtown shopping. Various suggestions were circulating through redevelopment circles. These included the idea of building a new baseball stadium for the Columbus Clippers, but the downtown redevelopment game had become stalled.

That situation resulted from a major change in several important matters since the Issue 1 battle. The main point is that the Arena District is not a general stimulus to the downtown. It will not provide customers for the small theater district and probably will not draw people to the major shopping mall. The district's restaurants compete with older restaurants in the downtown area. In other words, new revitalization efforts need to be made—no one project will provide an all-purpose cure.

The Stalled Downtown Revitalization

By January 2002, however, no serious downtown revitalization projects were on the table. The pro-growth coalition was drafting a new plan for downtown, but little beyond that was in evidence. Why was there such a change from all of the Arena District development? Several factors account for this.

First, the extralocal factors had changed. The question of reshaping downtown for big time sports had been resolved with the building of the arena. Professional sports leagues were no longer targeting Columbus as a new place to do business. Also, the national economy had been in decline for more than a year, and the Columbus economy was reflecting national trends. Workers were getting laid off, and times were getting hard. Emblematic of these economic difficulties was the Columbus Center of Science and Industry—one of the jewels of downtown redevelopment. In January 2002 it laid off a large percentage of its staff. In addition, since the September 11 tragedy, a general societal malaise had set in. The nation had been knocked off its stride. By winter things had still not returned to normal. The resulting uncertainty, along with the national economic slump and the lack of interest by outside interests, dampened the whole process of downtown revitalization.

A second factor in the downtown revitalization trajectory change was the changing of the guard in downtown leadership. As we saw in last chapter, several of the political and economic leaders of the 1990s were either leaving active participation in the revitalization game or moving on to new things. With them went the drive, energy, and plans that had sustained the earlier revitalization game and the various projects that it spawned. New leadership was in the wings, but it might take years before they created a new agenda and set it in motion. The revitalization game in Columbus is likely to be suspended until these new agents and actors gain momentum and the economy improves.

A third factor in the decline in downtown revitalization action was the change in the city's accumulated sociocultural context. Many people saw the development of the Arena District as the major downtown revitalization effort, and that one project was enough for the present. However, other things that needed attention were coming to the fore. The Columbus city schools had been and still are in an academic emergency. In some schools more than half of the students did not graduate. Clearly the crisis in education had to be handled. Also, during the 1990s the city had become a major destination for immigrants and refugees. Columbus was regularly receiving refugees from a range of countries from Russia to Somalia to Vietnam. For instance, by the end of 2001 there were more than twenty thousand Somali refugees in Columbus. Next to Seattle, Columbus had the largest settlement of Somali refugees in the United States, and more than fifty languages were spoken in Columbus schools. The Somalis, along with other immigrant groups, needed health care, welfare, education, housing, and employment. In addition, the outer-city neighborhoods were demanding attention since their local shopping and employment were being killed by edge-city development. To many, these matters seemed much more important than the decline of downtown shopping. Without a comprehensive plan, local politicians, redevelopers, and community actors were at a loss to establish a clear direction for their downtown improvement efforts.

In sum, after Nationwide resolved the arena issue, the downtown revitalization game changed. The net effect of these changes brought a halt to major efforts at improvement. The revitalization game basically ceased as social actors changed roles, new agendas began to be established, external pressures for revitalization diminished, and local priorities shifted to human services and to the suburbs. What will it take to restart the downtown revitalization game? The answer is not readily apparent. For one, Doug Kridler, Columbus Foundation CEO and leader of the Issue 1 campaign, hoped that Titan Les Wexner might be the one to move the downtown ahead. Kridler said, "I believe that Les Wexner continues to care about and wants to make a contribution to the viability of downtown. . . . My hunch is he is where a lot of the energy of this initiative may have to come from."[7] Kridler was not alone in his hope.

Beyond Columbus other cities were also wrestling with the issues of building two new stadiums to keep their professional sports franchises. Columbus's neighbors—Pittsburgh and Cincinnati—faced the same decision: Who would pay for the stadiums? The Columbus answer was private sector entrepreneurs. The answer in both Pittsburgh and Cincinnati was the taxpayers. Those cities did not have an organization comparable to Nationwide that encompassed their stadiums into a larger, profitable, neighborhood redevelopment project. For contrast, in the next chapter we describe the Pittsburgh and Cincinnati scenarios.

8

Other Cities, Other Games (with Benjamin Cornwell)

The formula is simple: Devote ever-decreasing amounts of public wealth to support the services needed by the poor and helpless, and invest more and more in ways that will return increasing profits to the small numbers of rich and privileged.

—Joanna Cagan and Neil deMause

THE SUCCESS of the opposition in defeating Columbus's Issue 1 may be due to the experience of its leadership and the generally conservative nature of the city's voters, but it could also be the result of the fact that the professional teams in question were *new*. The Crew was not well established, and the Blue Jackets were just an idea when the tax initiative was proposed. In this chapter we examine two cities near Columbus where stadium controversies erupted over well-established teams. The first case is Pittsburgh; the second, Cincinnati.

Bending the Rules to Build Stadiums in Pittsburgh

In the mid-1990s two owners of major, professional sports teams in Pittsburgh demanded new stadiums, prompting city leaders to draft a half-cent, stadium-tax referendum to fund the massive civic project. Similar to Columbus, widespread opposition arose to stadium construction, forcing city leaders to find alternative solutions to a series of financial and bureaucratic challenges. In one scholar's words, "building sports stadiums can be a hard sell. Hence, those individual actors and groups who push hard for new stadiums may have to go to extreme ends to achieve success. . . ."[1]

Selling the Home Team

As is the case with many other cities that are building sports facilities, the stadium issue in Pittsburgh originated with professional sports team owners. In this instance, the owners of the Pittsburgh Pirates baseball team initiated the demand. Since 1985, a consortium of six corporations, including several banks, private individuals, and Carnegie-Mellon University, had owned the Pirates. This group organized itself for the purpose of keeping the team in the city.[2] This was seen as a necessary move because, from 1991 to 1994 alone, problems with declining attendance, bloated players' salaries, and poor media contracts escalated, contributing to a loss of over $50 million. In 1995, citing the team's poor financial outlook, the consortium decided to sell the Pirates, leaving the team's future in Pittsburgh uncertain.

Given the losses the team had incurred in recent years, city leaders knew that it would be difficult to find a buyer for the team. Pittsburgh's mayor, Tom Murphy, actively sought buyers to facilitate the process. Several buyers soon emerged who seemed interested in making an investment in the team. One was a local cable-television mogul named John Rigas, who agreed to pay approximately $85 million for the team. However, the city's hopes of keeping the team in Pittsburgh dimmed when, in June 1995, Major League Baseball (MLB) rejected the deal because of a poor "debt to equity" ratio.[3] Soon the city learned that the owners would place the team on the open market (outside of Pittsburgh) if no suitable buyer could be found. At this time, Murphy publicly scolded the team owners for acting so selfishly.[4]

The first hint of the need for a new stadium in Pittsburgh surfaced with the city's growing desperation to keep the Pirates in town. After MLB rejected Rigas's offer, a wealthy California newspaper heir, Kevin McClatchy, stepped in to make an ambitious bid for the team. The owners of the Pirates warned that if this deal were unsuccessful, the team would have no other choice but to look for out-of-town ownership. McClatchy gathered forty investors to propose a final offer. The deal included taking over the team's current debts and making a $25-million payment to the current owners. McClatchy would also receive $40 million in credit from several local banks, as well as $32 million in lease concessions at Three Rivers Stadium. Finally, the tentative agreement required financing for a new baseball-only stadium to be in place by February 1998, which pressured the city's leaders to devise a plan. Again, Mayor Murphy pledged his support for the deal and urged the Pirates' board to accept the offer, which it did.

Major League Baseball accepted the deal on the strength of the promise of a new stadium.[5]

Leaving Three Rivers Behind

In years past, city leaders had considered building a new stadium for the Pirates. City council members had been discussing the idea since 1991, when a new stadium seemed to offer the only cure for the team's faltering financial outlook. Mayor Murphy played perhaps the most important role in making the stadium proposal a reality. As mayor, Murphy was concerned with keeping the city economically competitive, which, to him, meant keeping the professional sports teams in town and, more importantly, retaining the popularity necessary for reelection. Murphy argued that the stadiums would give Pittsburgh an air of civic pride and provide a shot in the arm for the local economy. For the teams, a new stadium seemed a profitable venture because it would allow for the addition of expensive luxury boxes, procurement of fresh advertising contracts, and profits gleaned from newly designed parking, concessions, and other amenities.[6] At one point in 1994 Mayor Murphy indicated that building a new stadium was feasible within the next three or four years, though he never explained how such a project would be financed.[7]

Now that a deal was in place, Murphy organized a task force made up of twenty-seven Pittsburgh business and civic leaders to explore possible locations for a new stadium and to investigate options for financing. The task force faced a difficult assignment because the project was likely to require many funding sources, including precious public dollars. In 1996 the group published its recommendations, which suggested locating the stadium near Three Rivers Stadium and stated that public dollars would be needed, along with the formation of a group to direct the financing efforts.[8] Furthermore, the task force said that a new, publicly funded stadium would be a good financial investment for the city. City council members expressed concern over these comments, citing the well-known lack of economic development generated by the current stadium over the past twenty-five years. Their doubts foreshadowed a deeper disapproval that existed among Pittsburgh residents. Moreover, Pittsburgh's inner core would not be improved by locating the new stadium near the site of Three Rivers.

The Pittsburgh stadium issue escalated when, in 1996, the Steelers football team began making its own demands. Steelers' officials took a more novel approach than simply arguing that a new stadium would be necessary to generate more profit. Of course, like McClatchy and his supporters, financial interests motivated Steelers officials, such as president Dan Rooney. However, they framed their request as a desire for *political fairness*. Steelers' officials claimed that, given the generous deals the Pirates received, they deserved their fair share from the city, also.

At first, the Steelers entertained the idea of making their own renovations of Three Rivers Stadium. However, as talks progressed, it became clear that they would settle for nothing less than a new, football-only stadium. They reasoned that "[a] new facility would cost only $75 to $100 million more [than] renovating Three Rivers, and more importantly, the Steelers could make more money at a new facility."[9] If the Pirates were guaranteed such a great deal, why should the Steelers be passed over for an equivalent financial opportunity? As an attorney for the Steelers stated, "We salute the city's efforts to keep the Pirates in the city. But we must reserve our rights to seek comparable concessions."[10]

Steelers' officials also made a veiled threat to the city of Pittsburgh. Though never actually saying they would move out of the Pittsburgh area, they did say the team would consider moving to the suburbs if the city did not meet its demands. Considering itself to be in financial competition with the suburbs, the city took the threat seriously and eventually agreed to put a new Steelers stadium in its civic improvement plans.

Following the additional demands that the Steelers placed upon the city, the city of Pittsburgh found itself facing the task of funding two new professional sports stadiums and the more daunting task of determining the best way to generate public funds. Perhaps noting the difficulty of justifying such use of public dollars, city officials put an interesting spin on the financial demands they were placing before Pittsburgh residents. They repackaged the two stadiums together with several other civic projects and presented them in one bundle as a comprehensive regional-development plan. In 1997 city leaders formed the Regional Renaissance Partnership (RRP), composed of representatives from the two teams, three Pittsburgh civic groups, and the Allegheny Conference on Community Government (which represented primarily the corporate community of the Pittsburgh region). Publicly, the RRP claimed that its goal was to make Pittsburgh a "world-class visitor destination," thereby making for a "bright[er] future" for the city's children.[11] The city's major paper, the *Post-Gazette*, supported the RRP's work. Headlines from the newspaper were nostalgic, supporting the half-cent tax increase with headlines like "Building the Region a Half-Cent at a Time," reflecting the theme of both civic pride and economic development.[12]

The Referendum

Pro-stadium leaders proposed to fund the projects using public dollars generated by a half-cent sales tax. The proposed sales tax would remain in effect for seven years and would be levied in ten southwestern Pennsylvania counties. Officials estimated that the tax would generate more than $600 million during that period. After aggressive lobbying by city representatives, state legislators in Harrisburg finally agreed to allow the referendum on the November 1997 ballot. The RRP's most difficult task, however, was to get the voters to approve the tax, as opposition had become more vociferous after leaders introduced the referendum to the ballot. Several obstacles stood in the way of securing voter approval. For one, opposition was embedded in Pittsburgh's populace. Polls consistently indicated that about two-thirds of residents in Pittsburgh's home county (Allegheny) opposed tax increases. This was partially because the county is home to a large number of elderly residents (in fact, the second-highest percentage of elderly residents in the United States). Furthermore, the county's population (and tax base) had diminished considerably in recent years, and Pittsburgh already had the fourth-highest tax rate of any city in the country.[13]

Other forms of opposition also surfaced. For instance, Richard Mellon Scaife sponsored research with the Allegheny Institute, a local think tank, that informed residents of the irresponsibility of publicly funding such projects. These opposition members wanted to keep local elites from benefiting at taxpayers' expense and aimed to prevent any new taxes. Together they published information in the *Pittsburgh Tribune-Review* showing that stadiums often have negative economic impacts on cities. Before the referendum vote, the paper "consistently informed its readers that new stadiums seldom bring prosperity and hammered home the idea that the tax increase was nothing more than welfare for the rich."[14] The Allegheny Institute stated that it supported private financing and maintained that cities without professional sports teams had the highest rates of economic development.

Nonetheless, stadium supporters composed mainly of members of the RRP continued to fight for the passage of the tax referendum. In addition to saturating local media outlets with pro-stadium propaganda, the Allegheny Conference on Community Development funded a study conducted by several local universities that showed that the referendum's proposed regional improvements would generate as many as thirty thousand jobs by 2006.[15] Rounding out the RRP's efforts, the Steelers agreed to chip in $50 million over twenty-five years for their stadium, while the Pirates would contribute $35 million to theirs.

To the disappointment of pro-development leaders in Pittsburgh, residents voted down the referendum by a margin of 3 to 2 in November 1997. The referendum's failure caused key pro-development players to search for other solutions. Refusing to back down, pro-stadium leaders like Mayor Murphy began to consider a Plan B, even though, like Columbus, they had earlier stated that no possible alternative to the sales tax plan existed. Several city council members, however, continually pressured pro-development leaders to supply additional evidence of a new stadium's utility, for they were not convinced that economic development would result. After the tax-referendum failed, city council president Jim Ferlo expressed a need for more input by local politicians. He stressed that "I want this to be an open and democratic participating process."[16] Thus, the city council passed a bill requiring Mayor Murphy to appoint a thirty-person panel to investigate other funding sources. However, since McClatchy's deadline was only a few months away, there was scarcely time for such a bureaucratic solution. Mayor Murphy and two Allegheny County commissioners threw together Plan B before the February deadline. This plan involved reallocating funds from the regional-asset district tax, which provided funds to cultural activities as well as Three Rivers Stadium. Plan B would reallocate $13.4 million a year for thirty years to pay for the bonds that would finance the stadium projects.

Yet Plan B brought with it several inherent complications. First, one of the county's commissioners, who was opposed to stadium funding, demanded that the two professional teams contribute more funds to the stadium projects—which they eventually did. The tax reallocation also required the approval of six of the seven regional-asset district board members, whose funds were being reappropriated.

At first, two of the board members opposed reallocation. However, one of these resigned his position. Finally, presumably anchored by a more sympathetic addition to the board, the reallocation measure passed on July 10, 1998, by a vote of 6 to 1.[17]

The state government of Pennsylvania offered the final obstacle confronting the stadium-funding scheme. During his reelection campaign, Governor Tom Ridge had promised to pay for one-third of the cost of new stadiums in Pittsburgh and Philadelphia. To do so, however, the state would have to raise its debt ceiling, an action that required the state legislature's approval. Many Pennsylvania residents resented the state government's spending of so much money on Philadelphia and Pittsburgh, especially for projects such as stadiums, which many rural residents would never get a chance to enjoy. Since it was apparent that the legislature would not vote for such a measure, even after intense lobbying efforts, local leaders changed their approach. Soon a Pittsburgh lobbyist urged the introduction of an amendment to a bill that would alter the Allegheny County code. After this, the governor would be clear to pass on funding without the approval of the state legislators in Harrisburg.

The Pennsylvania house and senate routinely approved the bill, even though lawmakers were not aware of the amendment's implications. They were incensed upon hearing that they had basically given away their veto rights. Supposedly recognizing that the move had been somewhat under-handed and in an attempt to avoid public disapproval, Governor Ridge refused to sign the bill.

Then he, along with house and senate leaders, drafted a plan that enabled the state to lend interest-free money to the teams. To accommodate these plans, on February 3, 1999, the state of Pennsylvania increased its debt ceiling to $650 million, which also allowed numerous local projects that state legislators supported to continue. State politicians had cleared the road to stadium construction in Pittsburgh, and groundbreaking ceremonies for the construction of the new Pirates' and Steelers' stadiums took place on April 7 and June 18, 1999, respectively. Despite the fact that so many residents had opposed the stadium tax, the public did not express any consistent outrage over the projects themselves once they had begun. Perhaps their passivity was due to the fact that the politicians found a way to fund the projects without obvious additional costs to the public.

As they relate to the Columbus case, the events in Pittsburgh reveal how powerful professional sports teams can make influential people go to great lengths to get stadiums built. Even though many Pittsburgh residents were against public funding of these structures, politicians found a way to raise the money. Here we see that, after the referendum failed, the political actors ignored democratic processes, thus negating any sense of pluralism. It remains to be seen how the Pittsburgh voters will ultimately respond to the two new stadiums, but clearly, in this case, pro-development forces won out by disregarding the rules and outmaneuvering the public.

The Cincinnati Stadium Fiasco

Around the time that the Baltimore Ravens were playing their first game in their new home and construction companies were breaking ground for the new Pittsburgh stadiums, Cincinnati was recovering from its own drawn-out debates over the future home of its two professional sports teams—the Bengals football team and the Reds baseball team. A period of intense controversy was ending (or so most Cincinnatians thought) following a series of demands made by the Bengals' owner, Michael (Mike) Brown, and the infamous Reds' owner, Marge Schott. In an unprecedented display of governmental ineptitude, a splintered set of local politicians quibbled for years with the owners and with each other over the planning, placement, and funding of two new stadiums. The previous cases had not provoked this degree of dispute. This case study shows how, without a healthy, well-supported opposition, the stadium game can spin completely out of control, costing the public hundreds of millions of unanticipated dollars.

The seeds of controversy were planted in the early 1990s, when members of Cincinnati's city government were discussing the refurbishment of several segments of the city's riverfront along the Ohio River. Riverfront Stadium, which both the Reds and the Bengals were using, overlapped these segments. At that time Mike Brown, then the assistant manager of the Bengals, began hinting that he was not happy with Riverfront Stadium. Beginning in May of 1990, he argued that the Bengals needed a larger stadium in order to remain competitive in the NFL. At first his comment went virtually unacknowledged by city leaders. By 1993, however, Brown had become the team's general manager, giving him the authority and political clout to strengthen his call for a larger stadium. He employed his new powers almost immediately. Not only was he one of Cincinnati's professional sports team managers, but his family had also been a prominent fixture in the Cincinnati area for some time; as a result, people listened to him. In fact, the Brown family has a long history in football in the entire state of Ohio. Paul Brown (Mike's father) coached the Cleveland Browns football team from 1944 to 1963, only to be fired by Art Modell. Four years later Paul Brown founded the Bengals, an American Football League (AFL) expansion team brought into the National Football League through its merger with the AFL.[18] Paul Brown died in 1991 and left the team to his son, Mike. Mike Brown's primary financial interest was, and still is, the Bengals, so he concentrated on making sure the Bengals' financial position was a good one.

As we will see, Brown's persistent demands for a new stadium during the early to mid-1990s and his concurrent threats to move the Bengals out of the city pressured politicians from Cincinnati, Hamilton County, and, more indirectly, the state of Ohio to make costly stadium-related deals with the Bengals. He framed the issue as Cincinnati's last chance to keep its professional football team, consistently taking a "meet this deadline, or else" position. In the end, this stance, combined with support from key local politicians, proved too powerful for local leaders to ignore.

Brown Turns Up the Heat

In November 1993 Mike Brown began responding to offers from other cities that were trying to attract football franchises. Like Modell, Brown saw Baltimore as an attractive option. He publicly proclaimed that the Bengals could earn three to five times more revenue in Baltimore than in Cincinnati, given the fan capacity of Riverfront Stadium at that time. The interest he expressed in moving the team, though, was more of a ploy to capture the attention of local politicians than it was a truthful effort to explore options elsewhere. Whatever the case, it was clear to city leaders that Mike Brown was unhappy with Riverfront Stadium and that he was determined to carve out a more satisfactory situation for the Bengals.

Eventually responding to Brown's persistence, the city made a tentative agreement with the Bengals by guaranteeing them more income with a renovated Riverfront Stadium and possibly a brand new stadium. Citing the limited scope of the city's resources, city manager John Shirey called for a regional approach to keeping the Bengals in Cincinnati. In December 1993, in a speech given to the Greater Cincinnati Convention and Visitors Bureau, Shirey indicated that an estimated $150 million would be needed from the greater Cincinnati area to fund a stadium project.[19] Unfortunately, the regional approach never materialized.

In December 1993 the city tried to finalize a deal with the Bengals by guaranteeing that the team would earn more income in a renovated Riverfront Stadium. The city council agreed to install an 6,000 additional seats in the stadium and to build a 1,000-seat stadium club restaurant. The council also proposed to make other improvements to the stadium and to Spinney Field, the Bengals' practice facility. The proposal committed the city to paying $30.5 million in support of the Bengals over the next four years.

Little progress was made on this deal, though, after Marge Schott, the owner of the Cincinnati Reds, voiced objections. Schott exercised virtual veto power over such deals because the Reds were also leasing the stadium and had equal interest in its fate. Her lease agreement curbed the city's bargaining power and, perhaps more importantly, antagonized Mike Brown, who was already disenchanted with his situation at Riverfront Stadium. Schott's primary interest, like Brown's, was financial. However, since Brown shared the stadium with her and drew on the same fan base, she viewed Brown and the Bengals as potential competition for revenue.

In June 1995 a Maryland group began asking the frustrated Mike Brown whether he was still interested in the construction of a new stadium facility in Baltimore. On June 6, 1995, Brown stated that he was going to inspect the new stadium as a possible future home for the Bengals. Two days later he flew to Baltimore with several other Bengals' officials to formalize his interest. That same month, concerned local politicians responded immediately to the possibility of a Bengals move, just as Brown had intended.

Local and state politicians held the key to Brown's chances of a new stadium for the Bengals. Cincinnati's mayor, Roxanne Qualls, along with city manager John Shirey, the city council, and Hamilton County commissioners, soon played major roles in scraping together funding for the new stadium and convinced others to contribute to the construction costs. Just two days after Brown's visit to Baltimore, Mayor Qualls publicly announced that Cincinnati would make a strong proposal aimed at ensuring that the Bengals would stay in Cincinnati for some time.

Hamilton County commissioner Bob Bedinghaus played perhaps the most crucial role in organizing funding for a stadium. Twelve days after Qualls's announcement, Commissioner Bedinghaus drafted a tax proposal to cover the cost of two stadium projects, which relieved some of the pressure on the city to appease Brown and the Bengals. Bedinghaus's proposal consisted of a twenty-year, one-cent, sales-tax increase for Hamilton County that was to generate roughly $100 million a year. The county would sell bonds to finance the construction and repay the bonds with the sales-tax revenue. A stadium-financing report revealed that it would cost roughly $545 million to build separate baseball and football facilities on the city's riverfront. Recognizing how useful these tax funds would be, city council and county commissioners promptly approved the proposal.

Forcing a Referendum

Citizens challenged this deal in August 1995 with a petition, compiled largely by Tim Mara, a lawyer affiliated with Citizens for Choice in Taxation. The petition forced the issue into a countywide vote. Thus, the referendum was born. Throughout Hamilton County the petition was eventually signed by more than ninety thousand people. "They were demanding that we build a stadium and that we not have a say in it," Mara said. "It was like a stick-up, just give us your money and don't think about it. We decided that, damn it, the people should have a say."[20]

Mara and other antistadium activists believed that the facility was not likely to stimulate much economic development or downtown revitalization for Cincinnati, and that it would instead benefit business owners such as Mike Brown. At the time, the activists suggested that the politicians consider other options before implementing a tax to build a new stadium. A week before the vote, Tim Mara stated, "There is a better way. I'm convinced Plan B exists."[21] Overall, though, the opposition appears to have been relatively unstructured. That is, it does not appear that highly organized interests backed the people who challenged public funding for the stadium.

The Hamilton County residents' main source of information regarding the sales-tax increase was media coverage. The key media in Cincinnati during this period were the major newspaper, the *Cincinnati Enquirer,* and to a lesser extent, the *Cincinnati Post,* as well as local radio and television stations.[22] Throughout this ordeal the media focused on reporting interesting news regarding negotiations and complications as the stadium game progressed. In doing so, local newspapers and radio and television stations succeeded in tracking public opinion of the stadium tax and in keeping residents abreast of changes in stadium-related plans. The *Cincinnati Enquirer,* in particular, updated residents on issues surrounding the stadium tax during the period just before the vote on March 19, 1996. In the two weeks prior to the vote, the *Enquirer* published nineteen articles that directly addressed the stadium tax, nine (forty-seven percent) of which appeared on the front page. Thus, during this period the actions of key players received a great deal of public attention.

Throughout this episode many local politicians involved in the game, particularly commissioner Bedinghaus, found themselves walking a thin line between trying to keep the Bengals in Cincinnati and protecting their reputations as responsible public officials. Local politicians passed off the stadium-tax proposal to local residents as a key to generating local development and as a way to increase civic pride. The *Cincinnati Enquirer* took the same line ten days before the vote: "Armed with a University of Cincinnati study, pro-tax leaders predict a $1.1 billion economic boost to the regional economy as the stadiums are being built. They also say 1,100 jobs will be created, another 5,700 will be retained. And when built, the stadiums, teams and tourists they draw will have an annual impact of $296 million."[23]

The public initially viewed the stadium-tax proposal in positive terms. A poll of eight hundred Hamilton County residents was conducted just days before the vote and published in the *Enquirer.* It indicated that 59 percent of the respondents supported the tax, while 38 percent opposed it. Those results closely paralleled the actual vote. Analysis of the poll results showed that the public had apparently accepted the concept of economic development, as 46 percent gave that as their primary reason for support. In contrast, of those opposing the tax, only 36 percent believed that the owners and big businesses should pay more.[24]

Just prior to the vote, many leading politicians, including some at the state level, voiced their views on the issue. Ohio senate president Stanley Aronoff, a Cincinnati native, voiced his support for the deal, stating publicly that the stadium-tax plan was needed to keep the Bengals in Cincinnati. Governor George Voinovich gave his spin on the issue just five days before the vote by warning that Cincinnati would become "minor league" if the proposal were to fail.

Only a few local politicians, such as city council member Tyrone Yates, characterized the stadium tax as a mistake. Four days prior to the vote, he publicly debated Commissioner Bob Bedinghaus on the merits of the proposal. Yates questioned statements made by pro-tax figures, such as Voinovich, who claimed that the city's status as a "world-class city" was at stake. As Yates put it, "I'm not persuaded that if this fails that Cincinnati will fall off the edge of the world as a world-class city."[25]

Without an effective opposition, many questions about the financing of the stadiums and other difficult issues were left unresolved. Instead, threats to leave the city dominated the discourse. In March 1996, four days before the vote, Mike Brown stated that if the measure failed, there would be little chance of his keeping the Bengals in Cincinnati. Hamilton County residents responded by passing the proposal in a 61 percent to 39 percent vote, the reverse of the margin of support in Pittsburgh.

The passage of the referendum in Cincinnati relieved its supporters but opened the door to many problems that would follow. The first one was deciding on a location for the new football stadium. In June 1996, county commissioners, together with city council, pushed to have the Bengals' stadium become a major revitalization project by building it in an area called "Broadway Commons," close to the city's urban core and working-class neighborhoods. This choice proved unpopular with Mike Brown and the Bengals, who preferred a site on the city's riverfront. After an architectural firm hired by the county stated that the Broadway Commons site was not feasible for a new stadium, county commissioners unveiled a costly plan that would keep the Bengals in Cincinnati for roughly thirty years—on the riverfront. To support the deal, the team would have to sell millions of dollars in season tickets, and other amenities would have to be sold by the following

April. The final deal did not appease Mike Brown, who thought that the proposed site was too far west by a couple of blocks. After months of heated negotiations, the county conceded to Brown by agreeing to build the Bengals a three-field practice facility near the stadium. In late May 1997 the county and the Bengals signed the deal, settling on a "maximum price" of $287 million (not including property costs or infrastructure expenses). The Bengals agreed to pay $44 million to fund the project, while the county agreed to pay $36 million for 12.5 acres of property on the riverfront.

More problems soon emerged. In July, city officials began to complain about several aspects of the plan. For one, they said that the proposed facility was too large and would take up too much of the part of the riverfront area that they had been hoping to refurbish. They also argued that the lease deal that the county had offered to the Bengals would give them virtual veto power over the city's riverfront development plans. Mayor Roxanne Qualls publicly denounced the deal, saying that county officials had given away the city's riverfront. Others did not agree. County Commissioner Bob Bedinghaus, for instance, offered a stinging response to Qualls's criticisms: "Normally, I'd attribute this kind of silly nonsense to a full moon . . . but it's this time of year in every council election when council takes a month break that a lot of these shenanigans tend to happen. I'm not going to overreact to Miss Qualls's obvious election year political pandering."[26]

In September, city manager John Shirey told city council not to transfer the 12.5 acres of land to the county until they could make a deal that was mutually satisfactory. On December 30, 1997, Brown threatened to move the Bengals if the city did not transfer the land within one month. In the early morning hours of February 1, 1998, after a night of eleventh-hour bargaining, the city finally agreed to transfer the land to the county. Stadium construction then began in April 1998.

Financial Fiasco

The city's most substantial problems did not surface until long after stadium construction had actually begun. In February 2000, after twenty-two months of stadium construction, an outside auditor informed Hamilton County commissioners that they had failed to ensure that the stadium's design plans were sufficiently complete for the proper scrutinizing of the costly changes in the project. They went on to say that, as a result, stadium construction could cost an *additional* estimated $45 million.

The budget overruns are perhaps the most telling evidence of the extent of the disorganization in the stadium negotiations. Prior to the passage of the half-cent tax, the most often-quoted stadium price tag was $184.5 million (which did not include the $60.5 million that was detailed in a 1995 task-force report as being necessary for parking, design fees, and other costs). From the time residents voted for the tax to the time construction was completed, the cost had climbed by more than $200 million—to more than $415 million. The increase can be attributed to several factors. For one, the task force had based their estimate on the construction costs of a stadium that was built in Charlotte, North Carolina, in 1995. No one took into account, however, that, unlike Ohio, North Carolina is a prevailing-wage state. This meant that a stadium project in Ohio would require union wage rates for construction workers—an additional $15 million. Second, the task force failed to figure in a three-percent annual inflation rate—an additional $31 million. Third, several deals made during the negotiation period (including the addition of practice fields and training facilities for the Bengals and agreeing to move the site several blocks west along the riverfront) further elevated the cost of the stadium (adding $75 million). Additional costs were incurred due to budget overruns caused by concrete, electrical, plumbing, and structural-steel contracts.

Figure 6 illustrates the cost increases for Paul Brown Stadium from the time of its inception in 1995 to 2001. The budget overruns cap an already drastic trend of cost increases. We compare this trend to that of the Great American Ballpark, the new Reds stadium, which was constructed shortly after Paul Brown Stadium. Clearly, Paul Brown Stadium was a much costlier project, but it is equally apparent that the Reds' stadium costs ballooned in almost as unruly a fashion. This is a further testament to the absence of a healthy opposition and of proper oversight in Cincinnati during this period.

Controversy surrounding the stadium-funding issue subsided slightly when the Bengals played their first game in Paul Brown Stadium on August 19, 2000 (against the Chicago Bears). The budget issue was revisited in January 2001, though, when an auditor examined what had grown to be a total of $51 million in budget overruns since the start of the project. The auditor examined more than 430 changes that had been made to the original guaranteed maximum price of $287 million and concluded that the most that taxpayers could recover from the budget mess was $18.5 million (due to "insufficient documentation" of the changes).[27]

Furthermore, problems with the stadium tax itself were compounding these financial worries. In February 2001 the *Enquirer* reported that revenue from the sales tax was growing at only about half the rate that was

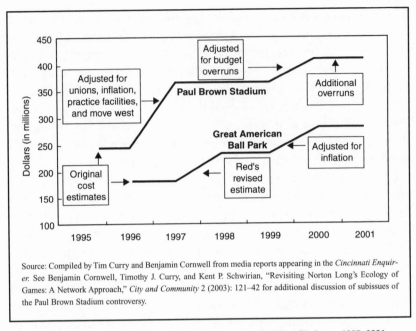

Figure 6. Changes in Taxpayer Costs for Cincinnati Stadium Projects, 1995–2001.

needed to pay for the riverfront stadiums and parking, a potentially long-term problem.[28] Amid growing economic concerns, the region began searching for new solutions.

Even though most Cincinnati residents still supported the stadium tax and remained interested in events as they unfolded, the mood of the general public shifted when construction began and the financial commitments became apparent. Disbelief over the accumulating costs and administrative bungling was the prevailing sentiment, as evidenced by comments made on the *Enquirer*'s web site, calls to radio talk shows, and newspaper editorials. The *Enquirer* steadily reported budgetary overruns and miscalculations that were costing taxpayers dearly. Eventually the public came to realize that not only had they voted for a tax proposal that set no limit on the amount of money that citizens could be obligated to pay, but there was also no coherent plan for the project. The sites and stadium designs had not been agreed upon beforehand, and the respective team owners bickered between themselves after the referendum was passed. Ultimately, public dissatisfaction ended the career of Bedinghaus, the politician most directly connected with the stadium game, and contributed to the mistrust and alienation of members of Cincinnati's inner city. These residents, mostly African American, saw the city court the middle-class suburbanites through public financing of a vast entertainment district on the riverbank, while their own pressing needs for better schools, better housing, and more effective government services went unheeded. Ironically, having built the stadiums, the city was required to invest heavily in maintaining that space as an attractive tourist district, potentially diverting even more of the city's resources to the riverfront, away from the core urban population's needs.

As a final capstone to an ill-planned project, Cincinnati was rocked by racial unrest in April 2001 after a white Cincinnati police officer shot and killed an unarmed African American man. Following the killing, protests escalated into riots and looting that lasted for several days. During this period, over 850 people were arrested, and by one estimate, more than $1.5 million in damage was done.[29] In response, Cincinnati mayor Charles Luken appointed a commission to explore the roots of racial tensions within the city. Doubtless, the city's flagrant misuse of public dollars and the fact that city leaders put economic interests ahead of race relations were partly responsible. During an interview with the *Cincinnati Enquirer,* one of the city's most active African American leaders, Reverend Damon Lynch III, offered a suggestion. When asked what the "true" problem facing Cincinnati was, Lynch responded: "We talk about the light rail, expanding the convention center, the 2012 Olympics, The Banks riverfront development. Let's get real. We've got racial problems. We can build stadiums. But can we deal with our human relations?"[30] His criticism of the city's more comprehensive development project for the city's riverfront (e.g., "The Banks") is clear.

An important point that emerges from this case is that, when public financing for stadiums is brought into play, economic restraint may fly out the window. To avoid a fiasco, a vocal and determined opposition needs to make the financial and human capital costs transparent to the public. In Columbus, the opposition forced the Titans to justify every expense and ultimately to become so familiar with the project cost that they determined that they could build the stadium and arena with much less taxpayer involvement. In Cincinnati, the popularity of the Reds and the Bengals allowed a massive project to go forward without adequate planning and with no actual limit on the costs that the public might have to absorb. Meanwhile, the valid educational, housing, and safety concerns of Cincinnati's urban population were left unaddressed.

National Patterns: A Critical View

State and local expenditures for stadiums and arenas escalated from $700

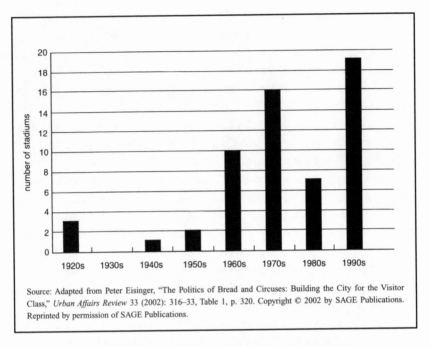

Source: Adapted from Peter Eisinger, "The Politics of Bread and Circuses: Building the City for the Visitor Class," *Urban Affairs Review* 33 (2002): 316–33, Table 1, p. 320. Copyright © 2002 by SAGE Publications. Reprinted by permission of SAGE Publications.

Figure 7. Public Financing of Urban Professional Sport Facilities by Decade.*

million in the mid-1970s to more than $2 billion in the early 1990s.[31] To illustrate, Figure 7 shows the dramatic increases in the numbers of facilities for professional sport teams that have been constructed with greater than fifty percent public funding.

Critics of such public funding have noted that of the 30 cities that undertook stadium or arena construction after 1970, only fifty-seven percent were growing in population. Thirteen of the 30 were actually experiencing sharp *declines* in population. Moreover, 26 of those 30 cities were experiencing an increase in the number of people living in high-poverty neighborhoods. In Cincinnati, for instance, the number of people living in high-poverty neighborhoods increased more than tenfold from 1970 to 1996.[32]

As cities decline in population and lose their middle-class residents to suburbia, they seek ways of attracting well-heeled visitors. Convention centers and massive stadium projects are devices for attracting wealthy people from outside the city limits. As one observer states, "The city as a place to play is manifestly built for the middle-classes, who can afford to attend pro-

---

* Note: Professional sport facilities include stadiums for baseball and football and arenas for basketball and hockey that received at least fifty percent public financing. Suburban facilities are excluded. The "1990s" bar does not include 1999.

fessional sporting events, eat in the new outdoor cafés, attend trade and professional conventions, shop in festival malls, and patronize the high- and middlebrow arts."[33]

Unfortunately, when cities use their resources to plan and build massive sport facilities to entertain free-spending visitors, basic services that residents need are given lower priority. For example, greater attention is given to policing the tourist areas than to protecting nearby residential areas, and funds for youth programs and loans for small businesses are diverted into acquiring land for stadiums, chain restaurants, and so on.

In addition, commitment to financing a stadium or other large capital expenditure may constrain a city's fiscal flexibility. When citizens are asked to raise their taxes for such expenditures, they may be unwilling to raise them again for better public transportation or other needed services and facilities. Similarly, large government bond issues to finance stadiums may dominate the bond market for years, forcing other borrowers to raise interest rates to attract buyers. Hence, taxpayers may pay more to retire school bonds or highway bonds that are competing with stadium bonds.

Critics also point out that the costs of providing entertainment facilities are frequently underestimated. In Cincinnati, the final cost of the two stadiums was far in excess of the original estimates. The same has been true in other cities once construction got underway. To illustrate, Coors Field in Denver ended up costing $215 million, rather than the $141 million originally estimated. Miller Park in Milwaukee cost $398 million—whereas the estimate was only $250 million.

Once the facilities are in place, city officials are inclined to value sports stadiums, arenas, and other entertainment facilities for what they *represent* rather than for what they cost. Emotional arguments about the prospect of losing the home team to another city carry great weight.[34] We saw this in Pittsburgh and Cincinnati, where local leaders did all they could to keep owners from relocating their teams to another city. Cities are highly competitive in their attempts to obtain or retain professional sports teams, and they must try very hard to look attractive to these teams. This competition puts home team owners in a position to threaten to move in order to get new facilities. As one observer remarks, "For places with teams, these trends offer scant comfort. Fewer teams may move, but more threaten to relocate, and places cannot ignore the possibility that a team will carry through on its threat."[35]

In Pittsburgh, Cincinnati, and many other cities with a resident professional sport team, the intangible benefits of keeping the home team have inspired city officials to manipulate public opinion, bend rules, and engage in other practices that strain "the links between the leaders and the led."[36] Between 1984 and 1997 there were at least 30 sports facilities referenda— 19 of them produced negative votes in 14 different cities. Remarkably, in 7 of these 14 cities, new stadiums and arenas were subsequently initiated anyway, using public funding other than local levies.[37]

Scholars have given little attention to the social and political implications of bypassing the popular will and of building sports entertainment districts designed for the "visitor class" rather than for locals. At the very least, such practices must introduce some cynicism among residents. In the case of Cincinnati, for instance, it may have even contributed to racial disturbances.

More cutting criticism sees professional owners who threaten to leave cities as swindlers.[38] In this view, neither the owners of sport teams nor the city officials who agree to their demands are behaving in ways that improve the lives of those who actually live in the city. These critics claim that cities that cater to tourists and suburbanites by building sport entertainment districts that are surrounded by impoverished neighborhoods are similar to third-world nations that try to attract tourists by building lavish hotels in the middle of poverty-stricken communities. In both cases, funds that might be spent to improve the residents' everyday lives go toward enhancing the spectacle for tourists.[39]

Finally, we turn to the matter of urban redevelopment. In Columbus, Nationwide's plan was not simply to build an arena. The arena was tucked into Nationwide's entire redevelopment of the north end of the central business district. The Arena District was built around the arena and included businesses, offices, residences, and other entertainment venues. After Issue 1's failure, downtown interests dropped the soccer stadium from their plans, and Hunt was left to his own devices. The soccer group eventually secured their stadium, but the new facility had no impact on urban redevelopment in general or, for that matter, on the improvement of the nearby neighborhoods. The stadium is isolated on the state fairgrounds and disconnected from the normal flow of city life.

One would think that two new stadiums would have been catalysts for urban redevelopment in Pittsburgh. That was not the case, however. They are located on the north side riverfront across from the downtown's Golden Triangle. When one strolls along the riverwalk in downtown's Point Park, the stadiums create an interesting view—much like two aircraft carriers docked in a single quay. However, freeways and railroads separate them from nearby neighborhoods, some of which are showing signs of gentrification. Pittsburgh has been a leader in urban redevelopment—but not through these stadiums. Although the new facilities kept the city's professional franchises in town, they added little to the rebuilding of the urban core.

The same can be said about the two new stadiums in Cincinnati. Hugging the north side of the Ohio River, they provide a view of downtown's skyscrapers and the hills of suburban northern Kentucky, but they are removed from the actual core of downtown. The stadiums in Cincinnati and Pittsburgh are simply not about downtown redevelopment. They are about the cities' wanting desperately to cling to their professional baseball and football franchises. The stadiums were not part of the redevelopment game but became part of the city leadership's ploy to keep the city "big time." As local elites saw it, this meant that they had to have big time sports. To keep these, they needed new stadiums for the teams—even if it meant doing so at the expense of redevelopment and urban residents.

The issues and events we describe in this book have significance for the sociology of urban redevelopment. In the following appendix, we discuss the connections of these case studies to several basic theories of the city. We also propose a new model that should prove useful in studying community issues in general. The appendix was written primarily for urban researchers, but we invite all of our readers to sample the richness of the sociology of cities.

Appendix: The Ecology of Games Social Action Model (with Benjamin Cornwell)

The notion of [an ecology of games] highlights the role played by those who shape the rules of the game . . .

—*William H. Dutton,* Communication Theory

OUR STUDY EXAMINED a large, complex community issue involving the interaction of numerous individuals, groups, interests, and institutions, as well as the convergence of massive social and economic trends. The analysis of the events growing out of this study demanded a theoretical perspective that helped us to understand the complexity of the interrelationships among the various parties as well as the form and direction that their actions take within a specific territory. Thus we decided on a combination of an ecological framework that is sensitive to the role of economic and political power and the sociopsychological dynamics of the interactions that took place.

For our analytical strategy we selected Norton Long's paper (1958) on "The Local Community as an Ecology of Games." Long's framework is both old and venerable. However, it offers a way of looking at community issues that captures the complexity of such systems in action that other frameworks today do not. Written at a time when functional analysis was at the height of its popularity, the ecology of games model has only seen occasional use as contemporary researchers of community issues have employed other perspectives. We view the application and extension of Long's approach to be a major contribution of our study.[1]

Long conceptualized a community as a territorial system in which order prevails mainly through historical traditions and arrangements. His views were based largely on one year of fieldwork he conducted in the Boston metropolitan area. In it, he studied interactions that took place in the community and focused his attention on the structure, goals, roles, strategies, and tactics of major players as they went about their business. He did not presume, as did many other theorists, that a group of actors masterminded community affairs; indeed, his investigations convinced him of just the opposite.

For some it may be intuitive to think that a community is controlled by a group of people—the power elite in Mills's theory, the bourgeoisie in Marx's scheme, or the Titans in our study. However, Long claims that local communities tend to be pluralistic. He observes that a great number of community activities consisted of "undirected co-operation of particular social structures, each seeking particular goals and, in doing so, meshing with others."[2] From this view flowed his apt phrasing of the community as an "ecology of games."[3]

To Long, games were not trivial, leisure time events, but serious activities that gave people meaningful roles and a satisfying sense of significance. Games played within the community follow institutional arrangements. Thus, in a large community one may find a political game, a banking game, a newspaper game, a civic organization game, and others. In our updated version of Long's work, this scheme includes a professional sports facility game and a downtown redevelopment game. Within each one, the achievement of goals indicates success or failure, and both the elites and the wider public recognize the winners. Within each game, the players may be as rational as the structure permits, but at the very least they know the rules of that game, which tell them how to behave and gain information.

Where Long's framework distinguishes itself is in its recognition of the consequences of overlapping games. Long realized that individuals may participate in a number of games, but for the most part they focus on one major contest. Still, it is possible for individuals to transfer from one game to another and to simultaneously play roles in two or more. In fact, this concurrent role playing is crucial for the linking of separate games. Thus, players in one game make use of the players in another. They all are intent upon furthering the success of their own game, and other players may use them also. For example, as we saw in Columbus, the owners of a professional sports team who intend to have a successful franchise may become linked to the owners of newspapers who aim at success in the newspaper game. In this case, the newspaper, as a business, finds itself promoting the success of another business, while also taking on a crusading role to promote a new stadium or arena.

Long's framework, while published more than three decades ago, is very contemporary in two respects. First, it highlights the fact that many Americans experience cynicism about the government's and big business's interest in the public. This cynicism runs deeper today than it did back when Long wrote his paper.[4] By looking at the community as an interplay of games, Long struck a cynical stance and suggested that political and business leaders were more concerned with their own success in the political and economic games than with the long-term success of their community—the public interest.

The second way that Long's model is contemporary is in its argument that community actors achieve integration through social acceptance or prestige. In modern sociology this approach is termed *network analysis.* Sociologists who use this approach believe that we may view communities as vast structures of interconnections among people and that these networks provide clues to the distribution of power and decision making in society. In some ways, one could argue that Long anticipated contemporary network analysis by several decades. By stating that success in each of the separate games can result in general social acceptance, Long provides a sociopsychological motivation for community involvement. He argues that such acceptance gives players a sense of vaguely shared aspirations and common goals. While the social game is no substitute for a structured government, it does enhance cooperative action. As Long writes, "The custodians of the symbols of top social standing provide goals that in a sense give all the individual games some common denominator of achievement. While the holders of social prestige do not necessarily hold either top political or economic power, they do provide meaningful goals for the rest."[5]

In sum, we believe that Long's view of the community as an ecology of games, while not well known by contemporary researchers, is still relevant as a general framework. However, we believe that we can enhance his approach by adding insights from contemporary urban and sociopsychological researchers. We call this refurbished perspective the "ecology of games social action model" (EGSA) (see Figure 8). These include frame analysis, the growth machine, the sociospatial perspective, symbolic economies, action theory, and the city character and urban tradition paradigm. In the conclusion, we discuss how these additional perspectives help to defend against weakness inherent in Long's original formulation.

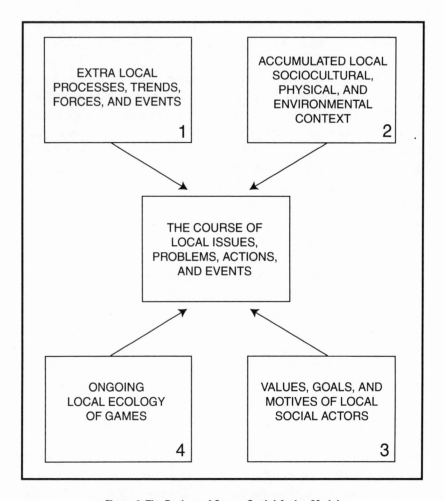

Figure 8. The Ecology of Games Social Action Model

The model posits the following: 1. that local issues, problems, actions, and events to some extent reflect extralocal (regional, societal, and global) social, political, and economic processes, trends, events, and issues; 2. that local issues are played out in the unique and historically accumulated local sociocultural, physical, and environmental context; 3. that local actors drive local events and issues through their values, goals, and motives; and 4. that action takes place through the local ecology of games.

The EGSA model makes four claims. First, it states that local issues, such as stadiums, ballparks, and arenas reflect extralocal trends, processes, forces, events, and other matters to a significant extent. For sport facilities issues these include the growth of big time sports, the decline of the inner city, the emergence of the urban redevelopment game, the decline in federal support for downtown revitalization, and the turning to entertainment ventures as a way of saving downtowns. Second, the model posits that local issues are played out in the unique and historically accumulated social, economic, political, and environmental contexts of the locality. Issues tend to spill over into each other, so that what has gone before shapes what follows. Third, the model proposes that local actors drive local events and issues through their values, goals, and motives. At times actors are willing to form coalitions to attain their goals. At other times they will engage in conflicts with each other if doing so will advance their agendas. Finally, the model submits that action takes place through the local ecology of games. Some games may go on for generations, while others may play out in the short run. Actors come and go, and new actors often change or deflect the course of ongoing games. They may also initiate new games and end old ones.

In addition to these postulations, the action model implies that even if several cities are exposed to the same national trends and forces, local issues tend to have different outcomes in different cities. This is because of variations among them in local history, leadership, and opposition motivations and because the structure of each community is itself an ongoing and ever-changing ecology of games.

Analysis of the Arena District

Extralocal Matters

By the mid-1990s several extralocal matters were impinging on local community activities. First, big time sports was in a period of rapid expansion, and leagues were increasing the number of franchises. Accordingly, sports entrepreneurs were selling franchises for unprecedented sums and large profits. Often leagues relocated franchises to other cities. Big time sports was demanding that cities provide new stadiums, ballparks, and arenas that would be more profitable than the older structures. The cities were threatened with either the loss of a franchise or the denial of a new or relocated franchise. Second, federal support for urban redevelopment had greatly declined from what it was in the heyday of urban renewal. Some federal programs remained, such as empowerment zones for neighborhood improvement, but on the whole, cities were left to their own devices to formulate downtown revitalization plans and come up with funds. Third, the national culture of urban administrators had settled on a strategy of revitalizing downtown that called for transforming these areas into entertainment districts. Presumably, new or refurbished theaters, auditoriums, and sport venues would attract more people to downtown, where they would shop, eat, and drink while also attending entertainment events.

By the mid-1990s, however, Columbus, like so many other older cities, was experiencing a decline in its downtown. Compared to twenty-five years earlier, fewer people were working, shopping, playing and living there. Politicians and business leaders alike saw the downtown as being in trouble. Even with a declining city core, big time sports leagues had targeted Columbus as a market for their product. Major league soccer had already located a franchise there. Its principal owner was a community outsider—Lamar Hunt from Dallas. The National Hockey League was also interested in Columbus as a site for a franchise but only if the locals would pay for an arena built to NHL standards. The city's downtown redevelopment group shared the view that sport entertainment would bring people back to the downtown, so for them, the need to build an arena to attract a professional sports franchise was obvious.

Accumulated Local Contexts

The totality of local contexts (sociocultural, environmental, and physical) is what gives each community its distinctiveness. To fully describe any city's cumulative contexts would require a comprehensive study along the lines of the Lynd and Lynd's (1929) Middletown or Warner's (1963) Yankee City.[6] Yet, for any given course of local events, it is possible to identify aspects of the accumulated contexts that are most relevant to understanding it. We suggest the following three as the most relevant.

PENITENTIARY SITE

In Columbus, a major physical context was the abandoned state penitentiary site in the northwest corner of downtown. It had defied revitalization efforts for many years, so it would take a unique and publicly funded action for this eyesore to be brought into positive and profitable development. The idea of developing a sports complex on the site was attractive to many. However, there were many obstacles to development there. There was concern that there might be toxic contamination on part of the site from former prison manufacturing conducted there. There was a general local assumption in redevelopment circles that if contamination proved to be the case, the city government would have to fund most, if not all, of the site clean-up.

STATE GOVERNMENT

A major sociocultural context factor is the location of the state government in Columbus. The governor and the legislators live in Columbus for a major part of each year. They have to work in downtown Columbus because the state capital and office buildings occupy the core of the central business district. Living and working there gives the politicians a stake in the well-being of downtown. In addition, the Republican administration of the 1990s was very favorable toward assisting downtowns in revitalization through the construction of sports and entertainment facilities. This favorable stance is evident in the fact that the state was willing to contribute to the funds for building the arena.

OHIO STATE UNIVERSITY

Another important contextual matter is Ohio State University. For decades, Ohio State's football teams filled the local entertainment gap because Columbus had no professional team. Many believed that new professional sports franchises were likely to have to compete with Ohio State for fan interest and support. During the 1990s the university launched a major construction project that included a new basketball arena; a new track, field, and soccer stadium; and a new baseball stadium. All of these were close to the Woody Hayes Center, a mammoth indoor football practice facility. In addition to this burgeoning sports campus, the Jack Nicklaus golf museum was added to the area. To top all of this, the university undertook a major expansion and renovation of its classic football stadium. This involved the expensive addition of an upper deck, as well as corporate luxury boxes comparable to those found in newly constructed professional stadiums.

After a brief, unproductive consultation with the downtown pro-redevelopment group, OSU, with the blessing and financial assistance of the state legislature, undertook the construction of a state-of-the-art arena. The facility was built for the university's basketball and ice hockey teams as well as for entertainment events of general interest to the students and the wider Columbus community. The downtown interests were not at all happy with the university's plans because they feared that sooner or later the two arenas would be competing for acts and attendance.

An Ongoing Ecology of Games

As in many large cities, a large number of games were underway in

Columbus in the mid-1990s. Those most relevant to the arena issue were the sports entrepreneurs' game; the downtown revitalization game; the anti-tax and fiscal responsibility game; and the community benefactor game.

THE SPORTS ENTREPRENEURS' GAME

Columbus's sports entrepreneurs' game involved two goals. First, entrepreneurs wanted to bring professional sports teams to Columbus. Second, as local leaders, they wanted to become owners of big time sports franchises. Bringing sports to Columbus and/or becoming an owner of a professional team (especially a Columbus-based professional franchise) would confer a great deal of prestige in the more general "community prestige" game. As we have seen, the entrepreneur group consists of both politicians and business leaders. During the Issue 1 battle, they felt that the city definitely needed a professional franchise to become a "big league town." When the sales tax increase was voted down, they worked around the clock to come up with an alternative. Fortunately for them, Nationwide Insurance intervened and agreed to fund the arena. Nationwide's motivation for rejoining this game (they had been a minority owner of the Cleveland Browns many years before) was to win the revitalization game.

THE DOWNTOWN REDEVELOPMENT GAME

Government and corporate groups with a stake in the downtown had been working very hard to redevelop the urban core for twenty years. They had completed several successful projects—new office buildings, a new shopping mall, a new science and industry museum on the riverfront, a successful convention center, restored theaters, and several new hotels. As valuable as these successes were, many people, including the downtown revitalizers, sensed that they were losing the game because people, businesses, and entertainment continued to move to the suburbs. To win this game, they had to demonstrate that people were coming back to downtown to shop, have fun, work, and live. There were constantly on the lookout for new projects. As Chapter 7 explains, Nationwide was one of the redevelopment leaders. As the company saw it, the voters' rejection of the tax increase threatened to halt the revitalization in the Nationwide area. Thus, Nationwide agreed to finance the arena because they wanted to make profits off of the other developments in the area. Still, many in Columbus declared Nationwide's leader, Dimon McFerson, a visionary and community benefactor. The Arena

District redevelopment largely completed the revitalization of the northwest corner of downtown, making Nationwide a winner in the redevelopment game. The *Columbus Dispatch* was now a winner, too, having partial ownership of the arena.

THE ANTITAX GAME

In Columbus an aggressive antitax-increase coalition now exists. It brings together people from all political points of view—liberal Democrats, socialists, balanced-budget Republicans, Libertarians, Green Party members, historic preservationists, and political gadflies of all sorts. What these factions have in common is a strong opposition to taxes that support private businesses and their wealthy owners. They believe that the public is always being asked to pick up the tab for things that help business—to the detriment of the taxpayers. Calling these tax burdens corporate welfare, they win the antitax game every time they block a proposed increase.

THE COMMUNITY BENEFACTOR GAME

This is a time-honored game in many cities. Those with money from business or industry use their wealth to invest in community projects. One wins the benefactor game by making splashy financial contributions to the city. Les Wexner is an example of a Columbus resident who plays this game successfully. He is the owner of The Limited and one of the wealthiest people in the United States. He is a well-known patron of the arts, particularly for the internationally renowned Wexner Center for the Arts. Overall, Wexner is one of the biggest winners in Columbus's benefactor game. Another one is John McConnell, who announced that he was buying the hockey franchise, not for the money, but to help put Columbus on the map. He also said that any profits that he made from the team would go to charity. He was rewarded with admittance to the Columbus Hall of Fame for his efforts. Similarly, Dimon McFerson of Nationwide was widely hailed as a top backer of the community even though Nationwide would profit from the venture.

Goals and Values of Community Actors

Individuals' goals, values, and motivations are complex matters to identify, and, more often than not, they are intertwined. In looking at the games under discussion, one may identify some basic values operating in each. In the sports entrepreneurs' game all of the players valued the notion of Columbus's obtaining a professional franchise of big time sports. For most, this was the key to enhancing the city's image. For them, such a franchise would mean that Columbus was a big time city. Others in the group wanted to enter the world of professional sports ownership. They had the money to do so, and they would thus put another feather in their cap within the local status system. It would also mean that they were now "players" at the national level.

Several values and motives, one of which is *capital accumulation,* are central to the downtown redevelopment game. Developers make their money from developing land. Land acquisition, site preparation, and building construction are highly profitable undertakings. Without revitalization projects, developers must search elsewhere for projects.

Another motive in the downtown redevelopment game is *political electability.* For politicians to be politically viable, they must demonstrate that they are actually working in visible projects that will benefit the city. Urban redevelopment is a splendid arena in which to demonstrate their actions. The politicians make allies of the redevelopers, but they must also give the impression that they are fiscally responsible. That is one reason they always claim that the redevelopment projects they choose to support will contribute to the city's economic well-being.

A third crucial motive in the redevelopment game is the *downtown rescue* motive. The phrase "saving downtown" has almost become a mantra for downtown interests. Indeed the daily newspaper, the *Columbus Dispatch,* is a principal advocate of that view. Since it is place bound, its well-being depends on a viable downtown. For Nationwide, economic considerations and professional creativity were also motives. The opportunity to revitalize the whole Arena District was a great chance to show Nationwide's vision and ability. Columbus is only one of many cities in which Nationwide funds revitalization projects, so a major success in Columbus would help that company consolidate its position in the *national* game of major redevelopment. Nationwide's decision also reflects a major element of corporate beneficence. The top executives actually express a sense of corporate responsibility for the downtown because they have been a major employer there for many years.

The antitax game focuses on two values: ending corporate welfare and promoting fiscal responsibility. This game brings together people from all parts of the political spectrum. It is interesting to note that in the Columbus antitax issue, many of the players were actually fans who wanted to see a new arena built for professional sports. The catch is that they opposed forcing the public to pay a sales tax for a facility that would generate profits for private businesses but serve only a small percentage of Columbus residents.

Now we turn to frame analysis. This is a general paradigm of communication that is not limited to the sociology of cities. However, it is useful for the analysis of debate over community issues and makes a good supplement to the EGSA framework. Therefore we devote much attention to the nature of the framing model.

Extending the EGSA Model

The EGSA model readily extends to include the analytical insights of other sociological models. In this section we extend the model to frame analysis, the sociospatial perspective, growth machine, symbolic economies, action theory, and the city character and tradition. *Frame analysis* helps us to understand how the values, goals, and motives of local actors connect to the course and resolution of local issues. The *sociospatial* perspective helps us see how extralocal matters as well as the spatial and sociocultural environment influence the course of local events. The *growth machine* perspective helps us to see the importance of how the property developers' interests mesh with the needs of local government. The *symbolic economies* view explains how politicians, business people, and the media attempt to manipulate urban imagery to fit their needs and goals. *Action* theory provides a way of looking at the factors that lead to the success or failure of local actors as they pursue their goals. The *city character and traditions* outlook shows how each community develops its own character and traditions and how these accumulated contexts affect issues and events.

Frame Analysis

Frame analysis is a combination of elements of cognitive psychology and symbolic interaction theory.[7] It is based on the idea that people are consumers and processors of information. They organize information in existing or newly constructed "frames" of reference. Through these frames people make sense of their world, develop their expectations, organize their memories, plan their actions, and interpret feedback.[8]

Frames are socially constructed meaning systems. They arise out of social interactions and become significant components of culture that are shared and passed on to newer members of society. Since frames occur in this way, they may be contested by various social actors who are attempting to establish and promulgate frames supportive of their ends. Groups often become ideologically committed to certain frames and advance social policy arguments based on them.[9]

Frames exist at different levels of generality. *Master frames* are part of the culture, and are subscribed to by most members of the population. They organize ways in which people take in and evaluate a wide variety of information. An example is the frame of democracy in American culture, which contains themes such as "government by the people, for the people, and of the people."

Frames may also be more limited and may even be specific to a group or subculture. They set their subscribers apart from others in the way they see things. For example, the theme of the "middle passage" provides African Americans with a perspective on their history and current life not held by most whites.

Frames may also be both strategic and tactical. That is, they are adopted or constructed for the explicit purpose of justifying a particular social action or mobilizing support for action from members of the general population. For example, women's groups have advanced the theme of "a woman's right to privacy" in advocating the right to abortion.[10]

From the standpoint of social action, the actors have the task of mobilizing support for their efforts.[11] This support must come from both within and without the actors' group. In the context of community issues, this means that the frame developed in support of their goals is most effective if it can be aligned with three things: a general, well-respected, subscribed-to cultural frame that places the actors within society's respected mainstream; the frames held by the actors' associates and coworkers, thereby contributing to their morale and motivating them to assist; and the frames held by members of the population that the actors aim to mobilize in support of the cause, thereby making a positive outcome for the actors more likely.

Framing may be considered a primary task of social actors as they pursue their goals. In mobilizing support, the actor's frame must resonate with people's perceptions, beliefs, values, and past experiences, or else the attempt at mobilization will fail. In contested issues, the actors often engage in counterframing opponents' arguments in order to gain ideological or moral advantage. Successful frame alignment, reframing, and counterframing form a repertoire of behaviors necessary for social actors' success. In a sense, a community conflict may be seen as a competitive or combative framing process as social actors vie with each other in search of popular support.

Framing Issue 1

We now turn to a frame analysis of the Issue 1 battle. In that contest, the pro-development group drew upon the general frame of *urban redevelopment* in presenting the issue to the community. Urban redevelopment as a cultural frame states, in effect, that the proposed project will make new, valuable, and interesting what is now old, worthless, and dull. In that same conflict, this frame incorporated several ideas, including (1) the proposed project is a valuable brownfield development (that is, it takes abandoned, underused, or wasteland and converts it to a much better use for the community); (2) the proposed development will act as a priming activity by attracting further investment and upgrading to its area; (3) by expanding local businesses, the tax burden on residents could be lessened as the business sector increases its share of tax contribution; and (4) the project will create jobs much needed by the nearby population. The Columbus pro-development group added to this frame the argument that they would permit the convention center to expand its market and enhance its operation, thereby capitalizing on a past investment already made by the community.

Quality of life was the second general cultural frame the pro-development group employed. This frame asserts that the proposed action will promote and enhance the general well-being of the population. In the Issue 1 conflict this frame encompassed the arguments that the arena and stadium would (1) enhance family life by providing safe and enriching opportunities for family activities; (2) make downtown a livelier and more fun place to be for all Columbus residents; (3) expand entertainment opportunities for the young and socially active adults; (4) make downtown a more attractive place for middle- and upper-middle-class residents to spend their shopping and leisure time, thereby improving the ambiance of Columbus's business district; and (5) reinvigorate the surrounding inner-city neighborhoods by making them attractive places in which to live or visit.

The third major cultural frame employed by the pro-development group was *civic pride*. As a general frame, civic pride is based on the idea that the proposed action will both enhance the way people feel about their community and show that as good citizens they are ready to act to promote the commonweal. In the context of Issue 1 this frame encompassed the following: (1) having a professional major league sports team would make Columbus a big league city and make it part of the nation's network of leading urban centers; (2) the new arena and stadium would make the city's downtown more attractive and the envy of other cities; (3) the costs in tax dollars were well worth the results; (4) by voting for the tax, Columbus residents would show what farsighted and progressive people they really are.

The pro-development group felt these cultural frames were both respectable and convincing. They also believed that the frames in some combination could easily be aligned with those of the voters they were trying to mobilize. The group identified the following segments of voters as their targets: soccer moms and dads, African Americans, male sports enthusiasts, rock concertgoers, middle-class, tax-conscious citizens, and women. As the issue turned out, the pro-development group was unable to adequately mobilize any of these voter segments.

The Opposition: The Central Issue of Taxes

The oppositional coalition VAST in its planning for action drew a distinction between the ends of the project—the arena and soccer stadium per se—and the means of achieving those ends—the Issue 1 sales tax. The opposition's strategy was to attack the legitimacy of the means while largely ignoring the ends. In interviews with the opposition's leadership, the investigators were told repeatedly, "I have nothing against an arena but *I am opposed to public financing.*" In presenting this central argument to the voters VAST employed four general frames.

The first frame was *corporate welfare.* This included the themes that citizens were being asked to pay for a facility that would benefit corporations at the expense of the public, that the corporations were shirking their community social responsibility by exploiting the public, and that this issue was all about the egos of the Titans. Another theme was that the corporations were willing to damage the environment of nearby neighborhoods in order to attain their goal. The theme was also added that the owner of the soccer franchise had no ties to the community and would likely move and take his franchise to another city as soon as a better financial opportunity appeared.

Class privilege was the second frame. This included the themes that the sports in question—soccer and hockey—were those of the middle and upper-middle class, yet the lower-middle, working, and lower classes were being asked to underwrite them. Also, the sports that Issue 1 would subsidize were essentially those of the white segment of the population and not those of people of color. Another class privilege theme was that the pricing of the tickets to events held in these facilities—sports, concerts, and others—would be beyond the means of the average citizen, and thus the arena and the stadium would not expand entertainment opportunities for them. A third theme was that the best seats in the facilities would be taken by corporations and top-level executives since so much space was devoted to luxury boxes and suites and other expensive seats.

The righteous citizen was the third frame. It had two themes. First was the idea that the opposition's motivation was not personal gain but simply that is was morally correct to stand up for the rights of average citizens in the face of a blatant attempt to take advantage of them. The second theme was that the opposition was outgunned by the pro-development group's power and finances and thus resembled David facing Goliath.

The fourth oppositional frame was *fiscal irresponsibility*. The main theme of this frame was that there was no evidence from any city that had constructed stadiums, ballparks, or arenas that proved that such projects had produced any positive fiscal impact on their city. A second variation within this theme was that with the opening of Ohio State's new arena, it was doubtful that a community of the size of Columbus could support two such entertainment venues. As a result of Ohio State's two-year head start in operation, the Columbus tax payers would most likely be stuck paying for and maintaining a dark, underused, and expensive downtown facility.

Counterframing

The counterframing response by the pro-development group took three forms: *vilification, frame debunking,* and *frame repair.* Those spokespersons vilified the opposition by claiming that it was made up of small-minded, selfish people who were willing to sacrifice community advancement for their own ends. In addition, the group argued that the opposition leaders were only trying to make names for themselves and that they would use that name recognition in later attempts to run for local office. The group also argued that the opposition was lying to the people about the financial benefits of such projects; that is, an arena and a stadium would be good for downtown, as the pro-development consultants predicted.

Frame debunking took the form of the pro-development spokespersons asserting that the opposition had the facts wrong and that, in fact, the local citizenry had nothing to lose from their investment. For example, they brought in the president of Ohio State University to endorse Issue 1 by stating that the city was indeed large enough to accommodate two successful arenas. They also brought in the African American head of city council to say that the whole community—blacks and whites alike— would benefit from the arena and not just the affluent whites, as the opposition argued.

The pro-development group felt that the opposition had damaged them by raising fears that the soccer owner would pull out of the city at any time and leave the Columbus taxpayers with the financial burden of an expensive, unused facility. To do *frame repair* on this issue, Lamar Hunt (the principal owner of the soccer franchise) sent a letter to the Convention Facilities Authority asserting that he was making a long-term financial commitment to the project and to the city. He detailed the financial steps he would take so that the city would not lose money on the project. In exchange for this assurance, he specified the favorable financial deal that he expected in return. (VAST attempted to debunk this attempt at frame repair by claiming that the letter was illegal because it amounted to an unbid contract between a private party and a public agency for control and management of the arena and stadium.)

Beyond responding to the letter to the Convention Facilities Authority, VAST did little in the way of counterframing the pro-development arguments. The one thing that it did do came near the end of the campaign. To respond to the pro-development group's argument that the opposition was simply trying to block an arena for the community, the principal VAST spokesman presented an alternative plan for financing the project that did not involve a countywide sales tax. It was based largely on user fees. The pro-development group simply dismissed his idea as a harebrained scheme designed to confuse the voters. The rest of the opposition's coalition leadership were miffed by the proposal since they were not consulted ahead of time. They also felt that they had framed the issue well and needed no such repair.

The VAST leadership had little counterframing to do because, given their past experience in conflictive community issues and by consulting with oppositional groups in other cities fighting similar issues, they were able to anticipate the arguments of the pro-development group and to build responses to them into the initial framing of their points of view. The pro-development groups did not do this pre-issue homework since they thought they had the issue clinched. They thought everyone would want a professional sports franchise to the same extent that they did. They were surprised when that proved not to be the case.

Framing Outcomes

In addition to framing arguments and positions, participants in intergroup conflict also tend to frame the outcome of their efforts. This is a major way that actors come to terms with winning or losing. Through outcome framing, actors are able to define the result of action in a way that is understandable to both themselves and observers. It is a way of writing a history of the action that is most favorable to the actors' side.

Framing defeat is an exercise in the sociology of blame. Blame is socially constructed and functions to explain why an attempted social action fails.[12] It assigns the responsibility for a failure to a person, group, entity, or event, thereby defining the target for potential negative sanctions. It often deflects attention from the most powerful actors to the least powerful or to outside factors. If negative sanctions are levied, it is unlikely that the more powerful actors will pay a price if others are available.

In the Issue 1 defeat, the Titans initially targeted VAST and the voters as the objects of blame. They accused VAST of playing unfairly and confusing the voters. They charged the voters with being selfish and shortsighted. The initial blaming of VAST and the voters terminated quickly when the plan for the private construction of the arena came forth. It soon became clear to the Titans that the voters were the market for the tickets for events, including hockey, to be held in the downtown arena. The Titans could not afford to antagonize the public, especially since the NHL required that the Columbus hockey group sell twelve thousand season tickets before the finalized awarding of the franchise.

Still, blame had to be assigned somewhere in order to deflect attention from the pro-growth group's lackluster campaign, so an outsider became the target. During the arena campaign the owner of the Hartford Whalers NHL team came to Columbus to explore the possibility of moving his franchise to Columbus. He even floated the idea that he would work with the city to renovate an unused airplane hangar as a temporary home for his team while the downtown arena was constructed. As one might expect, the Columbus hockey group became enraged. If this were to happen, their attempt to become new franchise owners would be terminated. Adding insult to injury, the Columbus group had funded and worked for the passage of Issue 1. Should that referendum pass and the Whalers come to town and not only take up residence in the new facility but manage it as well, the outcome would be a total disaster for the Columbus group. With the defeat of Issue 1 the owner of the Whalers dropped Columbus from his list of possible sites and ultimately moved his team to another city that had a waiting new arena.

The Whalers' owner now became the object of criticism by the Titans. They argued that he had ruthlessly played one city against another as he worked to secure the most favorable deal for his team. They maintained that he was never really serious about bringing the Whalers to town. His actions so muddled the Issue 1 controversy that the voters became confused and as a result took the safe action of voting "no." So the essence of the Columbus group's blame frame was that the good local people were misled and confused by the shenanigans of an outside charlatan, and that is what led to the defeat of the referendum.

VAST framed their victory as a job well done and as a rare triumph over the Titans. The leaders rejoiced in their win since they had often been on the losing side in past battles with the Titans. They argued that they had provided the voters with the needed information, and the voters had then acted responsibly. Winners seldom need to do much in the way of outcome framing, and that was the case in Issue 1.

This application of frame analysis shows that it can contribute much to the ecology of games model. Frame theory offers important insights into how key actors play their games by manipulating public knowledge and tying it to personal and social interests.

The Sociospatial Perspective

The *sociospatial* perspective (SSP) is a second perspective that we can use to supplement the general EGSA model. It is rooted in the work of Henri Lefebvre and incorporates Weberian, Engelsian, and Marxian insights. However, it goes far beyond those original roots and provides a modern, comprehensive picture of urban growth and development that is not slavishly tied to crude, simplistic economic determinism. Most fully developed by Mark Gottdiener, SSP has come to be one of the most important emphases of the *new urban* sociology.[13]

Environment Structured by Interaction

SSP argues that the development and structuring of the urban environment is the outcome of the interaction of a broad set of economic, political, and cultural factors. Real estate transactions are central in urban development and become enmeshed with the interests of a wide variety of groups including politicians, entrepreneurs, developers, bankers, class factions, racial and ethnic groups, home owners, renters, landlords, historic preservationists, and so on. Different groups or networks of actors come to share common interests in growth and change. They develop their own perceptions of growth, their own aspirations or goals, and their own agendas for pursuing those objectives. They form coalitions with other networks for as long as they may benefit from such cooperation. They engage in conflict with other networks or coalitions to achieve their purposes. In sum, Mark Gottdiener argues, "[D]evelopment is a contentious process involving many groups in society that push for a variety of forms. Development represents the outcome of all these separate interests as they play themselves out."[14]

In the Columbus arena and stadium issue several different growth interests were active. First were the Titans. They have been strongly pro-growth for many years. But the type of growth and development they have sought is "clean" development. They have opposed dirty smokestack industries like those in Cleveland that pollute the air, degrade the cityscape, and bring hourly workers, ethnic groups, and unions to town. The Titans have opted instead for office developments, corporate headquarters, and upscale shopping. They have wanted the old downtown to become a center of life and entertainment for the white-collar and professional classes of the metropolitan area. These city leaders have wanted Columbus to get the national recognition and respect that they feel is its due. Professional sports franchises and new stadiums and arenas were consistent with their dreams.

Politicians made up the second group interested in growth and development. City, county, and state politicians wanted growth for Columbus because it was good for the tax base. Growth was also good for their own self-interests. Supporting initiatives was a way for them to demonstrate that they were exercising their leadership role appropriately. The third pro-growth interest consisted of the downtown merchants and the chamber of commerce. Traditional supporters of all attempts to expand downtown dev-elopment, they saw growth as a way to improve and expand business. So too have the professional developers, architects, construction firms, lawyers, and Realtors, whose professional livelihoods are tied to growth and development. They can always be counted on to support growth initiatives.

Nationwide was another growth interest active in the city. For years the company had been connected to the Titans through its top leadership, but it had no direct interest in hockey. However, it did have a direct interest in the redevelopment of the northwest corner of the central business district because it had already invested millions in several corporate headquarter towers there. The prospect of the arena opened the door for them to pursue the commercial, entertainment, and residential development of their neighboring area. In doing so, the eyesore of the old state penitentiary, which was adjacent to Nationwide's corporate headquarters, could be rebuilt with a modern, mixed development. When offered the opportunity to join the arena development coalition, Nationwide joined eagerly and took the lead.

Other interests were active in the Issue 1 conflict but were opposed to the development. Neighborhood groups and residents adjacent to the construction sight were afraid that the project would adversely affect their quality of life as noise and traffic increased. Historic preservationists opposed the destruction of the final remnant of the old penitentiary. Some even went so far as to put themselves in harm's way by standing in front of the bulldozers—but not for long, as good sense ultimately prevailed. They thought that the pen's remnant should be saved because of its historic merit. Also opposed to the referendum was the VAST coalition, made up of people with a wide variety of political, ethical, environmental, and economic viewpoints united by opposition to the tax, or, as they characterized it, corporate welfare.

Government Independence

The SSP model argues that government plays an active role in development issues as it pursues its own interests beyond simply supporting the economic elites. In the Issue 1 conflict we see this in the central role of the Convention Facilities Authority. Its overall goal was clear—to make its downtown convention center one of the biggest, best, and most attractive in the United States. The stadium and arena project fit well with their hopes and plans, so they spearheaded the early stages of the venture. They commissioned the feasibility studies and made the original proposal to county government. The CFA also had the power of eminent domain, which meant that it could acquire nearby property from local owners for projects improving the convention center.

The mayor had been highly active on the local sports scene. He had played football for Ohio State's legendary coach Woody Hayes, who had supported the mayor's political career until Hayes's death. The mayor established the sports committee that ultimately attracted the soccer franchise to the community. He also worked closely with the Titans to bring the hockey franchise to the city. When Issue 1 failed, he played a major role in bringing together Nationwide and the *Columbus Dispatch,* who developed the plan for the arena's construction. Upon completion of his term, the mayor was appointed as a vice president of Nationwide, where he could continue his contribution to the project's development. He also approved the public funding of the infrastructure improvements required by the arena's construction. The $10-million cost overrun that occurred as a result of that development was left to his successor to cover. This overrun created a serious fiscal problem for the city and meant that other projects had to be put off to a later time or go forward with reduced funding.

Finally, we saw that the state of Ohio was pursuing its own interests in growth and development when it sent the Hunt group to the Ohio Exposition Center's commission to seek accommodation for its stadium.

Temporary Coalitions

The SSP model maintains that growth coalitions may be temporary. This was clear in the case of Columbus. The pro-growth coalition of the Titans, the downtown business community, and the chamber of commerce had worked hard for a long time to see that their image of city development was achieved.[15] The proposed stadium and arena fit well with their conception of what the city should be. They eagerly formed a short-term coalition with the Hunt group when they thought that it would help them obtain a professional hockey franchise. The price to the Titans was not only an arena but a stadium for Hunt's soccer team as well. When Issue 1 failed, the Titans-Hunt coalition fell apart. They no longer saw things the same way. Because the Titans were not about to let the failed stadium prevent them from obtaining a hockey franchise, they dropped Hunt from the coalition, after which their relationship soured, and a lawsuit followed. Ultimately, Hunt, the outsider to the community, lost the suit and was excluded from the hockey operation. As we have already described, Hunt formed another coalition— this time with the controlling board of the state fairgrounds, an arrangement that was mutually beneficial.

Growth Coalitions and Cultural Norms

The SSP model maintains that pro-growth coalitions will manipulate cultural norms to support growth projects that benefit the coalition first and foremost. The Columbus elite did just this. As we described earlier, the Titans argued for Issue 1 in terms of several cultural frames in attempting to persuade voters to support the proposed tax increase. The frames they chose were these: redevelopment favorable for community residents; improved quality of life for all community residents, especially families; and enhanced civic pride. The Titans were unable to sell their project on the basis of its promised cultural contribution. VAST argued against the issue by challenging the Titans' frames, and they convinced all categories of voters that the issue was public taxes for private gain.

From the SSP model we have learned several things that help to supplement the EGSA model. First, the use of space by various city activities becomes translated into real estate issues, and these concerns are central to the redevelopment process. Second, people with similar interests in the community form action groups whenever their agendas may be advanced or protected. Third, interest groups form coalitions when it seems profitable to them, but these coalitions are only temporary and may change as objectives and circumstances evolve. Finally, pro-growth coalitions are not above manipulating general community norms to advance their own selfish agendas.

The Growth Machine Model

Two hypotheses are at the heart of the *growth machine* model. The first is that local pro-growth coalitions have pervasive influence in local government regimes.[16] The second is that pro-growth regimes make a significant difference to local development. While several groups, including bankers, Realtors, and contractors, may be joined in a pro-growth coalition, land developers, or the "rentiers" class, are at its heart.[17] These are the people that acquire land for development, prepare it for construction, and market it to consumers. Their economic well-being depends on an active pattern of development and redevelopment. Consequently, they continually attempt to push issues of growth to the top of the public agenda.

Many local politicians and government officials find their needs fit well with the interests of the pro-growth rentiers. They join informally with the developers in a regime that pursues their common interests. Local government continually needs additional tax revenues to provide basic services for the community's population. Development and redevelopment offer ways to enhance local property tax revenue. Development often means local population growth. Additional people mean that the government needs to provide additional services. Additional services require additional funds. Additional funds enable more development. This race-with-the-devil means that the local government needs to continually cooperate with developers by accommodating their requirements. It also means that issues of growth and development are central government concerns. Cities, then, become "growth machines." If the machine falters, local economic disaster becomes a distinct possibility.

In Columbus we saw how the mayor and city council pushed economic development for the city and cooperated with Nationwide and the Titans to bring hockey to town and to build an arena. They worked well together because they had worked with each other in the past and would do so again in the future. Indeed, they formed a classic pro-growth coalition.

The prospect of the Arena District was that it would provide the city with a potential tax windfall from the property, payroll, and sales taxes that would eventually be collected from activities in that renewed area. In effect, Nationwide's redevelopment efforts converted an unproductive brownfield into a high-activity area. However, the city had to pay a price in tax abatements and other arrangements to encourage Nationwide to pursue the project. It would be years before any conclusions could be drawn as to just how much city budgets were enhanced by the development.

As solid a redevelopment as the Arena District was, the city officials had to move on to other projects to meet people's needs and help solve city problems.

Symbolic Economies Model

The growth machine model helps us to see the major economic reasons for growth and development activities. The *symbolic economies* model helps us to see that there is another side to this.[18] The way a city looks to most people reflects both entrepreneurial capital and cultural symbols. A city's cultural symbols are important because people behave in terms of images, definitions, and frames. Places acquire cultural meanings that become important to their prospects and potential.

Cultural definitions of a city or of a portion of a city may develop extemporaneously as people experience the environment and come to share sentiments about it. Alternatively, cultural definitions may be contrived through the actions of groups pursuing their own agendas. Pro-growth interests actively attempt to establish the image of the city or a segment of it that is positive and thereby attractive to investors. It is not easy to establish or change a cultural definition of a place. It takes considerable economic, political, and media capital to convince enough people that the new image is accurate and represents the place well.

In Columbus, the Titans wanted to shed the city's "cow town" image. They wanted it to be "big time" and "major league." They felt that acquiring a professional hockey team would be a key factor in changing the city's image. With a professional franchise they would no longer have to identify themselves as being from Columbus, Ohio. They would be from Columbus, period—the Columbus that appeared on the sports pages every day.

The Titans also felt that the presence of the abandoned Old Pen site at the northwest entrance to downtown was degrading. A new arena and a new Arena District in its place would make a very different statement. Columbus would now be "a happening place." Downtown would be where the hip came to play and maybe live and work as well.

Action Theory

Action theory has a long history in sociology, and it may also be used as a supplement to the EGSA model. *Action* is defined as the behavior of a social actor (individual, group, or organization) that is directed toward attaining a defined goal and oriented toward other social actors. Action usually consists of a series of stages ranging from planning, to mobilization of resources, to acting and carrying out plans, to evaluating success or failure, to reformulation of plans and strategies.[19] We now draw upon three propositions of action theory.

Leadership

The first action proposition deals with leadership. *The more experienced the actor, the more likely the actor is to achieve the goal.* We have seen evidence of this in the Columbus conflict. The opposition to Issue 1 had savvy leadership that was experienced in the world of conflictive local politics. Many of them had been campus activists in the troubled times of the 1970s. They had learned how to confront the power structure. They had also learned that, in the world of local politics, voter mobilization was critical. Mobilization could be successful only when the actors were able to articulate their positions in a way that would resonate with the majority of the public. The fact that their organization was a temporary alliance of disparate political groups was seen as a strength. Being experienced, they knew that their coalition had to hold together for only a short time. They also knew that by agreeing on this one issue, they were not making a long-run commitment to one another that would require a difficult period of adjustment. But they also knew that by joining together they would reach a large segment of the electorate.

The pro-development leadership actors had not learned the same lessons as had the oppositional leadership. The world of the elite was one of vast economic power and political influence. They had resources sufficient to undertake large projects themselves. In fact, after their defeat in Issue 1, they went ahead and spent their own money for the arena construction. They were also used to wielding political power behind the scenes. Hunt did exactly that when he obtained a prime location at state expense for his soccer stadium. The local leaders were well adapted for working while out of the spotlight but poorly adapted for mobilizing civic support on the public stage.

Unanticipated Turns

The second action proposition is, *the greater the ability of a social actor to respond to unanticipated events during the course of action, the more likely the actor is to achieve the goal.* These actors see themselves engaging in a linear process of steps that move them from goal to result.[20] Things seldom proceed in such a simple fashion. Unexpected events, unanticipated opposition, outside interventions, and other factors tend to knock social action off its planned course. A test of the actors' ability is their capacity to recover from such factors and adjust their procedures so as to achieve their desired outcome. The pro-growth groups were seemingly derailed by the negative vote. Nonetheless, they were able to overcome the setback by enlisting other actors that could provide the resources required. Both the hockey group and the soccer group, even though they had parted ways, were able to find the necessary sponsors. In doing so they were successful in the end. Economic power, political power, and skill in backroom maneuvering contributed to their success as actors.

The third action hypothesis is, *the greater the economic and political resources an actor controls, the more likely the actor is to achieve the goal.* The Titans were the power elite of Columbus. They had the wealth, control of major media outlets, strong and sympathetic ties to the local political order, and the unwavering support of the business community. Even though they were unable to convince the voters of the value of their project, they ultimately used those economic and political resources to build the arena and the stadium. Economic power, political power, and skill in backroom maneuvering contributed to their success.

In sum, what have we incorporated from general action theory into the EGSA model? First, there is no substitute for high-quality leadership. Leaders and their skills do matter. The wrong leaders can bring about disastrous results. Second, action doesn't just happen. It tends to go through a predictable series of steps, and each step may be a branching point at which actors may go one way or another. This fact always lends social action a degree of unpredictability at the outset. Third, having ample resources gives actors a major advantage, but the sheer size of resources alone does not determine the results.

City Character and Urban Tradition

This perspective starts with the position that each city exhibits overarching characteristics that make it distinctly different from other cities, and it adds an important dimension to the EGSA model. To understand the etiology of city distinctiveness, Harvey Molotch, William Freudenburg, and Krista E. Paulsen argue that the concepts of "character" and "tradition" are fundamental.[21] *Character* refers to the particular "lash-up," or configuration, of local social structural elements at a given time. *Tradition* refers to the way that character changes over time. The fact that structure at one instant shapes structure at a later time is important. In effect, one moment's structure either constrains or enables structure at another time. In other words, today's structure is built upon the structure of the past, and the future's will be built upon the present's. According to this paradigm all of the realms of local life—the economy, politics, voluntary associations, the built and natural environments, and the like—are of similar importance in understanding the community's character and tradition. Since research focuses on the "connective tissues" between these realms, the issue is moot as to which of the realms is the most important in local life. The ultimate research goal is to find out how communities work rather than to attribute dominance in local matters to one or two variables.

Since tradition and continuity are the normal state of affairs, how is it that, according to this perspective, radical shifts can take place in the lash-up of local elements? Consider the example of the transition of Miami's

South Beach from a dull, run-down, and decayed area inhabited by poor pensioners to a hip and happening place for affluent young adults whose social life revolves around restored residences, swank bars, restaurants and clubs, and frenetic socializing. This paradigm suggests that such a major turn of events may come in large part from a decay of the community's social infrastructure and economic base. As these deteriorate, they erode the underpinnings of former lash-ups and create opportunities, and sometimes even imperatives, for a rebalancing of institutional realms. In Miami's South Beach, the system had wound down and become vulnerable to change. At the time revitalization and gentrification in the community invaded South Beach because of its proximity to the ocean, its glorious beaches, and its available but run-down buildings.

In terms of character and tradition, Columbus has historically been described as a quiet, affluent, conservative, middle-class, and Midwestern state capital and college town. Certainly an appellation of "The Quiet Place" would not be inappropriate for Columbus. The lash-ups among the institutional realms all reinforce this conservative image. Change comes slowly to the city. The press, the Titans, and the general public make much of small changes, such as the refurbishing of an old downtown theater. People regularly show their resistance to change at the ballot box. For example, voters defeated five separate attempts by the pro-growth coalition to raise public funds for the construction of a downtown arena. Similarly, several mass transit issues to support the development of light rail have met a negative fate. If ever a city's motto should be "if it ain't broke, don't fix it," Columbus should adopt it, according to many. Unfortunately for downtown beyond the Arena District, not enough people think it is "broke" and in need of "fixing."

How did this affluent, conservative, and stable lash-up persist through time or, in effect, become the traditional pattern of community organization? Inspection of Columbus's history reveals many changes over the last one hundred years, yet none of them were revolutionary. In addition, the city's social stratification system continually reproduced itself so that families and people sharing a conservative economic and political philosophy remained in influential positions.

So, what do the concepts of character and tradition add to the perspective of the ecology of games? Clearly, community character and tradition are two things that help form the sociocultural environment in which issues play out. In comparing Columbus to Pittsburgh and Cincinnati, we see vast differences in character and tradition. Pittsburgh and Cincinnati have been big league sports towns for decades. If any of their teams left for another city, the whole lash-up that supports major league sports there would change and so too would the city's fundamental and important tradition. Community actors in the two towns were not about to let that happen. Actors in each city found different ways to build their stadiums, and these dissimilar strategies reflected differences in the character of their ongoing institutional realms. For Columbus, big time sports was not a part of the tradition, nor did the institutional lash-up include a major league sports dimension. That is why it was so difficult for the pro-growth interests there to build the arena and stadium and capture the hockey franchise. The change in local social structure that it ultimately took to achieve these feats was revolutionary. Not only did a set of new organizational structures arise, but the portent was also real for a major change in community tradition.

Conclusion: The Issues of Structure versus Agency and Testability

Criticisms of Long's original ecology of games model reflect the long-standing debate in sociology between the opposing ideas of structure and agency. From the perspective of "structure," things happen as they do because of the way the needs, demands, power, and influence of established social institutions and structures drive the social, economic, and political system.[22] Broad processes of change sweep over individuals as forces shape and reshape society. Individual actors are really just agents of these institutions. Their opportunities for innovation, self-determination, and individualized behaviors are highly constrained by their position in the large institutions and organizations. An example of this view is found in Michael Kennedy's analysis of municipal fiscal health in the United States. He wrote: "A city's fiscal health should not be attributed to the quality of its management, or the composition of its budget. The fiscal health of a city is to a large extent beyond the control of its municipal government, and it is ultimately determined by the city's attractiveness as a site for continued private capital investment."[23]

The concept of "agency" sees things as happening because of the ways individuals perceive the world, form plans and strategies, accumulate resources, and act. Individuals are influenced, and perhaps even shaped, by institutions, but in the final analysis, they are free to a significant degree to pursue their goals and plans. Because different individuals have different agendas, values, and styles of behaving, events develop differently depending on the particular configuration of actors involved at any one time. Things happen—or don't happen—because individuals do (or do not do) things and not because of some disembodied process operating beyond human control.

We may view structure and agency as forming a continuum on which a given theoretical orientation may be plotted. Critics of the ecology of games model assert that the model is so far toward the agency end that it gives very little consideration to structure. Consequently, more macro-oriented scholars are bothered by the paradigm's focus on individuals and their varying roles. These theorists argue that the ecology of games attributes too much power to the individual and, as a result, places too much emphasis on differences among them in their roles and interests. One such scholar, Peter Shields, argues that the explanatory power of the role of social institutions and structures is marginalized in ecological game analyses.[24] That is, social institutions are denied their independent status. Noting the socially constructed nature of these macropresences, though, William H. Dutton responds: "Indeed, structures and institutions do not have an independent ontological status in the sense that they do not spring from the heavens!"[25] This is not to say that institutions do not structure human agency. The social institutions in which we live condition human action, but not to the extent that we can use them to predict a series of outcomes in a community without considering the full range of rules, roles, and relationships that govern individuals' behavior.

We believe that by adding insights from the perspectives of frame analysis—the sociospatial perspective, the growth machine model, the symbolic economies model, action theory, and the city and urban tradition paradigms—we may bypass the old debate about structure and human agency. Clearly, events happen in cities as a result of both human agency and the existence of social structures. In the case of Columbus, the Titans achieved some of their goals in an interplay of forces that involved several large organizations and many individuals. With a different constellation of forces, a different outcome would have resulted.

Testability

Beyond the issue of structure vs. agency, one major limitation of Long's original ecology of games model is that it is difficult to test empirically whether the model is more useful than any other given perspective in any given case study. This limitation is due to the fact that this paradigm has been used in the past mainly as a sensitizing concept, a tool for describing the local community to others and for metaphorically linking the social world to an understandable context—a game.[26] As a consequence, however, it is difficult to compare the usefulness of the ecology of games model to other sociological perspectives. Like other sensitizing concepts, various aspects of game playing in the ecology of the local community cannot be measured and have not been broken down into statistical categories or variables. In effect, no machinery is in place to systematically test its worth. This is problematic because it makes the theory unattractive to quantitatively oriented researchers who study meso-level processes, restricting its use mainly to qualitative field analyses and case studies.

We do not feel that these limitations are fatal to the ecology of games. Rather, by incorporating additional perspectives into the framework, we construct a greater empirical base for testing. The EGSA model provides future researchers with a framework that can help develop the perspective to a point that it contributes more to modern sociological theory. Our use of the framework contributes to a deeper understanding of the scope of the theory and its application across contexts, as well as to its usefulness as a sensitizing concept. We use the EGSA model to highlight the macrosocial, historical, and individual-level actions that shape local community outcomes. In doing so, we create a unique model of social action that can be applied to a wide range of community outcomes. We have demonstrated how it works by applying it to the recent sports facility construction activity in Columbus.[27] In doing so, we hope to show the analytical advantage of using multiple perspectives in combination in the study of the conflictive world of urban growth and development.

A Note on Research Methodology

For this study we used a traditional community studies approach and gathered data from three major sources. The first was media reports—including local and national newspapers, magazines, radio, and television programming, and the Internet. The second source of data was official documents: contracts, reports, files, and informant correspondence. The third source was a series of in-depth interviews conducted with thirty-four of the social actors directly involved in the issue, as well as those who are knowledgeable about their community, such as reporters, market researchers, political activists, and other inside observers. In all but a few of the cases, the three authors jointly conducted the interviews. For the most part, these interviews took place at the interviewee's office or at the authors' offices at OSU. A few of them were conducted in coffee shops and diners.

Before each one of the semistructured interviews, the three authors conferred about what information they needed from the particular interviewee. We developed a general division of labor in asking our questions. Kent Schwirian mainly asked questions on who did what, when, where, and why. Tim Curry inquired about issues of timing, resource allocation and organization, and linkages to other sports-related issues. Finally, Rachael A. Woldoff asked about the political dynamics of the issue, elements of conflict, and connections to groups and organizations within and outside the community, and she probed to learn about the informants' assessments of the turn of events and outcomes. Woldoff also kept track of any gaps in the knowledge that we gathered over the course of an interview and used the last segment of time to redirect the discussion and gather any missing information.

However, in a given session, we sometimes diverged from the tidy division of labor. In these situations we would each attempt to squeeze in questions that we believed had not been fully answered. The interviews lasted between 90 and 120 minutes each. Afterward we reviewed our individual field notes with each other and discussed our impressions. Then each of us immediately entered our notes into a word-processing program and circulated our versions. Thus, for each interview, we had three sets of notes compiled so that we could triangulate. In addition, after reading the collected notes, we held discussions to make sure we concurred about what we had learned in the interview. Although we did not always have perfect consensus, we generally agreed on most important points. When appropriate, we listed multiple perspectives or interpretations of interview material and events.

Notes

Notes to Preface

1. See Kevin Allen, "Unique New Arena Has Coyotes Licking Their Chops: First True Home Sits amid Stores, Eateries," *USA Today,* 20 February 2003, sec. 8C.

2. Todd Jones, "The Cold Facts: MLS Has Survived and Even Thrived." *Columbus Dispatch,* 6 April 2003, sec. E6.

3. See Norton E. Long, "The Local Community as an Ecology of Games," *American Journal of Sociology* 64 (1958): 251–61.

Notes to Chapter 1

1. Warren Cohen, "Oysters, Scotch, and Hoops: New Sports Arenas Are Dens of Luxury: They May Also Fail," *U.S. News & World Report,* 15 November 1999, 92–93.

2. Charles Euchner, *Playing the Field: Why Sports Teams Move and Cities Fight to Keep Them* (Baltimore: Johns Hopkins University Press, 1993).

3. Sports fans have observed several examples of teams deserting their communities to pursue better deals elsewhere. Among the most notorious of these relocations was the migration of the Baltimore Colts football franchise to Indianapolis. The Colts made a surprise move from Baltimore to Indianapolis in the middle of the night, thereby escaping massive fan outcries of indignation, anger, and hostility—and the threats of lawsuits or legislation that might have forced them to remain in Baltimore. Ironically, those same fans were delighted a few years later when a new Baltimore stadium deal lured the Cleveland Browns to Baltimore (see chapter 2).

4. Thomas R. Shannon, Nancy Kleniewski, and William M. Cross, *Urban Problems in Sociological Perspective* (Prospect Heights, Ill.: Waveland Press, 1991).

5. See Mark Ferenchik, "Arena-Area Expenses Increasing," *Columbus Dispatch,* 30 April 2000, sec. F1–F2.

6. Michael A. Pagano and Ann O'M. Bowman, *Cityscapes and Capital: The Politics of Urban Development* (Baltimore: Johns Hopkins University Press, 1995).

7. Minor league baseball thrived in Waterloo, Iowa, from 1904 until 1994. Its death resulted from the fact that this town of sixty-six thousand could not afford to make the upgrades to their old and venerable Waterloo Municipal Stadium. The major league organization demanded these upgrades for its minor league affiliates. As a result, just three weeks before opening day that would have marked ninety years of baseball in Waterloo, the Waterloo Diamonds folded. This pattern was repeated many times in many places across the country. See Jerry Klinkowitz, *Owning a Piece of the Minors* (Carbondale: Southern Illinois University Press, 1999). See also Richard Panek, *Waterloo Diamonds* (New York: St. Martin's Press, 1995).

8. We use the term "big time" sports to refer to the institution itself. It includes the professional, major league organizations; the large-scale college and university sport establishment as embodied in the National Collegiate Athletic Association; and the myriad sports organizations that control the worlds of individual amateur sports such as track and field, boxing, and swimming. They are "big time" in the sense of the massive financial resources they hold and control, their central position in the economy of the mass media, their political clout, and the scope of control they exercise over athletes, teams, and franchises.

9. Citizens who favor development often resist specific projects when such projects are located in their own or adjacent neighborhoods. Residents are often afraid that these projects will complicate or degrade the quality of local life or cause property values to decline.

10. This idea is at the heart of the sociological concept of metropolitan dominance. Accordingly, metropolitan communities dominate their hinterlands by organizing the scale, scope, and mix of activities that occur there. See Donald Bogue, *The Structure of the Metropolitan Community* (Ann Arbor: University of Michigan Press, 1950). See also Amos Hawley, *Urban Society: An Ecological Approach,* 2d ed. (New York: John Wiley and Sons, 1981).

11. See Saskia Sassen, *The Global City: New York, Tokyo, and London* (Princeton, N.J.: Princeton University Press, 1991).

12. Scott Greer pointed out that the scale of American society has increased with the processes of industrialization, urbanization, and bureaucratization. As a result, the local community has become dependent, lost its autonomy, and is no longer in total control of its own fate. Community residents are exposed to conflicting norms from afar that render old rules and conventions vulnerable to change and that fragment the local normative order. See Scott Greer, *The Emerging City* (New York: The Free Press, 1962). A more recent statement of this argument is found in Tim Curry, Robert Jiobu, and Kent Schwirian, *Sociology for the Twenty-First Century* (Upper Saddle River, N.J.: Prentice-Hall, 2002).

13. Not to be outdone by Chicago, the New York art community undertook its own cow parade in the summer of 2000 when five hundred humorously painted cow sculptures were scattered across the city's neighborhoods. That same summer, Toronto entered the outdoor animal sculpture game with a display of comically decorated fiberglass moose. Also, in Cincinnati, the residents were treated to a public art display of more than 360 colorful, flying pigs in their "Big Pig Gig."

14. See Kevin Fitzpatrick and Mark LaGory, *Unhealthy Places* (New York: Routledge, 2000).

15. Roland Warren argued that even though local communities were connected to

organizations and institutions in other places through a series of social, economic, and political relationships, community members formed their unique local system of relationships when people performed locality-relevant functions. These included production-distribution-consumption, socialization, social control, social participation, and mutual support. See Roland L. Warren, *The Community in American Society,* 3d ed. (Chicago: Rand McNally, 1978).

16. Migrants are among those who are most sensitive to intercommunity differences in local culture. It is common for recent migrants to a community to experience a period of behavioral adjustment as they assimilate, adapt, acculturate, and learn the ways locals live in the new place. Migrants often form ethnic colonies or enclaves in cities, and these serve as temporary home bases for them as they assimilate to the city's mainstream culture. Specialized stores and institutions tend to develop in enclaves. These institutions provide local support for the migrants' distinctive lifestyles. The greater the difference in culture and lifestyle between the migrants and the mainstream population, the more time migrants need to assimilate. As long as migrants continue to come into the area and need transitional services, there will be institutions and services that cater to them. For various reasons, some enclaves are very resistant to change and stand as a reminder of the city's ethnic past, indicating the city's current cultural diversity. One major way that cities differ from each other is in their migrant history and the related mix and persistence of ethnic and racial colonies, enclaves, and ghettos and their related institutions and organizations. See Mark Abrahamson, *Urban Enclaves* (New York: St. Martin's Press, 1996). See also F. W. Boal, "Ethnic Residential Segregation," in *Social Areas in Cities, Vol. 1: Spatial Processes and Form,* ed. D. T. Herbert and R. J. Johnson (London: John Wiley and Sons, 1976), 41–80.

17. For a review of inner-city problems at the end of the twentieth century, see Elvin K. Wyly, Norman J. Glickman, and Michael L. Lahr, "A Top 10 List of Things to Know about American Cities," *Cityscape* 3 (1998): 7–32.

18. Amy Nelson and her associates show that distress—as measured by unemployment, poverty, low income, educational problems, family disorganization, crime, and housing quality—has increased greatly in our cities, especially the larger ones. See Amy L. Nelson, Kent P. Schwirian, and Patricia M. Schwirian, "Social and Economic Distress in Large Cities, 1970–1990: A Test of the Urban Crisis Thesis," *Social Science Research* 27 (1998): 410–31.

19. See note 18 above.

20. See Sam Walker, "Building Boom Reshapes City Skylines," *Christian Science Monitor,* April 18, 1997, available online at http://www.csmonitor.com/durable/1997/08-/18/us/us.2html. Walker points out that in some cities, such as Denver, Cleveland, Pittsburgh, Cincinnati, Dallas, and Baltimore, downtown amenities center around new stadiums.

Notes to Chapter 2

1. Herberg Maps, *2000 North American Baseball Travel Map* (Minneapolis: White Star Press, 2000).

2. Between 1980 and 1997 the number of nonprofit sports organizations and governing bodies in amateur sports increased from 504 to 826. U.S. Bureau of the Census, *Statistical Abstract of the United States, 1999* (Washington, D.C.: 2000), Table 1299.

3. See Bill Bryson, "Sydney, on Top of the World down Under," *National Geographic* 198 (2000): 2–25.

4. See note 2 above, Table 452.

5. There are critics of the festival approach to downtown redevelopment. For example, Peter Eisinger argues that rebuilding downtown for visitors' entertainment can strain the bonds of trust between local leaders and the citizenry and so skew the city's civic agenda that basic municipal services are hurt. See Peter Eisinger, "The Politics of Bread and Circuses: Building the City for the Visitor Class," *Urban Affairs Review* 33 (2000): 316–33, discussed in Chapter 8.

6. See Nancy Kleniewski, *Cities, Change, and Conflict* (New York: Wadsworth Publishing, 1997). Among other factors, she discusses the federal government's decision in the1980s to shift income redistribution priorities from the poor to businesses. This government policy, known as recapitalization, involved reducing business taxes, shrinking the public sector, increasing support for exports, reducing inflation by holding wages down, reducing government regulation of business, and so on.

7. Shayla Shrieves, "Brownfields and Voters," *Columbus C.E.O,* 14–19 October 2000.

8. See Anselm Strauss, *Images of the American City* (New York: Free Press of Glencoe, 1961), 14.

9. See Kent P. Schwirian, "Internal Structure of the Metropolis," in *Contemporary Topics in Urban Sociology,* ed. Kent P. Schwirian et al. (Morristown, N.J.: General Learning Press, 1977), 152–215.

10. David M. Hummon, *Common Places: Community Ideology and Identity in American Culture* (Albany: State University of New York Press, 1990).

11. Randell Lane, "In the Oakland A's, Some Lessons for Silicon Valley," *The New York Times,* 1 October 2000, 7.

12. David Lieberman, "$1B Bid Draws Static," *USA Today,* 10 September 1998, sec. 3C.

13. Don Pierson, "Brown-Out in Cleveland: NFL Owners' Credibility Takes Hit," *Chicago Tribune,* 7 November 1995, sec. 4, pp. 1, 5.

14. Jon Morgan, *Glory for Sale: Fans, Dollars, and the New NFL* (Baltimore: Bancroft Press, 1997), 81.

15. Ibid. Eventually, the animosity generated by the move forced the National Football League to promise Cleveland that they would receive a replacement team. In addition, the NFL contributed $48 million to the cost of building a new stadium.

16. Gerry Brown and Michael Morrison, eds., *The 1999 ESPN Information Please Sports Almanac* (Boston: Hyperion ESPN Books, 1999).

17. Mark S. Rosentraub, *Major-League Losers: The Real Cost of Sports and Who's Paying for It* (New York: Basic Books, 1997).

18. Gil Stein, *Power Plays: An Inside Look at the Big Business of the National Hockey League* (New Jersey: Birch Press, 1997); John MacKinnon, *NHL Hockey: An Official Fan's Game,* 3d ed. (Chicago: Benchmark, 1998).

19. Jeff Z. Klein, "Sad Farewells to Gretzky and the Past," *New York Times,* 18 April 1999, 40.

20. John MacKinnon, *NHL Hockey: An Official Fans' Game,* 3d ed. (Chicago: Benchmark Press, 1998), 6.

21. Zander Hollander, ed., *The Hockey News Hockey Almanac 1999* (Farmington Hills, Mich.: Visible Ink Press, 1999).

22. John Wilson, *Playing by the Rules: Sports, Society, and the State* (Detroit: Wayne State University Press, 1994).

23. Dan Hodes, "Swimming in It," in *ESPN: The Magazine*, 10 July 2000, 72–74.

24. Kevin Allen, "NHL Backs LEMIEUX, Begins a Push to Solve Penguins' Bankruptcy," *USA Today*, 21 April 1999, sec. 9C.

25. Kevin Allen, "Canadian Clubs: Help!" *USA Today*, 9 April 1999, sec. 1C.

26. D. Stanley Eitzen, *Fair and Foul: Beyond the Myths and Paradoxes of Sport* (Lanham, Md.: Rowman and Littlefield, 1999), 17.

27. E. M. Swift, "Hey, Fans, Sit on It!" *Sports Illustrated*, 15 May 2000, 70–85.

28. Michael Hiestand, "Fox Folks Aim to End Tenure with Flourish," *USA Today*, 22 January 1999, sec. 5F.

29. Ibid.

30. See note 20 above, 384.

31. See note 27 above.

32. Jeff MacGregor, "Boom with a View," *Sports Illustrated*, 28 March 1999, 18. Interestingly, hockey's appeal to local cable systems may not be so dependent on generating large audiences. A local hockey team can be considered a reliable source of family entertainment, with a particular appeal to a difficult-to-reach male audience. Moreover, a seventy-channel cable system has a yearly programming need for 613,200 hours of television.

33. Dave Litterer, "An Overview of American Soccer History," 11 May 1999, available online at www.sover.net/-spectrum/overview.html.

34. Neil Campbell, "World Cup Was a Big Success, But Will Soccer Live on in the U.S.?" *Columbus Dispatch*, 19 July 1994, sec. 6F.

35. Knight-Rider Newspapers, "U.S. Soccer Win Draws Attention, *The Columbus Dispatch*, 4 July 1994, sec. 6D.

36. Major League Soccer, *1998 Major League Soccer Media Guide and Register* (New York: Major League Soccer, 1998), 12.

37. See note 34 above.

38. See note 33 above.

39. Ron Rapport, "New Soccer League Probably Can't Afford U.S. Cup World Stars," *Columbus Dispatch*, 4 July 1994, sec. 6D.

40. See note 34 above.

41. Craig Merz, " 'No Excuses' Is Cry as Topsy-Turvy MLS Enters Fourth Season," *The Columbus Dispatch*, 19 March 1999, sec. 13D.

42. Jay Coakley, *Sport in Society: Issues and Controversies* (St. Louis: Mosby, 1999).

Notes to Chapter 3

1. Haya El Nasser, "Is Pittsburgh's Revitalization out of Step?" *U.S.A. Today*, 27 June 2000, sec. 17a. Pittsburgh, more than any other rust-belt city, has made the transition from steel-manufacturing center to financial and corporate center. With the loss of steel production there has been a major loss of well-paid manufacturing jobs as well. That, in turn, has been accompanied by a population loss of thirty thousand in the 1990s. In attempting to remodel itself, Pittsburgh has undertaken major construction projects that have reshaped the whole downtown area. Some of these projects—a new convention center, a new football stadium for the Steelers, and a new baseball park for

the Pirates—have come at a considerable price. The public funding for these projects has greatly stressed the city's budget (see Chapter 8).

2. See Felix M. Keesing, *Cultural Anthropology* (New York: Rinehart, 1958). Keesing tells us that for some cultures, war and fighting were "a kind of game or competition or chivalrous exercise in which physical combat, man to man or group to group, defined success and enhanced prestige for the victorious party" (296).

3. We distinguish between urban *development* and urban *redevelopment*. Development is essentially a "greenfields" enterprise, that is, conversion of open spaces that previously had nonurban uses (such as farms and open spaces) to urban spaces—manufacturing plants, housing developments, shopping malls, office and medical centers, airports, stadiums, and ballparks. Redevelopment is a form of "brownfield" enterprise. It takes areas that had a prior urban usage and converts them into updated, modern, and alternative uses. The term *revitalization* is often used synonymously with *redevelopment*. When Dodger Stadium was constructed in Los Angeles, it was an urban *development* project. When the Giants' new ballpark was built in San Francisco, it was a *redevelopment* (or *revitalization*) project. The economics, politics, and sociology of development and redevelopment, while related in many significant ways, are sufficiently unique processes that they may be considered separately. There is a "development" game and there is a "redevelopment game." The degree to which they overlap varies widely from city to city.

4. See Norton E. Long, "The Local Community as an Ecology of Games," *American Journal of Sociology* 64 (1958): 251–61. Long argues, "Far from regarding games as trivial, the writer's position is that man is both a game-playing and a game-creating animal, that his capacity to create and play games and take them deadly seriously is of the essence, and that it is through games or activities analogous to game playing that he achieves a satisfactory sense of significance and a meaningful role" (252).

5. See C. Wright Mills, *The Power Elite* (New York: Oxford University Press, 1956); William Form, "Mills at Maryland," *The American Sociologist* 26 (1995): 40–67. Also, Long wrote: "A final game that does in a significant way integrate all the games in the territorial system is the social game. Success in each of the games can in varying degrees be cashed in for social acceptance. The custodians of the symbols of top social standing provide goals that in a sense give all individual games some common denominator of achievement" (260). See Appendix.

6. See Tim Curry, Robert Jiobu, and Kent Schwirian, *Sociology for the Twenty-First Century* (Upper Saddle River, N.J.: Prentice-Hall, 1997).

7. See Andrew Cuomo, "From the Secretary," *Cityscape* 4 (2000): iii.

8. See William H. Form, "The Place of Social Structure in the Determination of Land Use: Some Implications for a Theory of Urban Ecology," *Social Forces* 32 (1954): 418–29; also see Kent P. Schwirian, "Urban Spatial Arrangements as Reflections of Social Reality," in *Remaking the City,* ed. John S. Pipkin, Mark E. LaGory, and Judith B. Blau (Albany: SUNY Press, 1983), 121–47. The players in the redevelopment game come from the city's land market.

9. See John R. Logan, "Gambling on Real Estate: Limited Rationality in the Global Economy," *Sociological Perspectives* 34 (1991): 391–401. Also see John R. Logan, Rachael Bridges Whaley, and Kyle Crowder, "The Character and Consequences of Growth Regimes: An Assessment of Twenty Years of Research," *Urban Affairs Review* 32 (1997): 603–30.

10. Levitt and Sons is one of the most successful development teams ever assembled in the United States. The firm is among one of the two percent of developers that have built the lion's share of residential housing in the United States in the second half of the twentieth century. Indeed, "Levittown" has become the symbol of the mass-produced, packaged suburb. While much of the public credit for the firm's success has been given to William Levitt, it was his genius in putting his *team* together that lead to its ultimate success in the development game. "Using nonunion labor, Levitt and Sons pulled together in one corporation the various aspects of house manufacturing and marketing process, from controlling the source of nails and lumber to marketing the finished houses," in Joe R. Feagin and Robert Parker, *The Urban Real Estate Game,* 2d ed. (Englewood Cliffs, N.J.: Prentice-Hall, 1990), 16; also see J. John Palen, *The Suburbs* (New York: McGraw Hill, 1995).

11. See Arthur Lubow, "Rem Koolhass Builds," *New York Times Sunday Magazine,* 9 July 2000, available online at www.nytimes.com/magazine/home/20000709 mag-koolhass.html.

12. Gerald D. Suttles, *The Man-Made City* (Chicago: University of Chicago Press, 1990), 281.

13. See Anselm Strauss, *Images of the American City* (New York: Free Press of Glencoe, 1961).

14. See Amy L. Nelson and Kent P. Schwirian, "Social and Economic Distress in Large Cities, 1970–1990: A Test of the Urban Crisis Thesis," *Social Science Research* 27 (1998): 410–31; J. John Palen, *The Urban World* (New York: McGraw-Hill, 1997).

15. See Kent P. Schwirian and Gustavo S. Mesch, "Embattled Neighborhoods: The Political Ecology of Neighborhood Change," *Research in Urban Sociology* 3 (1993): 83–110.

16. See T. D. Allman, "The Urban Crisis Leaves Town," *Harper's,* December 1978, 5.

17. See Sharon Zukin, "Gentrification: Culture and Capital in the Urban Core," *Annual Review of Sociology* 23 (1987): 129–47. In the 1970s, as gentrification became a noticeable urban phenomenon, some scholars thought that it might become a mass movement of older suburbanites back to the city after their children were grown. That proved not to be the case. See *Back to the City: Issues in Neighborhood Renovation,* ed. Daphne Spain and Shirley B. Laska (New York: Pergamon, 1980).

18. See Phillip Clay, *Neighborhood Renewal* (Lexington, Mass.: Lexington, 1979). The interesting communitarian argument is advanced that gentrifiers can add to the city's "civil class." These are people living good, constructed lives who work for the betterment of the commonwealth.

19. See Kevin Fitzpatrick and Mark LaGory, *Unhealthy Places: The Ecology of Risk in the Urban Landscape* (New York: Routledge, 2000).

Notes to Chapter 4

1. The metropolitan areas for these cities are as follows: Columbus, 1,540,000; Cleveland, 2,946,000; Cincinnati, 1,979,000; Toledo, 618,000; and Dayton, 951,000 (U.S. Bureau of the Census, *Statistical Abstract of the United States: 2000.* Washington, D.C., 2001).

2. Jane Dockery and Kent P. Schwirian, "Service Center Edge Cities," in *Beyond Edge Cities,* ed. Richard D. Bingham et al. (New York: Garland, 1997), 129–42.

3. Shirley Laska and Daphne Spain, *Back to the City* (New York: Pergamon Press, 1980).

4. Richard D. Bingham et al., *Beyond Edge Cities* (New York: Garland, 1997).

5. The city's population of 711,470 made Columbus the 15th largest city in the United States. Cleveland ranked 33rd and Cincinnati ranked 55th. . Columbus was actually larger than many cities that are more widely recognized, such as Boston (589,141), Washington (572,059), Seattle (563,374), Atlanta (416,474), Miami (362,470), and St. Louis (348,189). Between 1990 and 2000, the city of Columbus added 78,560 people, a growth rate of 12.4 percent. Columbus was the only one of Ohio's fifteen largest cities to gain population. All of the rest lost people: Cleveland lost 27,213; Cincinnati, 32,755; and Toledo, 19,324 (U.S. Bureau of the Census: *Statistical Abstract of the United States, 2000.* Washington, D.C., 2001).

6. The mayor was very popular. When the first female gorilla born in captivity was born at the Columbus zoo, she was named "Emmy" in his honor.

7. See Gregory S. Jacobs, *Getting around Brown: Desegregation, Development, and the Columbus Public Schools* (Columbus: Ohio State University Press, 1998).

8. Paul Horning, *Woody Hayes: A Reflection* (Champaign, Ill.: Sagamore Publishing, 1991).

9. Editors, "Power: Who Runs This City?" *Columbus Monthly*, July 2000, 41.

10. C. N. Stone, *Regime Politics: Governing Atlanta, 1946–1988* (Lawrence: University of Kansas Press, 1989); R. S. Turner, "Growth Politics and Downtown Redevelopment: The Economic Imperative in Sun Belt Cities," *Urban Affairs Quarterly* 28 (1992): 3–21; Kent P. Schwirian, Timothy J. Curry, and Rachael A. Woldoff, "Community Conflict over Arena and Stadium Funding: A Combative Framing Analysis," *Sociological Focus* 34 (2001): 1–20.

11. Jeffrey Sheban, "John B.'s Exit Ends McCoy's 65-Year Run atop Banc One," *Columbus Dispatch,* 14 May 2000, sec. H1.

12. The list is created by a local magazine, *The Columbus Monthly.*

13. See note 11 above.

14. Ibid., 47.

15. Debbie Briner, "Happy Warrior," *The Other Paper,* 16–22 September 1999, 2.

16. It is not unusual for successful athletes on OSU teams to use their local connections to advance careers in business, the professions, and politics. For instance, Gregory Lashutka won letters in football on the 1963–1965 teams and went on to become a successful partner in a law firm, a city attorney, and then the mayor of Columbus.

17. Just before he left Colorado to come to Ohio State, Gee gave the head football coach, Bill McCartney, a fifteen-year contract because of the success he had enjoyed on the field. The contract was mostly symbolic, as McCartney retired from coaching shortly thereafter. At Ohio State Gee supported football coach John Cooper through several disappointing seasons in spite of thousands of negative letters and many loud complaints of local television commentators.

18. Bob Baptist, "Andy Geiger: Making It Happen at OSU," *Columbus Dispatch,* 7 December 1998, sec. 1A.

19. See note 9 above.

20. Scott Powers, "Donations Are the Ticket," *Columbus Dispatch,* 8 December 1998, sec. 1A; Scott Powers, "Dreams, Debts, and Doubts," *Columbus Dispatch,* 9 December 1998, sec. 1A.

21. The area took shape slowly, from the mid-1970s to the late 1990s. It is now well established with many expensive homes.

22. Jeff Long, "The Death of South Campus (As We Know It)," *Columbus Monthly,* 11 November 1997, 41.

23. Steve Wright, "Boston Developer Wins OSU Bid," *Columbus Dispatch,* 22 May 1999, sec. 1C.

24. Steve Wright, "City Might Help Group Take Land," *Columbus Dispatch,* 10 December 1999, sec. 1C.

25. Greg Davies, "The Town Gown Battle," *Columbus Monthly,* July 1997, 122.

Notes to Chapter 5

1. Mike Pramik, "Conventions Set Records Locally in '96," *Columbus Dispatch,* 24 January 1997.

2. Letter of agreement from George Skestos and Ron Pizzuti to Mayor Lashutka and President Gee, 13 September 1994.

3. John Futty, "Arena Debate Bounces Back," *Columbus Dispatch,* 6 February 1997, sec. 1A.

4. Ibid.

5. Ibid.

6. Ibid.

7. Quoted in Jeff Long, "Dream Team," *The Other Paper,* 7–13 November 1996, pp. 1–2.

8. Ibid.

9. In the spring of 1995, FCCFA staff attended meetings of the Governor's Sports Facilities Task Force and met individually with individual members. The governor's task force recommended that the state participate in sports facilities projects for Ohio's large cities. In 1994 the chamber of commerce contracted with KPMG Peat Marwick, an accounting firm, to research the possibility of a professional arena for Columbus. The Peat Marwick report concluded that Columbus could support a new arena. In the course of its work, Peat Marwick contracted with the world's leading sports facilities group—Hellmuth, Obata, and Kassabaum (HOK) Sports Facilities Group of Kansas City—to evaluate possible sites for a Columbus arena. When HOK recommended a site downtown near the convention center, the governor's work group studied these reports, which did not include a stadium site because the soccer franchise was awarded in 1994, after HOK's basic work had been done. So the task force contracted with HOK in June 1995 to develop the arena and stadium concepts together with a site plan. They also studied reports and exit polls for the defeated attempts to pass taxes for an arena. They concluded that the 1986 and 1987 issues had failed because they did not involve private funding. They thought that, by including private funding, voters would be more likely to approve an arena tax issue. They were dead wrong.

10. Deloitte and Touche, LLP, *Franklin County Convention Facilities Authority. Economic Impact Report. Proposed Stadium and Arena* (Los Angeles, 8 December 1995).

11. Multi-Purpose and Sports Facilities Work Group, *Report* (14 December 1995).

12. Dan Williamson, "Titans Get Cold Feet," *The Other Paper,* 13–19 February 1997, 1.

13. Kevin Maywood, "Friends, Foes Ready to Begin Arena Battle," *Columbus Dispatch,* 19 February 1997.

14. Jeff Long, "The Thrill of Victory," *The Other Paper,* 20–26 February 1997, 1.

15. Ibid.

16. Dan Williamson, "Arena Slayer," *The Other Paper,* 16–22 January 1997, 1.

17. John Futty, "Arena Opponent Slams Garage Plan," *Columbus Dispatch,* 13 February 1997.

18. Ibid.

19. Michelle Adkins, "Arena Is Rich Man's Folly," *Upper Arlington News,* 29 January 1997.

20. Kevin Maywood, "People of Many Stripes Unite in Opposition to Stadium/Arena Tax," *Columbus Dispatch,* 19 March 1997.

21. Ibid.

22. Ibid.

23. Steve Wright, "Hunt Signs On as Controller of Arena, Stadium," *Columbus Dispatch,* 11 April 1997.

Notes to Chapter 6

1. Kent P. Schwirian, Timothy J. Curry, and Rachael A. Woldoff, "Community Conflict over Arena and Stadium Funding: Competitive Framing, Social Action, and The Socio-Spatial Perspective," *Sociological Focus* 34 (2001): 1–20.

2. Steve Gambini, "Kridler, Sheir Put in Overtime for Arena Campaigns," *Upper Arlington News,* 16 April 1997, 32A.

3. Barbara Carman, "Lashutka Hopes Others Take His 2nd Chance to Heart," *Columbus Dispatch,* 13 April 1997, sec. 1C.

4. John Futty, "Issue 1 Battle Is Going Down to the Wire," *Columbus Dispatch,* 3 May 1997, sec. 1A.

5. Dan Williamson, "Mission Improbable: The Arena Boosters Admit Things Look Grim," *The Other Paper,* 10–16 April 1997, 1.

6. Bruce Cadwallader, "NHL Chief Had Doubts about Hunt," *Columbus Dispatch,* 13 May 1999, sec. 1A.

7. Steve Wright, "Issue 1 Falls Hard, 56% to 44%," *Columbus Dispatch,* 7 May 1997, sec. 1A.

8. See note 1 above.

9. Quoted in John Futty, "NHL Hockey Franchise Dead, But Crew to Stay," *Columbus Dispatch,* 7 May 1997, sec. 1A.

10. Editorial, "Down for the Count: Franklin County Voters Flatten Issue 1," *Columbus Dispatch,* 7 May 1997, sec. 8A.

11. See note 9 above, sec. 2A.

12. Quoted in Steve Wright, " 'No' to Arena Tax," *Columbus Dispatch,* 7 May 1997, sec. 2A.

13. Ibid., sec. 1A.

14. Ibid., sec. 2A.

15. John Futty, "Columbus' Hat Is Back in the NHL Ring," *Columbus Dispatch,* 3 June 1997, sec. 1A.

16. Quoted in Mike Curtin, "Private Arena Proposed," *Columbus Dispatch,* 2 June 1997, sec. 1A.

17. The Ohio Farm Bureau Federation founded Nationwide in 1926. Originally, it provided automobile insurance to Ohio farmers. Over the years Nationwide grew into a full-service insurance company and expanded its insurance operations across the country and internationally. It entered into real estate development, urban renewal, consumer financing, communications, and professional sports. During the 1950s and 1960s, Nationwide owned a one-third interest in the Cleveland Browns professional football team. In the 1970s Nationwide moved out of many of its far-flung activities to focus on insurance and financial services. Nationwide Development Company was organized in 1948 to build family housing, develop real estate, and to own and manage commercial properties. Nationwide Realty Investors, Ltd., was founded in 1997 as Nationwide's real-estate-equity investment and development operation. Today Nationwide is a Fortune 500 Company. Its assets exceed $117 billion, and it employs 35,000 workers: www.nationwide.com/about_us/profile/today.htm 2001.

18. Editors, "Power: Who Runs This City?" *Columbus Monthly,* July 2000. 40–51.

19. See note 16 above, sec. 2A.

20. Kent P. Schwirian and Gustavo S. Mesch, "Embattled Neighborhoods: The Political Ecology of Neighborhood Change," *Research in Urban Sociology* 3 (1993): 83–110.

21. John Futty, "Council Oks Arena Proposal," *Columbus Dispatch,* 3 June 1997, sec. 1A.

22. Quoted in John Futty, "NHL Hockey Franchise Dead, But Crew to Stay," *Columbus Dispatch,* 7 May 1997, sec. 1A.

23. Tim Doulin, "McConnell Says He Did It for the City," *Columbus Dispatch,* 9 May 1998, sec. 1A.

24. See Brent LaLond, "Lawsuit Filed over Hockey Team," *Columbus Dispatch,* 18 June 1997, sec. 1A.

25. What is a blue jacket? As they say in Columbus, it is a "bug with an attitude." An insect resembling a yellow jacket was selected as the creature logo and was named "Stinger." A contest open to the public was held for a team name. "Blue Jackets" was the winner. The name "Blue Jack" has a prominent position in Ohio history. Every Ohio elementary student learns that, in territorial days, Blue Jacket was the name of Ohio's famous Shawnee warrior chief. Children also learn that Ohio contributed more troopers, or "Blue Jackets," to the Union army during the Civil War than any other state. Creatively, the yellow-jacket creature was married to the Blue Jack image. "Stinger" is depicted in the tunic and cap of a Union noncommissioned officer.

26. Quoted in Craig Merz, "Time to Meet Crew's Needs, Rootes Says," *Columbus Dispatch,* 19 June 1997, sec. 1E.

27. In spite of the university's offer to the Crew, many local observers said that the university "kicked the Crew off campus." In reality, the Crew was committed to obtaining and managing its own facility—if someone else would pay for construction, so much the better.

28. Quoted in Matthew Marx, "Commission Members Say Fair Deal Sounds Promising," *Columbus Dispatch,* 5 April 1998, sec. 4D.

29. Quoted in Steve Wright and Craig Merz, "Board Oks Crew Stadium," *Columbus Dispatch,* 16 May 1998, sec. 2C.

30. Dan Williamson, "Yea, Dimon," *The Other Paper,* 30 November–6 December 2000, 1.

31. Steve Wright, "McConnell Joins Columbus Hall of Fame," *Columbus Dispatch,* 10 October 1998, sec. 1B.

32. Brian Ball, "$1B Portfolio Aim of Pizzuti-NRI Deal," *Cincinnati Business Courier,* 14 January 2000: http://cincinnati.bcentral.com/cincinnati/stories/2000/01/17/focus4.html.

33. Quoted in Doug Caruso, "Gee's New Post a New World," *Columbus Dispatch,* 28 June 1997, sec. 1A.

34. Shop Talk, "Texans' No. 1 Cheerleader: Jamey Rootes," *Business First of Columbus,* 29 June 2001.

35. Quoted in Barbara Carman, "Tax Fighter Leaving City, Activist Days behind Him," *Columbus Dispatch,* 1 June 1999, 1B.

Notes to Chapter 7

1. The Blue Jackets proved to be very popular. In the first three years of the franchise, they ran off a string of fifty-eight consecutive sellouts at Nationwide Arena. Of the thirty National Hockey League franchises, the Blue Jackets, in their first year (2000–2001) in the league were 11th (715,738) in total home attendance. In 2001–2002 they were 8th (743,576), and in 2002–2003 they were 11th (727,522). See http://sports.espn.go.com/nhl/attendance?year=2003.

2. The Gateway development project has been in the works for many years, though, and seemingly little progress has been made in the meantime.

3. Jen DiMascio, "Saving City Center," *The Other Paper,* 17–23 January 2002, 1.

4. Doug Buchanan and Kathy Showalter, "Jacobson's Closing at City Center; Will Be 'Sorely Missed,'" *Columbus Business First,* 15 January 2002. http://columbus.bcentral.com /columbus/stories/20022/01/14/daily9.html.

5. See note 3 above, p. 3.

6. Quoted in Kathy Hoke, "Coleman Pushes New Look at Downtown Development," *Columbus Business First,* 6 October 2000. http://columbus.bcentral.com/columbus/stories/2000/10/09/story7.html.

7. See note 5 above.

Notes to Chapter 8

1. William Beaver, "Building Sports Stadiums in Pittsburgh: A Case Study in Urban Power Structures," *Sociological Focus* 34 (2001): 21–32, 22.

2. Eric Heyl, "Pirates Go up for Sale One Year Ago," *Pittsburgh Tribune-Review,* August 3, 1995; available at http://www.triblive.com.

3. Steve Halvanik and Mark Belko, "Baseball Says No to Rigas," *Pittsburgh Post-Gazette,* 27 June 1995, sec. A1.

4. Kris Manula, "Mayor Blasts Owners," *Pittsburgh Tribune-Review,* February 3, 1995; available at http://www.triblive.com.

5. Mark Belko, Paul Meyer, and Bob Smizik. "It Seemed Like an Eternity but Kevin McClatchy Finally Owns the Pirates," *Pittsburgh Post-Gazette,* 14 February 1996, sec. A1.

6. Mark F. Bernstein, "Sports Stadium Boondoggle," *Public Interest* 132 (1998): 45–57.

7. Sam Ross Jr., "If We Build It, Will They Stay?" *Pittsburgh Tribune-Review,* 7 July 1995; available at http://www.triblive.com.

8. Forbes Field II Task Force, *Final Report* (Pittsburgh, 1996).

9. See note 1 above.

10. Eric Heyl, "Steelers Want in on Deal Too," *Pittsburgh Tribune-Review,* January 11, 1996; available at http://www.triblive.com, cited in Beaver 2001, 24 (note 1 above).

11. "Regional Renaissance Partnership Formed," press release, 20 February 1997, cited in Beaver 2001 (note 1 above).

12. Paul Flora, "Building the Region a Half-Cent at a Time," *Pittsburgh Post-Gazette,* 14 September 1997, sec. A1.

13. Paul Peirce, "RRP Tax Called Welfare for Rich," *Pittsburgh Tribune-Review,* 1 October 1997; available at http://www.triblive.com.

14. See note 1 above, p. 25.

15. Sandra Skowron, "Study Plots Impact of Sales Tax Hike," *Pittsburgh Tribune-Review,* 15 October 1997; available at http://www.triblive.com.

16. Rich Lord, "City Taskforce Closes Door on Plan B," *Pittsburgh Tribune-Review,* February 11, 1998; available at http://www.triblive.com, cited in Beaver 2001, 26 (note 1 above).

17. Tom Barnes and Rob Dvorchak, "Plan B: Play Ball," *Pittsburgh Post-Gazette,* 10 July 1998, sec. A1.

18. J. Morgan, *Glory for Sale: Fans, Dollars, and the New NFL* (Baltimore: Bancroft Press, 1997).

19. B. M. Horstman, "How It Was Built: A Timeline," *Cincinnati Post,* 19 August 2000, sec. 12A.

20. Dan Klepal, "The Deadline Deals That Built a Stadium," *Cincinnati Enquirer,* 13 August 2000, sec. A1.

21. R. Green and A. Michaud, "Poll: 59% Back Sales Tax Hike," *Cincinnati Enquirer,* 16 March 1996, sec. A1.

22. The two newspapers kept a close eye on stadium-related events as they unfolded (with a combined article archive amounting to nearly six hundred stadium-related articles since 1995), thus providing a rich source of information for our study. Because the *Cincinnati Enquirer,* the city's largest newspaper, reaches over half a million readers on a daily basis (compared to 845,203 residents in Hamilton County), its coverage of the stadium tax likely had a major impact on the public's understanding of the issue.

23. R. Green, "Intangibles May Decide tax Vote," *Cincinnati Enquirer,* 9 March 1996, sec. A1.

24. See note 22 above.

25. A. Michaud, "Two Wrangle over Tax Vote," *Cincinnati Enquirer,* 15 March 1996, sec. C6.

26. Lucy May, "Qualls Rips County's Deal with Bengals," *Cincinnati Enquirer,* 4 July 1997, sec. A1.

27. Dan Klepal, "The $18 Million Question: Who Will Pay?" *Cincinnati Enquirer,* 11 January 2002, sec. A1.

28. Dan Klepal, "Stadium Tax Revenue Slowing: If Trend Continues, Paying for Riverfront Is in Danger," *Cincinnati Enquirer,* 15 February 2001, sec. A1.

29. Ken Alltucker, "Adding Cost of Damage Comes Later," *Cincinnati Enquirer*, 13 April 2001, sec. A8.

30. Cliff Radel, "Protester Lynch Becomes Peacemaker Lynch," *Cincinnati Enquirer*, 15 April 2001, sec. A17.

31. Peter Eisinger, "The Politics of Bread and Circuses: Building the City for the Visitor Class," *Urban Affairs Review* 35 (2000): 316–33.

32. Ibid., 321.

33. Ibid., 317.

34. Michael N. Danielson, *Home Team: Professional Sports and the American Metropolis* (Princeton, N.J.: Princeton University Press, 1997).

35. Ibid., 167.

36. See note 31 above.

37. The seven cities were Pittsburgh, Chicago, Cleveland, Milwaukee, Phoenix, San Diego, and Seattle. See note 31.

38. From our theoretical stance, critics are valuable because they provide a framework and dramatic language for critiquing the excesses that city officials have gone to in pursuit of their dreams of urban entertainment districts. Such critiques help mobilize taxpayer resistance to these excesses. But as we explained in chapters 2 and 3, part of this trend in the construction of expensive sports-entertainment districts is due to the desire of the owners of professional sport teams to replace existing stadiums with newer ones that will increase revenue streams for themselves and their teams. Equally important, another part of this trend is due to the drying up of urban renewal funds from the federal government, which has forced city leaders to look elsewhere for resources to stimulate growth to prevent further decay in the urban core. In other words, both the owners of professional sport teams and city officials are doing what "comes naturally"—they are pursuing goals that are meaningful to them in the games in which they are involved.

39. Joanna Cagan and Neil deMause, *Field of Schemes: How the Great Stadium Swindle Turns Public Money into Private Profit* (Monroe, Maine: Common Courage Press 1998), 151.

Notes to Appendix

1. The ecology of games perspective is unique in sociology because, even though it has received little application in sociology over the past forty years, it has been applied in other disciplines. Particularly useful is Marilyn Gittell's study of school reform efforts in New York and Chicago, which looks at each city as an ecology of games, and William Dutton's study of the shaping of telecommunications policy in the United States from the perspective of the ecology of games. See Marilyn Gittel, "School Reform in New York and Chicago: Revisiting the Ecology of Local Games," *Urban Affairs Quarterly* 30 (1994): 136–51; William H. Dutton, "The Ecology of Games Shaping Telecommunications Policy," *Communication Theory* 2 (1992): 303–28.

2. Norton E. Long, "The Local Community as an Ecology of Games," *American Journal of Sociology* 64 (1958): 251–61.

3. The term *ecology* was borrowed from biology. Very broadly, it focuses on the relationships between organisms and their environments. In urban studies, ecologists

study human populations and their reciprocal relations (competition, cooperation, dependence, autonomy, and interdependence). Human ecologists refer to a natural order that operates within a society—one in which people (and their environment) have conflicts and are in harmony at various times but are always in a state of interaction.

4. Several national surveys, such as the General Social Survey and the Gallop poll, indicate that confidence in government and business was at its highest point right after World War II and just before the Vietnam War. Confidence declined sharply in the 1970s. See Seymour Martin Lipset and William Schneider, *The Confidence Gap: Business, Labor, and Government in the Public Mind,* rev. ed. (Baltimore: John Hopkins Press, 1983).

5. See note 2 above, p. 261.

6. Robert S. Lynd and Helen Merrell Lynd. *Middletown: A Study in American Culture* (New York: Harcourt Brace, 1929); W. Lloyd. Warner. *Yankee City* (New Haven, Conn.: Yale University Press, 1963).

7. This discussion of frame analysis, social action, and the sociospatial perspective is from Kent P. Schwirian, Timothy J. Curry, and Rachael A. Woldoff, "Community Conflict over Arena and Stadium Funding: Competitive Framing, Social Action, and the Socio-Spatial Perspective," *Sociological Focus* 34 (2001): 1–20. See also Erving Goffman, *Frame Analysis: An Essay in the Organization of Experience* (New York: Harper and Row, 1974); Teun A. Van Dijk, *Macrostructures: An Interdisciplinary Study of Global Structures in Discourse, Interaction, and Cognition* (Hillsdale, N.J.: Lawrence Erlbaum, 1980).

8. Kimberly Fisher, "Locating Frames in the Discursive Universe," *Sociological Research Online,* 1997, http://www.socresonline.org.uk/2/3/4.html.

9. A. Triandafyllidou and A. Fotiou, "Sustainability and Modernity in the European Union: A Frame Theory Approach to Policy-Making," *Sociological Research Online* (1998), http://www.socresonline.org.uk/3/1/2.html.

10. Dawn McCaffrey and Jennifer Keys, "Competitive Framing Processes in the Abortion Debate: Polarization-Vilification, Frame Saving and Frame Debunking," *The Sociological Quarterly* 41 (2000): 41–61.

11. William A. Gamson, "Constructing Social Protest," in *Social Movements and Culture,* ed. Hank Johnson and Bert Klandermans (London: UCL Press, 1995).

12. Warren Cohen, "Oysters, Scotch, and Hoops: New Sports Arenas Are Dens of Luxury. They May Also Fail," *U.S. News & World Report,* 15 November 1999, 92; Randy Stocker, "The CDC Model of Urban Redevelopment: A Critique and an Alternative," *Journal of Urban Affairs* 19 (1997): 1–22.

13. Henri Lefebvre, *The Production of Space* (Oxford: Basil Blackwell, 1991); Mark Gottdiener and Ray Hutchison, *The New Urban Sociology* (New York: McGraw-Hill, 2000).

14. Ibid., 225.

15. William G. Holt III, "Distinguishing Metropolises: The Production of Urban Images," *Research in Urban Sociology* 5 (2000): 225–52.

16. John R. Logan, Rachael Bridges Whaley, and Kyle Crowder, "The Character and Consequences of Growth Machine Regimes: An Assessment of 20 Years of Research," *Urban Affairs Review* 22 (1997): 603–30.

17. John Logan and Harvey Molotch, *Urban Fortunes: The Political Economy of Place* (Berkeley and Los Angeles: University of California Press, 1987).

18. Sharon Zukin, *The Culture of Cities* (Cambridge, Mass.: Blackwell Publishers, 1995).

19. Tim Curry, Robert Jiobu, and Kent Schwirian, *Sociology for the Twenty-First Century* (Upper Saddle River, N.J.: Prentice-Hall, 2002); Kent P. Schwirian and Gustavo Mesch, "Embattled Neighborhoods: The Political Ecology of Neighborhood Change," *Research in Urban Sociology* 3 (1993): 83–110.

20. Alejandro Portes, "The Hidden Abode: Sociology as Analysis of the Unexpected," *American Sociological Review* 65 (2000): 1–18.

21. Harvey Molotch, William Freudenburg, and Krista E. Paulsen, "History Repeats Itself, But How? City Character, Urban Tradition, and the Accomplishments of Place," *American Sociological Review* 55 (2000): 791–823.

22. Nancy Kleniewski, *Cities, Change, and Conflict* (Belmont, Calif.: Wadsworth Thomson Learning, 2002).

23. Michael D. Kennedy, "The Fiscal Crisis of the City," In *Cities in Transformation: Class, Capital, and the State,* ed. Michael Peter Smith (Thousand Oaks, Calif.: Sage, 1984), 105.

24. Peter Shields, "Beyond Individualism and the Ecology of Games: Institutions, Structures, and Communication Policy," *Communication Theory* 5 (1995): 366–78.

25. William H. Dutton, "The Ecology of Games and Its Enemies," *Communication Theory* 5 (1995): 390.

26. Gary Alan Fine, "Games and Truths: Learning to Construct Social Problems in High School Debate," *The Sociological Quarterly* 41 (2000): 103–23.

27. See also Benjamin Cornwell, Timothy J. Curry, and Kent P. Schwirian, "Revising Norton Long's Ecology: A Network Approach." *City and Community* 2 (2003): 121–42.

Index

Arena District, vii–ix, 86, 96, 99, 100–112, 143, 157, 158, 161
Arena slayer, 56, 74, 99
Bedinghaus, Bob, 123, 124, 126, 128
Bettman, Gary, 69, 82, 84, 86, 90
Blue Jackets, vii–ix, 20, 98, 101, 105, 113
Boas, George, 76
Brown, Michael (Mike), 121, 122, 123, 124, 125, 126
Cincinnati: two stadiums, 120–23; referendum, 123–26; financial burden, 126–29
Coleman, Michael, 82, 106, 110, 111
Columbus Crew, 26, 27, 56, 64, 67, 68, 70, 76, 90–92
Community games, 29–32, 33–37
Dream Team, 4, 5, 68–70, 82–86, 88, 90, 95, 96, 99
Dutton, William H., 162
Ecology of games social action model: framework, 134–39; arena district application, 139–45
Extending the model: frame analysis, 145–52; sociospatial perspective, 152–56; growth machine, 156–57; symbolic economies model, 157–58; action theory, 158–60; city character and urban tradition, 160–62

Ellis, Brian J., 107
FCCFA (Franklin County Convention Facilities Authority), 65, 69, 70, 72, 76, 77, 78, 87, 96
Gee, E. Gordon, 55, 56, 57, 58, 59, 60, 66, 67, 68, 77–78, 99
Gehry, Frank, 35
Geiger, Andy, 58–60, 65, 68, 92, 99
Higdon, Mark, 75, 79, 84
Hunt, Lamar, 55, 56, 64, 68, 69, 70, 73, 76–77, 81, 82, 83, 86, 88–96, 99, 132, 140, 150, 155
Issue 1: planning, 70; battle, 71–82; voters decide, 82–83; aftermath, 84–88; elite fall out, 88; McConnell and Nationwide to the rescue, 88–90; soccer stadium odyssey, 91–96; moving on, 98–100
Jennison, William, 72
Karmanos, Jr., Peter, 81
Kessler, Jack, 55
Kirwan, Brit, 97
Knepley, Dennis, 75
Koolhaas, Rem, 35
Kridler, Doug, 36, 72, 76, 80, 100, 113
Lashutka, Greg, 55, 66, 67, 77, 80, 84, 86, 87, 89, 94, 98, 106, 110
Long, Norton, 134, 136, 137, 162, 163
Loughley, Heather M., 75, 84

Lynch III, Damon, 120
Major League Soccer (MLS), vii, ix, 3, 23–27, 68
Mara, Tim, 123, 124
Marsh, Ty, 111
McClatchy, Kevin, 115, 116, 119
McConnell, John H., 42, 55, 69, 72, 73, 80, 82, 86, 88–91, 98, 106, 143
McConnell, John P., 55, 106
McCoy, John B., 54, 55, 72, 88
McFerson, Dimon, 55, 72, 85–87, 97, 98, 106, 108, 142, 143
Modell, Art, 10, 17, 18, 121, 122
Murphy, Tom, 28, 115, 116, 119, 127
Nationwide Arena, vii, 3, 90, 96, 97, 101, 105–8
Pittsburgh: two stadiums, 114–18; referendum, 118–19; plan B, 119–20
Pizzuti, Ron, 55, 66, 68, 69, 73, 84, 98, 99
Qualls, Roxanne, 123, 126
Redevelopment: local pride and redevelopment, 14–16; redevelopment game, 36–37, 49; urban crisis and redevelopment, 37–38; gentrification and redevelopment, 40–41; economy and redevelopment, 44–47; redevelopment game players, 51–57; Ohio State and redevelopment, 59–61; hard times for downtown, 109–13
Research methodology, 164–65

Ridge, Tom, 119, 120
Rigas, John, 115
Rooney, Dan, 117
Rootes, Jamey, 95, 98, 99
Scaife, Richard Mellon, 118
Schott, Marge, 121, 122
Sheir, Richard, 56, 57, 74, 75, 76, 77, 80, 81, 99, 100
Shirey, John, 123, 126
Shumate, Alex, 55
Skestos, George, 66
Stadium game, 16–20
Tavares, Charleta, 82
Titans, x, 53–56, 60, 61, 63, 64, 65, 69, 71, 72, 73, 78, 83, 89, 90, 98, 129, 136, 148, 151, 152, 153, 154, 155, 156, 157, 158, 159, 161, 163. *See also* E. Gordon Gee; Jack Kessler; Greg Lashutka; John B. McCoy; Dimon McFerson; Ron Pizzuti; Alex Shumate; Les Wexner; Frank Wobst; John F. Wolfe
VAST (Voters Against the Stadium Tax), 56, 75, 76, 77, 79, 84, 105, 148, 150, 151, 152, 154, 155
Wexner, Les, 54, 55, 111, 112, 143
Wobst, Frank, 55
Wolfe, John F., 55, 67, 73, 74, 86, 89, 90, 106
Wolfe, John W., 54, 55
Yates, Tyrone, 125

URBAN LIFE AND URBAN LANDSCAPE SERIES

Zane L. Miller, General Editor

The series examines the history of urban life and the development of the urban landscape through works that place social, economic, and political issues in the intellectual and cultural context of their times.

Cincinnati, Queen City of the West, 1819–1838
DANIEL AARON

Domesticating the Streets: The Reform of Public Space in Hartford, 1850–1930
PETER C. BALDWIN

Proportional Representation and Election Reform in Ohio
KATHLEEN L. BARBER

Fragments of Cities: The New American Downtowns and Neighborhoods
LARRY BENNETT

The Lost Dream: Businessmen and City Planning on the Pacific Coast, 1890–1920
MANSEL G. BLACKFORD

Merchant of Illusion: James Rouse, American's Salesman of the Businessman's Utopia
NICHOLAS DAGEN BLOOM

Suburban Alchemy: 1960s New Towns and the Transformation of the American Dream
NICHOLAS DAGEN BLOOM

Planning for the Private Interest: Land Use Controls and Residential Patterns in Columbus, Ohio, 1900–1970
PATRICIA BURGESS

Cincinnati Observed: Architecture and History
JOHN CLUBBE

Lancaster, Ohio, 1800–2000: Frontier Town to Edge City
DAVID R. CONTOSTA

Suburb in the City: Chestnut Hill, Philadelphia, 1850–1990
DAVID R. CONTOSTA

Main Street Blues: The Decline of Small-Town America
RICHARD O. DAVIES

For the City as a Whole: Planning, Politics, and the Public Interest in Dallas, Texas, 1900–1965
ROBERT B. FAIRBANKS

Making Sense of the City: Local Government, Civic Culture, and Community Life in Urban America
EDITED BY ROBERT B. FAIRBANKS AND PATRICIA MOONEY-MELVIN

The Mysteries of the Great City: The Politics of Urban Design, 1877–1937
JOHN D. FAIRFIELD

Faith and Action: A History of the Catholic Archdiocese of Cincinnati, 1821–1996
ROGER FORTIN

Cincinnati in 1840: The Social and Functional Organization of an Urban Community during the Pre–Civil War Period
WALTER STIX GLAZER